CALIFORNIA

100 BEST PLACES TO VISIT

BUCKET LIST

Copyright © 2024

ISBN: 9798303259126

ABOUT CALIFORNIA

California, a state in the United States of America, became the 31st state of the union on September 9, 1850. By the early 1960s, it had become the most populous state in the U.S. The exact origin of California's name remains uncertain, but many believe it came from a 16th-century Spanish novel called "Las sergas de Esplandián" ("The Adventures of Esplandián"), which described a mythical island rich in gold and precious stones called California. The influence of Spanish settlers during the 18th and 19th centuries is visible in California's architecture and place names. The capital city is Sacramento.

California is bordered by Oregon to the north, Nevada and Arizona to the east, Baja California (Mexico) to the south, and the Pacific Ocean to the west. The state boasts diverse geography, ranging from the rainy northern coast to the arid Colorado Desert in the south, and from the Mediterranean-like central and southern coastline to the volcanic plateau in the far northeast. California is home to both the highest point (Mount Whitney) and the lowest point (Death Valley) in the contiguous United States. Mount Whitney is the highest peak in the Sierra Nevada range, one of North America's major mountain ranges.

The dynamic character of the state's social, economic, and political landscape—largely shaped by the continuous influx of people from other states and nations—has long made California a testing ground for new lifestyles. California's population, primarily concentrated along the coast, ranks as the most urbanized in the United States, with over three-fourths residing in metropolitan areas such as Los Angeles, San Francisco, and San Diego. Despite its urban development and the conversion of land for industrial use, California remains the leading agricultural producer in the nation. Approximately half of the state's territory is under federal ownership, with national parks spread across it dedicated to preserving nature and natural resources. Its area spans 163,695 square miles (423,967 square km), and its population stood at 39,538,223 in 2020, estimated to be 38,965,193 in 2023.

The core of California is the Central Valley, stretching 450 miles (725 km) through the middle of the state, forming a basin between the Coast Ranges to the west and the Sierra Nevada to the east. This valley serves as the agricultural hub of the state, with its sole outlet being the delta where the Sacramento and San Joaquin rivers flow into San Francisco Bay. Bounded by the Cascade Range to the northeast and the Klamath Mountains to the northwest, the valley exhibits varied terrain, from rugged, forested landscapes in the far north to drier, barren areas in the higher northeast.

Eastern California is predominantly desert, with the northeastern region characterized by sparse settlements amidst barren plains, mountains, and a volcanic plateau. In the east-central area lies the Trans-Sierra desert, running along the steep eastern face of the Sierra Nevada range and forming part of the expansive interstate Great Basin within the Basin and Range Province. Elevations in the Trans-Sierra desert range from 2,000 to 7,400 feet (600 to 2,300 meters) above sea level. Major settlements are situated in the Owens Valley, once fertile farmland until its water flow was redirected to Los Angeles via an extensive series of conduits constructed between 1908 and 1913.

To the west of the Trans-Sierra desert lies the Sierra Nevada mountain range. Its eastern face is steep, plunging around 10,000 feet (3,000 meters) within a 10-mile (16-km) span near Owens Lake. On the western side, the range gradually slopes down into the foothills leading to the Central Valley, encompassing the valleys of the San Joaquin and Sacramento rivers. Stretching from the vicinity of Lassen Peak in the north to the outskirts of Los Angeles in the south, the Sierra Nevada spans approximately 430 miles (700 km). Besides Mount Whitney, towering at 14,494 feet (4,418 meters) above sea level, there are ten other peaks in the Sierra Nevada surpassing 14,000 feet (4,200 meters). Passes traversing the range from east to west are limited but high, with some reaching elevations of over 9,000 feet (2,700 meters). Three national parks—Kings Canyon, Sequoia, and Yosemite—are nestled within the Sierra Nevada. Yosemite, designated a UNESCO World Heritage site in 1978, emerges from the purplish foothills of the Mother Lode Country and extends across the ice-carved valleys of the Merced and Tuolumne rivers, boasting stunning waterfalls and granite domes.

In the southeastern part of the state lies the Mojave Desert, covering over 25,000 square miles (65,000 square km), which constitutes approximately one-sixth of California's land area. The Mojave Desert is characterized by vast basins, eroded mountains, fault blocks, and alluvial plains, many of which sit at elevations exceeding 2,000 feet (600 meters) above sea level. Vegetation in the Mojave includes the resilient creosote bush, yucca, saltbush, burroweed, encelia, cottonwood, and mesquite, while higher elevations are home to juniper and piñon pine.

Just below the Mojave Desert lies the lower Colorado Desert, which is an extension of the Sonoran Desert and begins in the Coachella Valley. This desert region descends into the Imperial Valley near the Mexican border, renowned for its extensive irrigation and cultivation of winter crops. Over 4,000 square miles (10,500 square km) of the desert are situated below sea level, including the Salton Sea, a 300-square-mile (800-square-km) lake formed between 1905 and 1907 when the nearby Colorado River breached its banks.

California's coastline stretches approximately 1,100 miles (1,800 km) and is predominantly mountainous. This rugged terrain is most striking in the Santa Lucia Range, located south of San Francisco, where towering cliffs loom about 800 feet (240 meters) above the Pacific Ocean. Lower hills mark the entrances to the three major natural harbors along the coast at San Diego, San Francisco, and Eureka. Coastal mountains, comprising numerous interwoven chains, range from 20 to 40 miles (30 to 65 km) in width and elevate from 2,000 to 8,000 feet (600 to 2,400 meters) above sea level.

Southern California's dense urbanization is concentrated along a coastal plateau and within valleys extending roughly 10 to 60 miles (16 to 100 km) inland. As one moves north along the coast beyond the Tehachapi Mountains, population density diminishes, although growth has accelerated in the central coastal region since the 1990s. The heavily populated coastal region around San Francisco Bay transitions into the less-developed northern coast, characterized by lumbering and fishing communities nestled beside streams and rivers flowing from the Coast Ranges. This area is renowned for its coastal redwood forests and is home to Redwood National Park, designated a UNESCO World Heritage site in 1980.

The San Andreas Fault, extending over 800 miles (1,300 km), is a significant geological fault line traversing much of California. Tectonic activity along this fault has led to major earthquakes, including the devastating San Francisco earthquake of 1906. Other prominent fault lines, such as the Hayward Fault in the San Francisco Bay Area and the San Gabriel fault zone in metropolitan Los Angeles, have also produced significant earthquakes, with the destructive 1994 Northridge earthquake occurring along one of the San Andreas's larger secondary faults. Additionally, separate fault systems in the Sierra Nevada and the Klamath Mountains remain tectonically active.

In southern California and the desert areas, water is consistently scarce, while in the northern coastal regions, excess rainfall and snowmelt often lead to winter flooding along rivers. Elaborate networks of dams and aqueducts have been established to transfer water from north to south. However, this practice faces opposition from those who view it as hindering future growth or disrupting environmental equilibrium. One such system, the Colorado River Aqueduct near the Arizona border, conveys water from the Colorado River across the desert and mountains of southern California to supply the Los Angeles metropolitan area. Another significant initiative, the California State Water Project initiated in 1960, represents the largest water transfer scheme ever attempted. Its objective is to transport water daily from the Feather River in north-central California, a tributary of the Sacramento River, to communities as far south as the Mexican border.

The primary lake within the Sierra Nevada is Lake Tahoe, straddling the California-Nevada border at an elevation of 6,229 feet (1,899 meters). This mountain-enclosed alpine lake spans approximately 193 square miles (500 square km), boasting one of the world's greatest average depths and reaching a maximum depth of about 1,640 feet (500 meters). Throughout the Sierra Nevada, numerous smaller lakes are scattered, some situated above the timberline amidst regions of rugged granite and steep-walled canyons. Clear Lake, located west of the Sierra Nevada, covers an area of 67 square miles (174 square km) and stands as the largest natural lake entirely within California. On the eastern flank of the Sierra lie Mono Lake and Owens Lake, both of which have long been imperiled by agricultural development.

California experiences two distinct seasons—a wet season and a dry season. With the exception of the coastal areas, the aridness of the air and subsequent rapid evaporation significantly mitigate the intensity of summer heat. Precipitation varies widely, ranging from over 170 inches (4,300 mm) in the northwest to negligible amounts in the southeastern desert regions, while the coast generally enjoys moderate temperatures and rainfall. The climate undergoes rapid changes with elevation, with Death Valley, situated at 282 feet (86 meters) below sea level, being the hottest and driest location in North America. Summer temperatures in Death

Valley frequently exceed 100°F (about 48°C), with an average annual rainfall of only around 2 inches (50 mm). The nearby Colorado Desert experiences scorching summer temperatures, sometimes reaching approximately 130°F (54°C), with annual precipitation averaging just 3 to 4 inches (75 to 100 mm). In the higher eastern desert regions of California, summer temperatures are more temperate. Winters in the Sierra Nevada can bring near-freezing temperatures. Los Angeles maintains an average annual temperature in the mid-60s°F (about 18°C), with an average annual precipitation of approximately 14 inches (350 mm). San Francisco experiences average temperatures in the mid-50s°F (about 14°C), with an annual precipitation average of about 20 inches (508 mm). Along the coast, temperatures rarely surpass 90°F (32°C) or drop to freezing, and humidity remains low.

California stands out as the most biologically diverse state in the United States, boasting over 40,000 plant and animal species, some of which face endangerment or threat. Nearly a quarter of all plant species found in North America naturally inhabit the state. Among its notable features are the iconic redwood trees, which once covered roughly 2,000,000 acres (800,000 hectares) of California before European colonization. While many redwood forests have suffered destruction or alteration due to logging activities, approximately 200,000 acres (80,000 hectares) of redwoods are safeguarded within state and national parks. Other distinctive plant species, emblematic of various regions in the state, include the bristlecone pine, palm trees, creosote bushes, and Monterey cypress. However, some of California's characteristic landscapes, particularly along the central and southern coastal regions, are dominated by plant species introduced from other countries, such as Bermuda grass from southern Africa, the tree of heaven from China, the thistle from Central Asia, and the giant reed from southern Europe.

The diversity of animal life in California mirrors its varied geography, with approximately 400 species of mammals and around 600 species of birds identified. Many of these species are extinct or at risk of extirpation. For instance, the California grizzly bear is extinct, and the bighorn sheep primarily inhabit remote desert mountains. Some species have been reintroduced or granted protected status, including the California condor, whose population has gradually increased thanks to zoo breeding programs and protected wilderness areas. Wildcats and pumas (cougars) are commonly found in remote mountainous regions, although they increasingly encounter humans as urban and suburban development expands. Deer, bobcats, coyotes, skunks, raccoons, and black bears are prevalent in various habitats. In arid and desert regions, squirrels, jackrabbits, and chipmunks are common, while desert tortoises, horned toads, and rattlesnakes thrive in desert climates. Common bird species include California jays, thrashers, juncos, mountain bluebirds, and hermit thrushes. The Pacific Ocean off California's coast is home to bass, perch, rockfish, and tuna, along with numerous species of marine mammals.

Although agriculture contributes less than one-tenth of California's income, the state is responsible for over half of the nation's vegetable and fruit production. California's fields and orchards yield an astonishing array of agricultural products, largely from irrigated farmland. Major cash crops include cattle, milk, cotton, and grapes. Approximately half of the state's agricultural output originates from the Central Valley, which is irrigated through an intricate network of dams, canals, and power and pumping facilities. Periodic droughts have impacted agricultural production, and the conversion of farmland for commercial and residential purposes has led to a decline in acreage.

California's agricultural dominance dates back to 1947 when its farm production surpassed that of any other state. The Fresno, Kern, and Tulare areas boast growing seasons of 9 to 10 months, ranking them among the top in the country in terms of the value of farm produce. Many large landholdings stem from federal land grants to railroads, resulting in farms characterized by absentee owners, high mechanization, and persistent labor disputes. Most farms specialize in one or two crops: almonds thrive north of Sacramento, while Fresno is known for cotton, forage crops, figs, and grapes. In the fertile delta region, crops like asparagus, tomatoes, rice, safflower, and sugar beets are prevalent. Research conducted at the University of California, Davis, has contributed to agricultural specialization and advises the state's wine industry, which produces the majority of wine in the United States. Despite nearly being decimated by a virus in the 1940s, the citrus industry remains a significant contributor to California's agricultural output.

The premium wine grape industry flourishes in the Napa and Sonoma valleys north of San Francisco and neighboring areas. The Imperial Valley in the southern Colorado Desert, albeit smaller in size compared to the Central Valley, boasts around 500,000 irrigated acres (200,000 hectares) of farmland. Other notable farming regions include the Coachella Valley, renowned for dates and grapefruit, and the Salinas Valley and Monterey Bay region.

Approximately one-tenth of California's workforce is employed in agriculture, comprising low-income laborers, including migrants and Mexican nationals who migrate during harvest seasons. Migrant laborers, historically subjected to exploitation, organized under the leadership of Cesar Chavez in the late 1960s, staging prolonged strikes that garnered nationwide support through consumer boycotts. However, the United Farm Workers union, led by Chavez, subsequently lost much of its membership to the Teamsters Union, which organized agricultural and industrial labor forces to such an extent that California is now one of the most heavily unionized states in the country.

California's forestlands are a mix of private and public ownership, with logging activities occurring as part of state and federal land-management policies emphasizing multiple uses.

The state also boasts a significant commercial fishing industry, with seafood from the Pacific Ocean including tuna, mackerel, sole, squid, and sardines. Trout and salmon are predominantly farm-raised.

California's cultural landscape is characterized by extensive public engagement with the arts and a fervor for cultural symbols of achievement, often manifested through extravagant investments in the construction of galleries, museums, and concert halls.

Cities like San Francisco have nurtured notable painters such as David Park, Elmer Bischoff, and Richard Diebenkorn, while Los Angeles has flourished as a thriving art marketplace, boasting a vibrant community of galleries along La Cienega Boulevard. Other locales like Carmel, Big Sur, Ojai, and Sausalito have served as havens for diverse artistic communities.

Early literary figures associated with California hailed from outside the state, including Bret Harte from New York, Mark Twain from Missouri, Joaquin Miller from Indiana, and Ambrose Bierce from Ohio. Yet, the Gold Rush era in San Francisco provided a receptive audience for their works, as well as for theater and music. Subsequent writers contributed to the establishment of a regional literary tradition. Jack London, known for his narratives set amidst frontier violence, was born in San Francisco. Native Californians like Frank Norris and Upton Sinclair addressed social issues of their time, foreshadowing the later works of John Steinbeck and William Saroyan. John Muir, a Scottish naturalist, celebrated the state's natural marvels, while Robinson Jeffers, a prominent poet, spent much of his life in California. The San Francisco Beat movement included poets like Kenneth Rexroth, Lawrence Ferlinghetti, Denise Levertov, Michael McClure, and William Everson.

However, Hollywood's influx of literary figures, both American and European expatriates, during the 1930s and '40s did not establish a strong regional cultural tradition. Instead, the California milieu became a favored subject of satire in novels like Nathanael West's "The Day of the Locust," Aldous Huxley's "After Many a Summer Dies the Swan," and Evelyn Waugh's "The Loved One," as well as in works by F. Scott Fitzgerald, Budd Schulberg, and Ross Macdonald. The hard-boiled fiction of authors like Raymond Chandler, Dashiell Hammett, and James M. Cain also depicted aspects of California life.

However, California's most renowned industry is undoubtedly that of movies and television, centered in and around Hollywood. The pioneers of the motion picture industry found Southern California exceptionally well-suited to their needs due to abundant sunshine, mild temperatures, diverse terrain, and a highly skilled and diverse labor force.

Hollywood has traditionally been seen as the epicenter of a global movie industry, particularly during the 1920s, '30s, and '40s, when real estate thrived and opulence was flaunted. However, the studios were caught off guard by the upheaval brought about by the emergence of television after World War II. Millions of Americans chose to stay home, opting to watch television rather than frequenting movie theaters. Simultaneously, legal rulings deemed major production companies as monopolies due to their control over not only film production but also distribution and exhibition. Despite the introduction of new features such as widescreen projection, vibrant color, advanced lenses, and stereophonic sound, the industry suffered significant losses. Major studios began offloading their film inventories and leasing their facilities to television entities. Some studios, like Universal, transitioned into massive television production. With a restructuring of the studio system in the 1990s and a heightened focus on international markets, Hollywood's film industry experienced a revival by the close of the 20th century.

The music industry, centered in Los Angeles, also wields considerable influence in California, although its prominence emerged more recently compared to the film industry. Capitol Records, founded in 1942, was California's first major record label, and independent labels like Specialty and Modern played crucial roles in shaping rhythm and blues and rock and roll during the 1950s. Before California left its indelible mark on rock music, Cool Jazz, also known as West Coast Jazz, gained traction in the late 1940s. In the 1960s, as the music industry shifted from New York to Los Angeles, the Beach Boys pioneered California's distinctive sound, sparking a wave of successful popular music genres ranging from folk rock, country rock, and singer-songwriters to punk and gangsta rap. Concurrently, San Francisco became the hub of psychedelic rock, while Bakersfield emerged as a significant center for country music.

Given California's vast size and the rich diversity of its landscapes and communities, the state offers a plethora of popular recreational activities and sports. From skiing in the Sierra Nevada mountains, extending south to destinations like Big Bear Mountain near San Bernardino, to surfing along California's renowned beaches, particularly those stretching from Santa Barbara to San Diego, the state boasts a wide array of options. Additionally, California is a hub for surfing-inspired activities such as skateboarding, with the inaugural major contest held in Hermosa Beach in 1963.

For hiking enthusiasts, the trails of the High Sierra are especially popular, including the iconic 211-mile (340-km) John Muir Trail traversing the heart of the Sierra Nevada, as well as the Pacific

Crest Trail, which spans the entire length of the state. Anglers and hunters also find ample opportunities throughout California, with notable fishing spots including Trinity and Shasta lakes in the north, Lake Havasu in the south near the Arizona border, and the Salton Sea, which includes designated national wildlife refuge areas. Numerous reservoirs scattered across the state, particularly in the arid southern regions, also attract visitors for recreational pursuits.

History of California

In 1542, Spanish navigator Juan Rodríguez Cabrillo became the first European to see what is now California, where around 130,000 Native Americans were living at the time. However, Spain ignored the region for over two centuries due to reports of its poverty and a general decline in Spanish exploration. In 1602, merchant Sebastián Vizcaíno sailed along the southern California coast, naming locations such as San Diego, Santa Catalina Island, Santa Barbara, and Monterey. Using inaccurate maps, Vizcaíno and later explorers mistakenly believed California was an island, which discouraged them when they failed to chart its surrounding waters.

Pressure to settle came from Spanish missionaries eager to convert Native Americans to Christianity, as well as Russian and British traders seeking sea otter pelts and a desire to find the Northwest Passage. In 1769, the Spanish viceroy sent both land and sea expeditions from Baja California. The Franciscan friar Junípero Serra established the first mission in San Diego, while Gaspar de Portolá set up a military post in Monterey in 1770. After 1773, colonization expanded with an overland supply route designed to connect Spanish settlements in what are now Arizona and New Mexico to the coast.

The 21 missions established by Serra and his successors were central to California's development. While attempting to Christianize the Native Americans, the padres taught them farming and crafts. The padres also used forced labor to irrigate large ranches and traded goods like hides, tallow, wine, olive oil, and leather for manufactured items brought by Yankee vessels.

After Mexico gained independence from Spain in 1821, Spanish settlers, known as Californios, pushed for the secularization of the missions. From 1833 to 1840, the Mexican government divided the mission lands among political allies, leading to the padres' departure and the exploitation of Native Americans. In 1841, the first wagon train of settlers departed from Missouri for California. The colony grew slowly, but in 1846, during the Bear Flag Revolt, settlers at Sonoma declared California an independent republic. When the United States declared war on Mexico, U.S. forces raised the flag in Monterey, and by January 1847, California had surrendered to U.S. troops. The Treaty of Guadalupe Hidalgo, signed by Mexico, ceded California to the United States.

In early 1848, carpenter James Wilson Marshall discovered gold at Sutter's Mill near Coloma, just days before the Mexican-American War ended. By August, thousands of gold miners arrived, and others traveled from the East, enduring dangerous conditions. Around 40,000 people arrived in San Francisco by boat in 1849, while many others used the California Trail to reach the area. Few struck it rich due to the challenging work and high prices. Many settlers shifted to farming or opening businesses instead.

The Gold Rush sped up California's statehood, which was granted in 1850 as part of the Compromise of 1850. Although the Gold Rush peaked in 1852, the settlement momentum continued, and nearly $2 billion worth of gold was extracted before mining activity began to decline.

The Compromise of 1850 did not resolve the slavery debate in California, as political factions were split over whether the state should be free or allow slavery. One proposal, supported by

California Senator William M. Gwin, suggested dividing California into two states—one for slavery and one free. Another plan aimed to establish a Pacific Coast republic. However, when the Civil War began, California sided with the Union, providing troops and supplies.

After the war, the governor's office switched between Democrats and Republicans until the century's end. Following 1876, the state's political landscape was marked by labor unrest, and there were efforts to control industries like mining and irrigation through state support. The 1870s saw an economic downturn, leading to labor union dissatisfaction, one of the results of which was a push to exclude Chinese workers, who were paid less than "white" laborers.

This period of turmoil led to the 1879 California Constitution, which included reforms but discriminated against the Chinese. A law passed by the U.S. Congress that year was vetoed, but a treaty with China in 1880 gave the U.S. authority over Chinese immigration, leading to the Chinese Exclusion Act of 1882. The law suspended Chinese immigration for ten years, and in 1902, exclusion laws were reenacted. The restriction of Chinese workers contributed to the decline of large single-crop ranches and the rise of smaller, more diverse farms.

As Japanese laborers replaced Chinese workers, anti-Japanese sentiment grew, especially in San Francisco. The Gentlemen's Agreement between Japan and the U.S. in 1907 halted Japanese immigration, and in 1913, the Webb Alien Land Law was enacted to prevent Japanese landownership, marking the peak of anti-Japanese lobbying.

In the early 20th century, reform movements focused on increasing public influence in governance. California's economy was less affected by the Great Depression than other parts of the country, though migrant farmworkers from the Dust Bowl region swelled the state's population, creating social unrest. The

Depression gave rise to welfare movements like EPIC (End Poverty in California), led by author Upton Sinclair. During this period, the Democratic Party gained strength, though Republicans controlled the state government for most of the early 20th century, with notable governors like Earl Warren, who later became Chief Justice of the U.S. Supreme Court.

In 1958, the Democrats won the governorship with Edmund Brown, and for the first time in the 20th century, they also gained majorities in both houses of the state legislature. However, in 1966, Ronald Reagan, a Republican, became governor. From the 1960s onward, California's leadership alternated between Democrats and Republicans.

Throughout this period, California's economy grew, and its population increased. Immigrants began arriving in Southern California around 1900, attracted by the region's citrus, oil, and opportunities after the 1906 San Francisco earthquake. Agriculture and industry flourished, particularly in the cities. During World War II, aircraft and shipbuilding industries expanded, and by the 1950s and 1960s, the West Coast saw an influx of scientists and academics, many of whom had migrated during the war.

The 1970s and 1980s saw demographic changes, with new urban centers emerging and smaller cities experiencing rapid growth. San Diego's metro area surpassed two million residents and had the highest proportion of college graduates among North American cities. Suburban areas near San Jose, Sacramento, and Riverside also grew quickly. By the late 1980s, major corporations had moved their headquarters to Southern California, marking the decline of San Francisco as the state's financial center.

California's population continued to grow rapidly throughout the 1980s, but by the early 1990s, a national economic recession impacted this growth. The U.S. government reduced defense spending, which affected the state's large aerospace and military industries. In addition, California faced a series of natural disasters, including floods, fires, droughts, and earthquakes, which diminished the state's appeal. However, by 1994, California began recovering economically, following the trend of the rest of the country.

This recovery was driven by the rise of the high-tech industry, which initially took hold in Silicon Valley and then spread across the state, and by the influx of highly educated workers from across the U.S. and other countries to fill jobs in this sector. This brought a more diverse and cosmopolitan population to California, with prosperity benefiting many, but also highlighting the growing divide between the wealthy and the working class, many of whom were immigrants.

California's diverse ethnic and racial makeup has often led to tensions. In the 19th century, Chinese immigrants faced discrimination, a trend that continued into the 20th century. Tensions grew as other ethnic groups settled in the state. During World War II, nearly 100,000 Japanese Americans, including many U.S. citizens, were placed in internment camps due to fears about their loyalty. In 1988, the U.S. government formally apologized and provided reparations to those affected. After World War II, the African American population in California grew significantly. The state saw significant riots in 1965 and 1992, the latter sparked by the acquittal of several white police officers in the beating of an African American motorist. Additionally, the large Hispanic population often faced difficult working conditions, and many were undocumented. In 1994, California voters approved Proposition 187, which aimed to deny social services to illegal immigrants, though the law was later overturned.

The political landscape in California has often been shaped by direct democracy, with the state seeing a significant increase in ballot initiatives since the 1960s on issues like healthcare, taxes, and the environment. In 2008, the California Supreme Court ruled to legalize same-sex marriage, only for voters to overturn the decision in November 2008 with the passage of Proposition 8, which banned same-sex marriage. After years of legal challenges, the California Supreme Court ultimately overturned Proposition 8 in 2013, declaring it unconstitutional.

California's economy was once again hit by a financial crisis in 2008-09, following the global economic downturn. Faced with a large budget deficit, Governor Arnold Schwarzenegger declared a fiscal emergency in December 2008. In May 2009, voters rejected most of the ballot measures aimed at addressing the budget crisis, further complicating the state's financial situation.

REGIONS

Shasta Cascade

North Coast

San Francisco Bay Area

Gold Country

Central Valley

High Sierra

Central Coast

Deserts

Los Angeles County

Orange County

Inland Empire

San Diego County

COUNTIES

CITIES

Crescent City

Alturas

Eureka
Redding
Red Bluff
Susanville
Chico
Mendocino
Healdsburg
Santa Sacramento
Rosa
Oakland
Stockton
San Francisco
Mariposa
San Jose
Modesto
Bishop
Santa Cruz
Furnace
Creek
Fresno
King City
San Simeon
Ridgecrest
San Luis Obispo
Bakersfield
Santa Maria
Pasadena
San Bernardino
Santa Barbara
Santa Monica
Riverside
Los Angeles
Palm
Springs
El Centro
San Diego

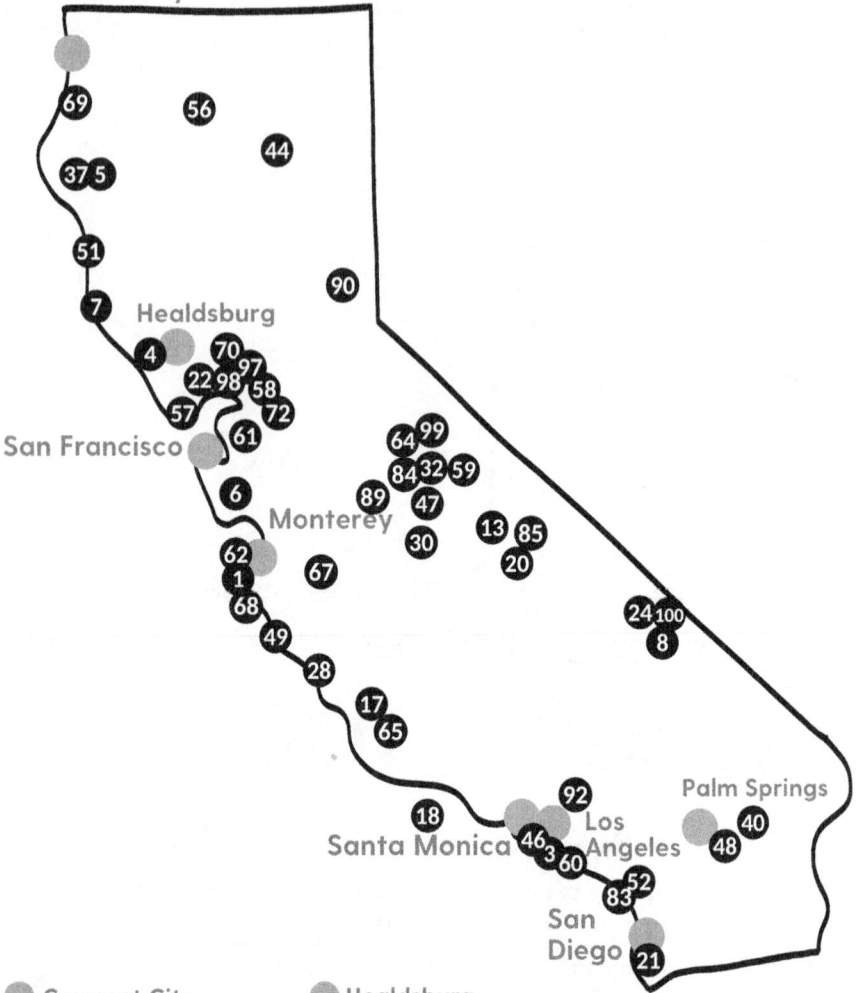

Crescent City

Healdsburg

San Francisco

Monterey

Los Angeles

Santa Monica

Palm Springs

San Diego

Crescent City
23 39 71 87

Healdsburg
31 35

Los Angeles
10 11 27 36 50 73 81 91 93 96

Monterey
25 54 55

Palm Springs
14 38 86

San Diego
9 12 16 26 41 42 74 75 76 82 88 94 95

San Francisco
2 15 19 29 33 34 43 45 53 63 66 77 78

Santa Monica
79 80

★The city where the place is located or the nearest city.

65 PCPA - Pacific Conservatory Theatre

66 Pier 39

67 Pinnacles National Park

68 Point Lobos

69 Prairie Creek Redwoods State Park

70 Pride Mountain Vineyards

71 Redwood National Park

72 Robert Biale Vineyards

73 Runyon Canyon Park

74 San Diego Harbor Cruise

75 San Diego Sand Castles

76 San Diego Zoo

77 San Francisco Bay

78 San Francisco Magic Theater at the Marrakech

79 Santa Monica Pier

80 Santa Monica State Beach

81 Scot Nery's Boobietrap

82 SeaWorld

83 Self Realization Fellowship Hermitage & Meditation Gardens

84 Sentinel Dome

85 Sequoia & Kings Canyon National Parks California

86 Smoke Tree Stables

87 Stout Grove

88 Sunset Cliffs Natural Park

89 Taft Point

90 Tahoe Treetop Adventure Parks

91 The Getty Center

92 The Huntington Library, Art Museum and Botanical Gardens

93 The Nethercutt Collection

94 Torrey Pines State Natural Reserve

95 USS Midway Museum

96 Venice Beach

97 VGS Chateau Potelle

98 Wellington Cellars

99 Yosemite National Park

100 Zabriskie Point

PLACE NAME	COUNTY	CITY	✓
17-Mile Drive	Monterey	Pebble Beach	
Alcatraz Island	San Francisco	San Francisco	
Aquarium Of The Pacific	Los Angeles	Long Beach	
Armstrong Redwoods State Natural Reserve	Sonoma	Guerneville	
Avenue of the Giants	Humboldt	Fortuna	
AxeVentures	Santa Clara	San Jose	
B Bryan Preserve	Mendocino	Point Arena	
Badwater	Inyo, San Bernardino	Furnace Creek	
Balboa Park	San Diego	San Diego	
Battleship USS Iowa Museum	Los Angeles	Los Angeles (San Pedro)	
Bhagavad-gita Diorama-Museum	Los Angeles	Los Angeles	
Black's Beach	San Diego	San Diego (La Jolla)	
Boyden Cavern	Fresno	Fresno	
Brandini Toffee	Riverside	Palm Springs	
Cable Car Museum	San Francisco	San Francisco	
Cabrillo National Monument	San Diego	San Diego	
Chamisal Vineyards	San Luis Obispo	San Luis Obispo	
Channel Islands National Park	Ventura	Ventura	
Club Fugazi	San Francisco	San Francisco	
Congress Trail	Tulare	Visalia	
Coronado Island	San Diego	Coronado	
Coursey Graves Estate Winery	Sonoma	Santa Rosa	
Crescent Trail Rides	Del Norte	Crescent City	
Death Valley National Park	Inyo, San Bernardino	Furnace Creek	
Discovery Whale Watch	Monterey	Monterey	
Escapology San Diego	San Diego	San Diego	
Fantastic Race	Los Angeles	Los Angeles	
Fiscalini Ranch Preserve	San Luis	Cambria	

★The city where the place is located or the nearest city.

PLACE NAME	COUNTY	CITY	✓
Fisherman's Wharf	San Francisco	San Francisco	
Forestiere Underground Gardens	Fresno	Fresno	
Gary Farrell Winery	Sonoma	Healdsburg	
Glacier Point	Mariposa	Mariposa	
Golden Gate Bridge	San Francisco	San Francisco	
Golden Gate Park	San Francisco	San Francisco	
Gracianna Winery	Sonoma	Healdsburg	
Griffith Observatory	Los Angeles	Los Angeles	
Humboldt Redwoods State Park	Humboldt	Garberville	
Indian Canyons	Riverside	Palm Springs	
Jedediah Smith Redwoods State Park	Del Norte	Crescent City	
Joshua Tree National Park	San Bernardino	Twentynine Palms	
La Jolla Cove	San Diego	San Diego (La Jolla)	
La Jolla Sea Cave Kayaks	San Diego	San Diego (La Jolla)	
Lands End	San Francisco	San Francisco	
Lassen Volcanic National Park	Tehama	Mineral	
Lombard Street	San Francisco	San Francisco	
Manhattan Beach	Los Angeles	Manhattan Beach	
Mariposa Grove of Giant Sequoias	Mariposa	Mariposa	
Marvyn's Magic Theater	Riverside	La Quinta	
McWay Falls	Monterey, San Luis Obispo	Big Sur	
Medieval Torture Museum	Los Angeles	Los Angeles	
Mendocino Coast	Mendocino	Mendocino	
Miniature Engineering Craftsmanship Museum (MECM)	San Diego	Carlsbad	
Misalignment Museum	San Francisco	San Francisco	
Monterey Bay Aquarium	Monterey	Monterey	
Monterey Bay Whale Watch	Monterey	Monterey	
Mount Shasta	Siskiyou	Mount Shasta	

★The city where the place is located or the nearest city.

PLACE NAME	COUNTY	CITY	✓
Muir Woods National Monument	Marin	Mill Valley	
Napa Valley Balloons	Napa	Yountville	
Nevada Falls Loop	Mariposa	Mariposa	
Newport Beach	Orange	Newport Beach	
Oakland California Temple & Visitors' Center	Alameda	Oakland	
Pacific Grove Oceanview Boulevard	Monterey	Pacific Grove	
Palace Games	San Francisco	San Francisco	
Panorama Trail	Mariposa	Mariposa	
PCPA - Pacific Conservatory Theatre	Santa Barbara	Santa Maria	
Pier 39	San Francisco	San Francisco	
Pinnacles National Park	San Benito	Paicines	
Point Lobos	Monterey	Carmel-by-the-Sea	
Prairie Creek Redwoods State Park	Humboldt	Orick	
Pride Mountain Vineyards	Napa	St. Helena	
Redwood National Park	Del Norte, Humboldt	Crescent City	
Robert Biale Vineyards	Napa	Napa	
Runyon Canyon Park	Los Angeles	Los Angeles	
San Diego Harbor Cruise	San Diego	San Diego	
San Diego Sand Castles	San Diego	San Diego	
San Diego Zoo	San Diego	San Diego	
San Francisco Bay	San Francisco	San Francisco	
San Francisco Magic Theater at the Marrakech	San Francisco	San Francisco	
Santa Monica Pier	Los Angeles	Santa Monica	
Santa Monica State Beach	Los Angeles	Santa Monica	
Scot Nery's Boobietrap	Los Angeles	Los Angeles	
SeaWorld	San Diego	San Diego	
Self Realization Fellowship Hermitage & Meditation Gardens	San Diego	Encinitas	
Sentinel Dome	Mariposa	Mariposa	

★ *The city where the place is located or the nearest city.*

PLACE NAME	COUNTY	CITY	✓
Sequoia & Kings Canyon National Parks California	Tulare	Three Rivers	
Smoke Tree Stables	Riverside	Palm Springs	
Stout Grove	Del Norte	Crescent City	
Sunset Cliffs Natural Park	San Diego	San Diego	
Taft Point	Mariposa	Mariposa	
Tahoe Treetop Adventure Parks	Placer	Tahoe City	
The Getty Center	Los Angeles	Los Angeles	
The Huntington Library, Art Museum and Botanical Gardens	Los Angeles	San Marino	
The Nethercutt Collection	Los Angeles	Los Angeles (Sylmar)	
Torrey Pines State Natural Reserve	San Diego	San Diego	
USS Midway Museum	San Diego	San Diego	
Venice Beach	Los Angeles	Los Angeles (Venice)	
VGS Chateau Potelle	Napa	St. Helena	
Wellington Cellars	Sonoma	Glen Ellen	
Yosemite National Park	Mariposa	Mariposa	
Zabriskie Point	Inyo, San Bernardino	Furnace Creek	

★The city where the place is located or the nearest city.

COUNTY	CITY	PLACE NAME	✓
Alameda	Oakland	Oakland California Temple & Visitors' Center	
Del Norte	Crescent City	Crescent Trail Rides	
Del Norte	Crescent City	Jedediah Smith Redwoods State Park	
Del Norte	Crescent City	Stout Grove	
Del Norte, Humboldt	Crescent City	Redwood National Park	
Fresno	Fresno	Boyden Cavern	
Fresno	Fresno	Forestiere Underground Gardens	
Humboldt	Fortuna	Avenue of the Giants	
Humboldt	Garberville	Humboldt Redwoods State Park	
Humboldt	Orick	Prairie Creek Redwoods State Park	
Inyo, San Bernardino	Furnace Creek	Badwater	
Inyo, San Bernardino	Furnace Creek	Death Valley National Park	
Inyo, San Bernardino	Furnace Creek	Zabriskie Point	
Los Angeles	Long Beach	Aquarium Of The Pacific	
Los Angeles	Los Angeles (San Pedro)	Battleship USS Iowa Museum	
Los Angeles	Los Angeles	Bhagavad-gita Diorama-Museum	
Los Angeles	Los Angeles	Fantastic Race	
Los Angeles	Los Angeles	Griffith Observatory	
Los Angeles	Manhattan Beach	Manhattan Beach	
Los Angeles	Los Angeles	Medieval Torture Museum	
Los Angeles	Los Angeles	Runyon Canyon Park	
Los Angeles	Santa Monica	Santa Monica Pier	
Los Angeles	Santa Monica	Santa Monica State Beach	
Los Angeles	Los Angeles	Scot Nery's Boobietrap	
Los Angeles	Los Angeles	The Getty Center	
Los Angeles	San Marino	The Huntington Library, Art Museum and Botanical Gardens	
Los Angeles	Los Angeles (Sylmar)	The Nethercutt Collection	
Los Angeles	Los Angeles (Venice)	Venice Beach	

★The city where the place is located or the nearest city.

COUNTY	CITY	PLACE NAME	✓
Marin	Mill Valley	Muir Woods National Monument	
Mariposa	Mariposa	Glacier Point	
Mariposa	Mariposa	Mariposa Grove of Giant Sequoias	
Mariposa	Mariposa	Nevada Falls Loop	
Mariposa	Mariposa	Panorama Trail	
Mariposa	Mariposa	Sentinel Dome	
Mariposa	Mariposa	Taft Point	
Mariposa	Mariposa	Yosemite National Park	
Mendocino	Point Arena	B Bryan Preserve	
Mendocino	Mendocino	Mendocino Coast	
Monterey	Pebble Beach	17-Mile Drive	
Monterey	Monterey	Discovery Whale Watch	
Monterey	Monterey	Monterey Bay Aquarium	
Monterey	Monterey	Monterey Bay Whale Watch	
Monterey	Pacific Grove	Pacific Grove Oceanview Boulevard	
Monterey	Carmel-by-the-Sea	Point Lobos	
Monterey, San Luis Obispo	Big Sur	McWay Falls	
Napa	Yountville	Napa Valley Balloons	
Napa	St. Helena	Pride Mountain Vineyards	
Napa	Napa	Robert Biale Vineyards	
Napa	St. Helena	VGS Chateau Potelle	
Orange	Newport Beach	Newport Beach	
Placer	Tahoe City	Tahoe Treetop Adventure Parks	
Riverside	Palm Springs	Brandini Toffee	
Riverside	Palm Springs	Indian Canyons	
Riverside	La Quinta	Marvyn's Magic Theater	
Riverside	Palm Springs	Smoke Tree Stables	
San Benito	Paicines	Pinnacles National Park	

★The city where the place is located or the nearest city.

COUNTY	CITY	PLACE NAME	✓
San Bernardino	Twentynine Palms	Joshua Tree National Park	
San Diego	San Diego	Balboa Park	
San Diego	San Diego (La Jolla)	Black's Beach	
San Diego	San Diego	Cabrillo National Monument	
San Diego	Coronado	Coronado Island	
San Diego	San Diego	Escapology San Diego	
San Diego	San Diego (La Jolla)	La Jolla Cove	
San Diego	San Diego (La Jolla)	La Jolla Sea Cave Kayaks	
San Diego	Carlsbad	Miniature Engineering Craftsmanship Museum (MECM)	
San Diego	San Diego	San Diego Harbor Cruise	
San Diego	San Diego	San Diego Sand Castles	
San Diego	San Diego	San Diego Zoo	
San Diego	San Diego	SeaWorld	
San Diego	Encinitas	Self Realization Fellowship Hermitage & Meditation Gardens	
San Diego	San Diego	Sunset Cliffs Natural Park	
San Diego	San Diego	Torrey Pines State Natural Reserve	
San Diego	San Diego	USS Midway Museum	
San Francisco	San Francisco	Alcatraz Island	
San Francisco	San Francisco	Cable Car Museum	
San Francisco	San Francisco	Club Fugazi	
San Francisco	San Francisco	Fisherman's Wharf	
San Francisco	San Francisco	Golden Gate Bridge	
San Francisco	San Francisco	Golden Gate Park	
San Francisco	San Francisco	Lands End	
San Francisco	San Francisco	Lombard Street	
San Francisco	San Francisco	Misalignment Museum	
San Francisco	San Francisco	Palace Games	
San Francisco	San Francisco	Pier 39	

★The city where the place is located or the nearest city.

COUNTY	CITY	PLACE NAME	✓
San Francisco	San Francisco	San Francisco Bay	
San Francisco	San Francisco	San Francisco Magic Theater at the Marrakech	
San Luis	Cambria	Fiscalini Ranch Preserve	
San Luis Obispo	San Luis Obispo	Chamisal Vineyards	
Santa Barbara	Santa Maria	PCPA - Pacific Conservatory Theatre	
Santa Clara	San Jose	AxeVentures	
Siskiyou	Mount Shasta	Mount Shasta	
Sonoma	Guerneville	Armstrong Redwoods State Natural Reserve	
Sonoma	Santa Rosa	Coursey Graves Estate Winery	
Sonoma	Healdsburg	Gary Farrell Winery	
Sonoma	Healdsburg	Gracianna Winery	
Sonoma	Glen Ellen	Wellington Cellars	
Tehama	Mineral	Lassen Volcanic National Park	
Tulare	Visalia	Congress Trail	
Tulare	Three Rivers	Sequoia & Kings Canyon National Parks California	
Ventura	Ventura	Channel Islands National Park	

*The city where the place is located or the nearest city.

17-MILE DRIVE

COUNTY: MONTEREY   **CITY:** PEBBLE BEACH

DATE VISITED: **WHO I WENT WITH:**

RATING: ☆ ☆ ☆ ☆ ☆   **WILL I RETURN?** YES / NO

17-Mile Drive
Pebble Beach, CA 93953
800-877-0597

17-Mile Drive, located on the breathtaking Monterey Peninsula, is one of California's most iconic scenic routes. This 17-mile stretch weaves through the exclusive Pebble Beach community, offering a mix of rugged coastlines, enchanting forests, and glimpses of luxurious estates. A drive along this route promises an unforgettable journey through some of the most picturesque landscapes in the state. Visitors can start their journey from one of five entrance gates, paying a small toll to access this private roadway. Along the way, they are treated to stunning ocean views, windswept beaches, and natural landmarks that highlight the area's unique geography and history.

One of the most famous sights is the Lone Cypress, a 250-year-old tree perched dramatically on a rocky outcrop above the crashing waves. This tree has become a symbol of resilience and a widely recognized icon of Pebble Beach. Another notable attraction is Pebble Beach Golf Links, one of the world's premier golf courses, renowned for its challenging design and breathtaking coastal scenery. Wildlife enthusiasts will enjoy Bird Rock, a lively habitat for seals, sea lions, and various seabirds, while Spanish Bay offers a tranquil coastal landscape rich with history, named after the Spanish explorers who camped in the area centuries ago. Fanshell Overlook provides incredible views of white sandy beaches and is home to seals during birthing season in the spring. As the drive continues, travelers pass through Del Monte Forest, a serene enclave of towering Monterey pines and cypress trees that contrasts beautifully with the dramatic ocean vistas.

The drive is best experienced over a leisurely two to three hours, allowing visitors to fully appreciate the scenery and landmarks. Maps are provided at the gates to help navigate the 17 designated stops along the way. Travelers are encouraged to bring cameras to capture the spectacular views and binoculars for a closer look at the abundant wildlife. Dining options in Pebble Beach, such as The Bench or Stillwater Bar & Grill, offer a chance to enjoy a delicious meal with equally stunning views. Access to 17-Mile Drive is year-round, with spring and summer being the most popular times to visit. The route is easily accessible from Pacific Grove, Carmel-by-the-Sea, or Highway 1, and parking is available at many stops.

Whether exploring by car or bicycle, 17-Mile Drive is a journey that immerses travelers in the beauty of California's coastline, blending natural splendor with historical significance. From the dramatic waves crashing against rocky shores to the peaceful serenity of Del Monte Forest, this iconic drive is an experience that leaves a lasting impression.

ALCATRAZ ISLAND

COUNTY: SAN FRANCISCO   **CITY:** SAN FRANCISCO

DATE VISITED: **WHO I WENT WITH:**

RATING: ☆ ☆ ☆ ☆ ☆   **WILL I RETURN?** YES / NO

Alcatraz Island
San Francisco Bay, CA 94133
415-561-4900

Alcatraz Island, located in San Francisco Bay, is one of California's most iconic and historically significant landmarks. Just over a mile from the shores of San Francisco, the island is best known as the site of the infamous Alcatraz Federal Penitentiary, which housed some of America's most notorious criminals. Today, Alcatraz is part of the Golden Gate National Recreation Area and serves as a major tourist attraction, drawing visitors from around the world to explore its storied past and stunning natural surroundings.

The island's history stretches far beyond its days as a prison. Originally home to a lighthouse and later a military fortification, Alcatraz evolved into a federal penitentiary in 1934. Over nearly three decades, it held notorious inmates such as Al Capone, George "Machine Gun" Kelly, and Robert Stroud, known as the "Birdman of Alcatraz." Visitors can tour the remnants of the prison, including the stark cell blocks, solitary confinement cells, and the warden's office, while listening to captivating audio guides that bring the stories of former inmates and guards to life. The tales of daring escape attempts and daily prison life provide a haunting yet fascinating glimpse into the island's darker days.

Alcatraz also played a pivotal role in the Native American Red Power movement. In 1969, a group of Native American activists occupied the island for 19 months in a powerful protest to reclaim indigenous lands, leaving a legacy that is still celebrated today. The island's history is richly layered, offering insights into various eras of American history and culture.

In addition to its historical significance, Alcatraz Island boasts remarkable natural beauty. Surrounded by the sparkling waters of San Francisco Bay, the island offers panoramic views of the city skyline, the Golden Gate Bridge, and Marin County. Its rugged terrain is home to vibrant gardens and diverse wildlife, including seabirds such as cormorants and gulls. Guided tours and walking trails allow visitors to explore both the historic ruins and the natural landscapes at their own pace.

Access to Alcatraz Island is available via ferry from San Francisco's Pier 33, operated by Alcatraz Cruises. Tickets should be purchased in advance, as this popular destination often sells out, especially during peak travel seasons. The ferry ride itself is a memorable experience, offering picturesque views of the bay and a sense of anticipation as the imposing island comes into view.

Alcatraz Island is more than just a former prison—it's a place where history, culture, and nature converge. Whether you're captivated by its tales of infamous inmates, inspired by its role in social justice movements, or drawn to its rugged beauty, a visit to Alcatraz is a deeply immersive experience that leaves a lasting impression.

AQUARIUM OF THE PACIFIC

3

COUNTY: LOS ANGELES   **CITY:** LONG BEACH

DATE VISITED: _____   **WHO I WENT WITH:** _____

RATING: ☆ ☆ ☆ ☆ ☆   **WILL I RETURN?** YES / NO

100 Aquarium Way
Long Beach, CA 90802
562-590-3100

The Aquarium of the Pacific, located in Long Beach, California, is one of the largest and most diverse aquariums in the United States, offering visitors an incredible opportunity to explore the ocean's rich ecosystems and marine life. Situated on the beautiful waterfront of Long Beach, this popular attraction is dedicated to the conservation of ocean habitats and is an essential educational resource for ocean lovers and families alike.

The aquarium is home to more than 11,000 animals representing over 500 species from the Pacific Ocean, making it a must-visit destination for marine life enthusiasts. It features a variety of exhibits that showcase the diverse ecosystems found in the Pacific Ocean, from the chilly waters of the Alaska and Northern Pacific regions to the vibrant coral reefs of the Tropical Pacific and the deep sea. Visitors can explore interactive and immersive exhibits that take them on a journey through various aquatic environments, giving them the chance to see the stunning variety of marine life up close.

One of the aquarium's most popular exhibits is the Shark Lagoon, where visitors can see different species of sharks, rays, and other fascinating creatures of the deep. The lagoon is home to species like the Blacktip Reef Shark, the Leopard Shark, and the graceful Bat Rays, all swimming in a large, open-air habitat. Guests can even touch some of the creatures, such as rays and small sharks, in the interactive touch tanks, which adds an exciting hands-on element to the experience.

Another standout feature of the Aquarium of the Pacific is the Penguin Habitat, where visitors can observe a group of Magellanic Penguins. These playful and charismatic birds can often be seen waddling around, swimming, and interacting with one another. The exhibit is designed to replicate the penguins' natural environment, providing them with space to thrive while offering a unique chance to see these fascinating creatures in action.

For those interested in the more majestic creatures of the ocean, the aquarium's

Whale and Dolphin Exhibit is a must-see. This exhibit highlights the migration patterns and behaviors of marine mammals, and although you can't see whales and dolphins in the tanks, there are numerous informational displays, videos, and live feedings that showcase their fascinating lives in the wild. The aquarium also offers several live shows and programs, including special presentations about marine mammal conservation, giving guests a deeper understanding of the challenges faced by these incredible animals.

The aquarium's Tropical Pacific Gallery is another highlight, where guests can marvel at colorful coral reefs, see playful sea otters, and learn about the diverse species that inhabit the warm waters of the Pacific. The gallery features stunning, large-scale tanks filled with vibrant schools of fish, sea turtles, and other exotic marine life. The lush, beautiful coral environments and the varied colors and textures of the fish are not only visually captivating but also serve as an important reminder of the fragility of marine ecosystems.

In addition to its exhibits, the Aquarium of the Pacific offers numerous educational programs and activities designed to engage visitors of all ages. The Ocean Science Center offers hands-on science demonstrations and allows guests to participate in activities related to marine research, conservation, and oceanography. Children will love the interactive learning opportunities, including the Play Area where they can explore the world of tide pools, touch starfish and sea anemones, and learn about the delicate balance of marine ecosystems.

For those seeking an even more immersive experience, the aquarium offers behind-the-scenes tours and sleepovers, where visitors can explore areas not normally open to the public, observe feeding times, and interact with aquarists. The aquarium also hosts special events and temporary exhibits, often highlighting current conservation efforts or bringing attention to under-explored areas of the ocean.

The Aquarium of the Pacific is not just a place to admire marine creatures; it is a hub for conservation efforts, research, and public education. The aquarium plays a crucial role in marine animal rescue, rehabilitation, and research, and it is actively involved in global efforts to protect ocean habitats. Visitors can learn about the aquarium's role in these efforts through the many informational displays, videos, and programs focused on sustainability, climate change, and ocean conservation.
The aquarium's gift shop offers a wide range of ocean-themed merchandise, including toys, books, and eco-friendly products, making it a perfect place to pick up a unique souvenir. After visiting the exhibits, guests can relax at one of the aquarium's many cafes or restaurants, offering a selection of locally sourced,

sustainable food options with beautiful views of the harbor.

Whether you're a family with young children, a student eager to learn more about marine biology, or simply someone who loves the ocean, the Aquarium of the Pacific offers an unforgettable experience that combines entertainment, education, and conservation. It's a fantastic way to connect with the wonders of the ocean and become inspired to protect its delicate ecosystems. With its engaging exhibits, hands-on activities, and dedication to marine life conservation, the aquarium provides a truly immersive experience that fosters a deeper understanding and appreciation of the Pacific Ocean and its inhabitants.

4

ARMSTRONG REDWOODS STATE NATURAL RESERVE

COUNTY: SONOMA   **CITY:** GUERNEVILLE

DATE VISITED: **WHO I WENT WITH:**

RATING: ☆ ☆ ☆ ☆ ☆   **WILL I RETURN?** YES / NO

17000 Armstrong Woods Rd
Guerneville, CA 95446
707-869-2015

Armstrong Redwoods State Natural Reserve, located near the charming town of Guerneville in Sonoma County, California, is a serene and awe-inspiring destination that showcases the majestic beauty of coastal redwood trees. This ancient forest provides visitors with a tranquil escape into nature, where towering giants, some over 1,400 years old, stand as a testament to the resilience and grandeur of these magnificent trees.

The reserve is home to some of the tallest and oldest trees on Earth, including the Parson Jones Tree, which rises over 310 feet, and the Colonel Armstrong Tree, estimated to be more than 1,400 years old. Walking among these towering redwoods, with their thick trunks and sprawling canopies, offers a humbling reminder of nature's enduring power. The cool, shaded atmosphere of the forest, combined with the rich, earthy scent of redwood trees, creates a peaceful environment perfect for relaxation and reflection.

Armstrong Redwoods features well-maintained trails suitable for all skill levels, making it an ideal destination for hikers, families, and nature enthusiasts. The Discovery Trail, a flat and accessible path, leads visitors to some of the reserve's most iconic trees, while the Pioneer Nature Trail provides an easy loop through the heart of the forest. For those seeking more adventure, nearby trails extend into the surrounding Austin Creek State Recreation Area, offering opportunities for longer hikes and panoramic views.

The reserve also provides picnic areas and interpretive displays, where visitors can learn about the ecological significance of redwoods and the conservation efforts that have protected these trees for generations. Guided tours and educational programs further enhance the experience, making Armstrong Redwoods an excellent destination for both recreation and learning.

Located just a short drive from Sonoma County's wine country and about 75 miles north of San Francisco, Armstrong Redwoods is easily accessible for day trips or weekend getaways. Parking is available for a small fee, with free entry for those walking or biking into the reserve. Early morning and late afternoon visits are recommended for the most serene experience and to capture the magical light filtering through the forest canopy.

Whether you're marveling at the ancient giants, enjoying a leisurely hike, or simply soaking in the peace of the redwood grove, Armstrong Redwoods State Natural Reserve offers a truly unforgettable encounter with one of California's most cherished natural wonders. It's a place where the timeless beauty of the redwoods inspires awe and a deep appreciation for the natural world.

----

⑤ AVENUE OF THE GIANTS

COUNTY: HUMBOLDT   **CITY:** FORTUNA

DATE VISITED: _____   **WHO I WENT WITH:** _____

RATING: ☆ ☆ ☆ ☆ ☆   **WILL I RETURN?** YES / NO

Avenue of the Giants,
CA 95571

Avenue of the Giants, located in Humboldt County, California, is one of the most scenic drives in the United States, offering a breathtaking journey through towering old-growth redwood forests. This 31-mile stretch of Highway 254 winds through the heart of Humboldt Redwoods State Park, showcasing some of the tallest and oldest trees on Earth. As visitors drive along this magnificent route, they are treated to awe-inspiring views of the ancient redwood trees, some of which stand over 350 feet tall and are over 2,000 years old. The Avenue of the Giants is not only a visual masterpiece but also a testament to the power of nature and the importance of preserving these natural wonders.

The drive itself is an unforgettable experience, with the towering trees creating a canopy of green above, casting dappled sunlight onto the road below. The majestic redwoods, with their thick trunks and lush foliage, provide a sense of wonder and serenity, making it feel like a journey into another world. Along the way, visitors can stop at various points of interest, including scenic pullouts, hiking trails, and interpretive signs that offer information about the ecology and history of the redwood forests.

One of the most popular stops along the Avenue of the Giants is the Immortal Tree, a 1,000-year-old redwood that survived a lightning strike and continues to stand tall. Another must-see is the Tree Farm, where you can drive through a massive fallen tree trunk, offering a truly unique experience. For those interested in learning more about the redwoods, the Visitor Center near the Humboldt Redwoods State Park headquarters offers exhibits, maps, and helpful staff to guide you on your adventure.

Outdoor enthusiasts will find plenty of opportunities to explore the area on foot, with numerous hiking trails that wind through the ancient forest. The Avenue of the Giants Trail, for example, is an easy, paved path that allows visitors to walk beneath the towering trees, while the more challenging Bull Creek Flats Trail takes hikers deeper into the wilderness. These trails provide an up-close look at the incredible biodiversity of the region, including ferns, moss, and a variety of wildlife.

The Avenue of the Giants is easily accessible from nearby towns such as Garberville and Scotia, making it a popular stop for visitors traveling through Northern California's Humboldt County. It is particularly enchanting in the early morning or late afternoon when the light filters through the trees, creating a magical atmosphere. The drive is also an excellent way to experience the beauty of California's North Coast, offering both scenic beauty and an educational journey through one of the most impressive ecosystems in the world.

Avenue of the Giants is a must-visit for nature lovers, families, and anyone looking to experience the majestic beauty of California's redwood forests. Whether you're driving through, hiking the trails, or simply pausing to marvel at the towering trees, it's an experience that leaves a lasting impression, reminding visitors of the ancient and timeless power of nature.

6

AXEVENTURES

COUNTY: SANTA CLARA   **CITY:** SAN JOSE

DATE VISITED:	WHO I WENT WITH:

RATING: ☆ ☆ ☆ ☆ ☆	WILL I RETURN? YES / NO

850 Park Ave.
San Jose, CA 95126
408-477-2609

AxeVentures, located in the heart of California, offers an exciting and unique experience for those looking to try their hand at axe throwing in a fun and safe environment. This entertainment venue, with locations in cities like Anaheim and nearby areas, provides an adrenaline-pumping activity that is perfect for groups, families, corporate team-building events, and anyone looking to try something new. Axe throwing has become a popular trend in recent years, combining skill, strategy, and a bit of friendly competition. At AxeVentures, guests can enjoy this growing sport in a welcoming atmosphere, guided by expert instructors who ensure safety while helping everyone improve their throwing technique.

The venue features a variety of lanes where guests can practice their aim, compete in games, and take part in tournaments. Whether you're a first-time thrower or an experienced enthusiast, AxeVentures caters to all skill levels, offering a range of fun games and challenges that make the experience both thrilling and social. The venue's friendly staff is always on hand to offer tips and encourage guests to hit the bullseye, adding an extra layer of excitement to the activity. AxeVentures also offers customizable packages for special occasions such as birthdays, bachelor and bachelorette parties, or corporate events. Guests can reserve private lanes, enjoy exclusive access to the venue, and even arrange for catering and beverages, creating a memorable and enjoyable experience for everyone involved. For those new to axe throwing, AxeVentures provides detailed safety instructions before guests begin, ensuring a responsible and enjoyable experience. The staff emphasizes the importance of safety throughout the event, giving everyone peace of mind as they engage in this thrilling activity. Located in a lively area with a range of nearby dining and entertainment options,

AxeVentures is the perfect spot for an evening of fun and bonding. It's a great way to break away from traditional nightlife activities and try something that combines physical activity with social interaction. Whether you're looking to challenge friends, celebrate a special event, or simply try something out of the ordinary, AxeVentures offers an unforgettable experience that guarantees laughs, competition, and a whole lot of fun.

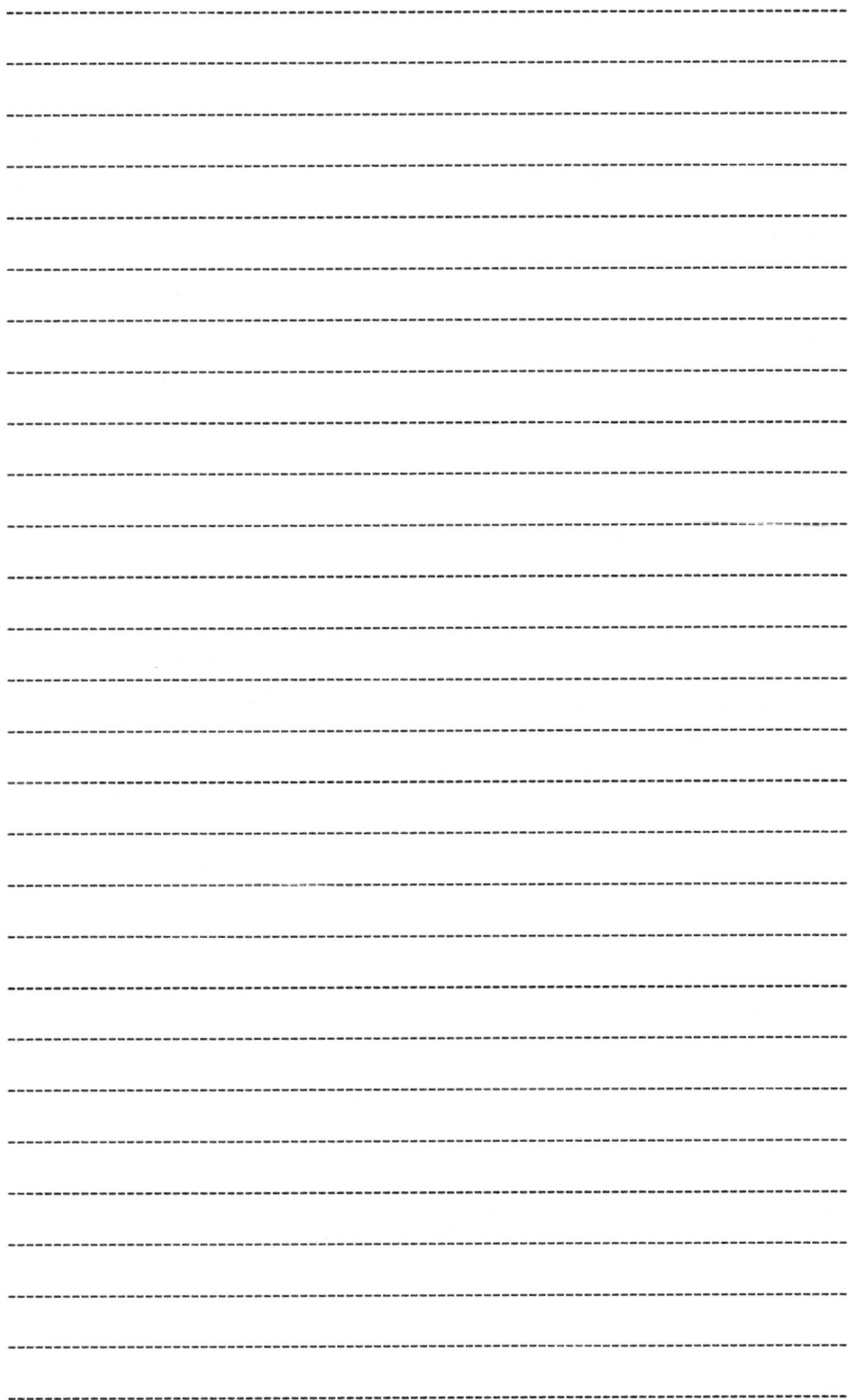

7

B BRYAN PRESERVE

COUNTY: MENDOCINO   **CITY:** POINT ARENA

DATE VISITED: **WHO I WENT WITH:**

RATING: ☆ ☆ ☆ ☆ ☆   **WILL I RETURN?**   YES / NO

130 Riverside Dr
Point Arena, CA 95468
707-882-2297

B Bryan Preserve, located in the scenic coastal town of Point Arena, California, is a unique and exciting wildlife sanctuary dedicated to the preservation of endangered African species, particularly zebras, antelopes, and giraffes. This privately-owned preserve offers visitors the rare opportunity to get up close and personal with some of the most majestic and endangered animals on the planet, all while learning about conservation efforts and the vital role these creatures play in our ecosystems.

Spanning over 1,000 acres of natural, rolling hills and lush grasslands, B Bryan Preserve provides a safe and spacious environment where animals roam freely. The preserve specializes in breeding and protecting endangered species, with a focus on rare African animals that are threatened in the wild due to habitat loss and poaching. The sanctuary is home to various species of antelope, including the Bongo and Greater Kudu, along with several species of zebra, such as the Grevy's zebra, and giraffes, which are some of the most iconic animals on the preserve.

Visitors to B Bryan Preserve can enjoy guided tours led by knowledgeable staff who share fascinating insights into the animals' behavior, history, and conservation efforts. The tours often include a chance to observe the animals in their natural habitat, offering a rare glimpse into their daily lives and interactions. As you walk or drive through the preserve, you'll be surrounded by stunning views of the countryside and wildlife, providing an immersive and educational experience.

In addition to its wildlife tours, B Bryan Preserve offers guests the chance to participate in special programs such as private tours, wildlife photography sessions, and even opportunities to feed and interact with certain animals under the supervision of staff. The preserve is particularly popular for educational field trips, as it offers a hands-on way for students and nature enthusiasts to learn about endangered species and conservation practices.

B Bryan Preserve is open by appointment only, ensuring a more intimate and personal experience for visitors. It is located just a short drive from the Pacific coast, making it an excellent stop for those traveling along California's scenic Highway 1. With its commitment to wildlife conservation, B Bryan Preserve offers a meaningful and unforgettable experience that not only showcases the beauty of African animals but also raises awareness about the importance of protecting these species for future generations.

For those looking to support the preserve's efforts, donations and membership programs are available, allowing individuals to contribute directly to the sanctuary's mission and the ongoing protection of endangered animals. Whether you're an animal lover, a photographer, or simply someone seeking a unique adventure, B Bryan Preserve offers a remarkable and enriching experience that connects visitors to nature in a deeply meaningful way.

8

BADWATER

COUNTY: INYO, SAN BERNARDINO   **CITY:** FURNACE CREEK

DATE VISITED: **WHO I WENT WITH:**

RATING: ☆ ☆ ☆ ☆ ☆   **WILL I RETURN?**   YES / NO

Badwater Rd. 19 mi south of Furnace Creek
Death Valley National Park, CA 92328
760-786-3200

Badwater Basin, located in Death Valley National Park, California, is one of the most unique and extreme natural features in the United States. Situated at 282 feet below sea level, it is the lowest point in North America, making it a significant geographical landmark. This extraordinary location in the Mojave Desert offers visitors a surreal landscape, marked by vast salt flats, an almost otherworldly stillness, and unparalleled views that stretch out to the distant mountains. Its extreme conditions and stunning beauty attract photographers, adventurers, and nature lovers from all over the world, making it a must-see destination for those exploring Death Valley.

The name "Badwater" is derived from the area's salty water, which is located in a small pool near the basin. Early travelers who encountered the water found it undrinkable due to its high salinity, leading to the "bad water" reference. This pool, however, is just a small feature of the larger Badwater Basin, which spans an expansive 200 square miles. The salt flats that cover the basin are the remnants of an ancient lake that once occupied much of Death Valley millions of years ago. As the lake dried up over time, the minerals and salts it contained were left behind, creating the distinctive salt crusts that cover the basin today.

Visitors to Badwater Basin are greeted by a stark, flat expanse that is often described as both beautiful and desolate. The ground is covered in salt polygons, creating a cracked surface that adds to the basin's otherworldly feel. The salt formations shimmer in the heat of the day, creating a shimmering mirage effect, especially in the late morning and afternoon hours. This unique salt crust is a testament to the extreme climate of Death Valley, which is known for its scorching summer temperatures that can exceed 120°F (49°C), making it one of the hottest places on Earth.

Badwater Basin is not just a place of striking natural beauty; it is also an important spot for those interested in the history and ecology of Death Valley National Park. The basin is located along the Badwater Road, which is one of the park's main thoroughfares, providing easy access to this remarkable site. Visitors can walk along a boardwalk and view the salt flats up close, or they can venture out onto the flats themselves, but it's essential to keep in mind the extreme desert conditions. Even during cooler months, visitors should bring plenty of water, wear sun protection, and be prepared for the rugged, desert terrain.

For those interested in exploring the area more thoroughly, the Badwater Basin Trail offers a chance to experience the basin's vastness firsthand. This trail is short but takes visitors onto the salt flats themselves, offering a sense of isolation and tranquility that is hard to find anywhere else. The journey across the salt crust is mesmerizing, and as you walk, you may feel as though you are traveling across a vast, white ocean with no clear destination. This immense open space allows for a sense of awe and reflection, as the overwhelming landscape makes visitors feel small in comparison to the natural world around them.

From Badwater Basin, visitors also get a fantastic view of the surrounding Black Mountains and the Panamint Range, including Mount Whitney, the highest peak in the contiguous United States, visible in the distance. This contrast between the lowest and highest points in the contiguous U.S. is one of the striking aspects of Death Valley. The vast distance between these two extremes highlights the park's incredible geological diversity.

While Badwater Basin is famous for its extreme conditions and desolate beauty, it is also home to some surprising and resilient wildlife. Despite the harsh environment, the basin and surrounding areas support a range of desert-adapted species, including creosote bushes, desert cacti, and small mammals like kangaroo rats and bats. Birdwatchers may spot species such as black-necked stilts and sandpipers near the pools that form around Badwater when rare rainfall occurs. During wetter years, a temporary phenomenon called the "Badwater Basin bloom" takes place, with wildflowers blooming across the basin's salty floor, adding a brief burst of color to the otherwise stark white landscape.

In addition to its natural beauty, Badwater Basin holds cultural significance. The area has long been a part of Native American lands, and the surrounding Amargosa and Timbisha tribes have a deep cultural connection to the land. The area has also been a key site for early explorers and settlers who braved the treacherous terrain of Death Valley. Despite the inhospitable conditions, people have managed to survive in the valley for thousands of years, and their stories are woven into the rich history of the region.

For those planning to visit Badwater Basin, the best times to go are typically during the cooler months, from October to April, as temperatures in the summer can be dangerously high. The basin is most striking during sunrise or sunset when the soft light casts a warm glow over the salt flats, enhancing the textures of the landscape. Photographers will find this to be the ideal time to capture the unique features of the area. Even at these cooler times, visitors should prepare for the extreme environment by bringing plenty of water, wearing a hat, and dressing in layers to protect against the sun's intense rays.

In conclusion, Badwater Basin is a must-visit destination for anyone traveling to Death Valley National Park. Its combination of stunning landscapes, extreme geography, and rich natural and cultural history make it one of the park's most iconic features. Whether you're exploring the salt flats up close, taking in the panoramic views, or simply reflecting on the stark beauty of the landscape, Badwater Basin provides a truly unforgettable experience that showcases the incredible power and resilience of nature.

BALBOA PARK

9

COUNTY: SAN DIEGO

CITY: SAN DIEGO

DATE VISITED:

WHO I WENT WITH:

RATING: ☆ ☆ ☆ ☆ ☆

WILL I RETURN? YES / NO

1549 El Prado
San Diego, CA 92101

Balboa Park, located in the heart of San Diego, California, is a cultural gem that offers visitors a rich blend of history, nature, and world-class attractions. Spanning over 1,200 acres, it is one of the largest urban parks in the United States and is often referred to as San Diego's cultural hub. Home to 17 museums, beautiful gardens, theaters, and the world-renowned San Diego Zoo, Balboa Park is a must-visit destination for anyone exploring the city.

The park's stunning architecture is a highlight, featuring Spanish-Renaissance style buildings that were constructed for the 1915 Panama-California Exposition. These historic structures, with their intricate facades and tiled arches, add a sense of grandeur to the park and provide a picturesque backdrop for visitors. As you stroll through the park, you'll encounter vibrant courtyards, fountains, and palm-lined promenades that invite exploration and relaxation.

One of the main attractions within Balboa Park is the San Diego Zoo, one of the most famous zoos in the world. Home to thousands of animals from around the globe, the zoo offers an immersive experience with its lush, naturalistic habitats and educational exhibits. Visitors can enjoy close-up views of rare and endangered species such as giant pandas, koalas, and African elephants, all while learning about conservation efforts and wildlife protection.

For those interested in art and culture, Balboa Park boasts several exceptional museums. The San Diego Museum of Art, with its vast collection of European, Asian, and American art, is a highlight for art lovers. The Museum of Man delves into anthropology and human history, while the Fleet Science Center offers hands-on exhibits for science enthusiasts of all ages. The Natural History Museum and the Timken Museum of Art are also noteworthy stops, providing insight into the region's history and artistic legacy.

Beyond its museums and attractions, Balboa Park is also a sanctuary for nature lovers. The park features several beautiful gardens, including the Botanical Building and Garden, the Rose Garden, and the Japanese Friendship Garden, where visitors can wander among vibrant blooms, tranquil ponds, and lush greenery. The park's wide-open spaces are perfect for picnicking, walking, or simply relaxing in a peaceful environment.

Balboa Park is also home to several theaters and performance venues, offering year-round entertainment. The Old Globe Theatre, a renowned regional theater company, stages classic plays, musicals, and new works, while the San Diego Civic Theatre hosts Broadway shows and concerts. Throughout the year, the park hosts a variety of cultural events, festivals, and outdoor performances, making it a lively and dynamic destination for both locals and tourists.

Easily accessible from downtown San Diego, Balboa Park offers free entry to many of its outdoor spaces, gardens, and attractions, while individual museums often have reasonable admission fees. With its stunning landscapes, cultural richness, and family-friendly attractions, Balboa Park is a place where visitors of all ages can immerse themselves in the beauty and history of San Diego. Whether you're exploring the world-class museums, enjoying the outdoors, or attending a live performance, Balboa Park offers something for everyone and remains one of the city's most beloved treasures.

BATTLESHIP USS IOWA MUSEUM

COUNTY: LOS ANGELES   **CITY:** LOS ANGELES (SAN PEDRO)

DATE VISITED: **WHO I WENT WITH:**

RATING: ☆ ☆ ☆ ☆ ☆   **WILL I RETURN?** YES / NO

250 S Harbor Blvd San Pedro
Los Angeles, CA 90731
877-446-9261

The Battleship USS Iowa Museum, located in the Port of Los Angeles in San Pedro, California, offers a captivating and immersive experience into the history of the U.S. Navy and the battleships that played a crucial role during World War II, the Korean War, and the Cold War. The USS Iowa, known as the "Battleship of Presidents," is a historic naval vessel that served as the flagship for several U.S. fleets and played a prominent role in multiple significant military engagements throughout its service.

The USS Iowa was commissioned in 1943 and became the largest and most powerful battleship in the U.S. Navy at the time. With its impressive 16-inch guns and advanced technology, the ship earned a place in naval history, and after decommissioning, it was transformed into a museum, allowing visitors to step aboard and explore its storied past.

Visitors to the USS Iowa Museum can enjoy a self-guided tour or participate in a guided tour led by knowledgeable docents, who share fascinating insights into the battleship's history, the role it played in various military conflicts, and the lives of the sailors who served aboard it. As guests explore the ship, they can see the massive guns on the deck, the vast corridors of the ship, the captain's quarters, and the engine rooms that powered this mighty vessel. The museum offers a detailed view of the battleship's operations, the technology of the time, and the history of naval warfare.

One of the most memorable aspects of visiting the USS Iowa Museum is the opportunity to experience what life was like for the sailors who served aboard. Interactive exhibits, artifacts, and personal stories from veterans provide an intimate look into the daily operations and challenges faced by those on board. The ship's decks offer stunning views of the harbor, making it a unique location for learning and reflection.

In addition to the historic battleship itself, the USS Iowa Museum also features exhibits on naval history, including the story of the ship's involvement in significant military operations. The ship's involvement in the Korean War, where it provided naval gunfire support for ground forces, as well as its role during the Cold War, are highlighted in exhibits and displays. The museum also offers educational programs, events, and activities for all ages, making it a great destination for families, history buffs, and those interested in military history.

The USS Iowa Museum is open year-round and provides a unique opportunity to walk through history on a ship that saw action in some of the most significant conflicts of the 20th century. Located in San Pedro, it is easily accessible from the greater Los Angeles area and is a must-see for anyone interested in military history, naval warfare, or the legacy of the U.S. Navy. Whether you're admiring the ship's massive size, learning about its rich history, or reflecting on the sacrifices of those who served aboard it, the USS Iowa Museum offers an unforgettable and educational experience for visitors of all ages.

COUNTY: LOS ANGELES   CITY: LOS ANGELES

DATE VISITED: WHO I WENT WITH:

RATING: ☆ ☆ ☆ ☆ ☆   WILL I RETURN?   YES / NO

3764 Watseka Ave
Los Angeles, CA 90034
310-845-9333

The Bhagavad-gita Diorama-Museum, located in the vibrant city of San Diego, California, offers visitors a unique and immersive cultural and spiritual experience. This museum is dedicated to showcasing the teachings and stories of the ancient Hindu scripture, the Bhagavad-gita, through a stunning collection of intricately designed dioramas. The Bhagavad-gita, considered one of the most important texts in Hindu philosophy, presents a dialogue between the prince Arjuna and the god Krishna, addressing complex themes of duty, righteousness, and the nature of existence.

The museum features a series of life-like dioramas that visually narrate the key teachings and stories from the Bhagavad-gita and other significant Hindu scriptures. Each diorama is meticulously crafted, capturing moments from the ancient text with vibrant colors, detailed figurines, and dramatic scenes that bring the teachings of the Bhagavad-gita to life. Visitors can walk through the museum, exploring the dioramas, which cover a range of themes such as the importance of selfless action, the struggle between good and evil, and the spiritual journey of the soul.

In addition to the dioramas, the Bhagavad-gita Diorama-Museum offers educational exhibits that explain the philosophical and spiritual concepts of the Bhagavad-gita in a way that is accessible to people of all backgrounds and beliefs. The museum provides a comprehensive introduction to the Bhakti-yoga tradition, which emphasizes devotion and the cultivation of a personal relationship with the divine. Visitors can learn about the significance of the Bhagavad-gita in Hinduism and its influence on various aspects of life, including ethics, meditation, and personal development.

The museum also serves as a center for spiritual enrichment, offering a peaceful atmosphere where visitors can reflect on the messages of the Bhagavad-gita and engage in discussions about philosophy, spirituality, and personal growth. It provides a welcoming environment for both those who are already familiar with the text and those who are new to its teachings. The museum often hosts workshops, lectures, and cultural events that further enhance the educational experience and allow visitors to deepen their understanding of the Bhagavad-gita and its relevance in today's world.

One of the highlights of the museum is its devotion to preserving and sharing the rich cultural heritage of India. The museum is part of a larger cultural complex that includes a temple, gardens, and a community space, offering visitors a holistic experience that connects them to the spiritual and cultural traditions of Hinduism. The serene environment and beautiful landscaping around the museum create a tranquil space for visitors to relax, meditate, and reflect on the teachings they have encountered during their visit.

Located near Balboa Park, the Bhagavad-gita Diorama-Museum is an ideal destination for anyone interested in exploring Hindu philosophy, spirituality, and culture. Whether you're a scholar of religion, a seeker of spiritual knowledge, or simply curious about one of the world's oldest and most revered scriptures, the museum provides an engaging and educational experience that offers profound insights into the human condition and the path to spiritual enlightenment.

BLACK'S BEACH

COUNTY: SAN DIEGO   **CITY:** SAN DIEGO (LA JOLLA)

DATE VISITED: **WHO I WENT WITH:**

RATING: ☆ ☆ ☆ ☆ ☆   **WILL I RETURN?**   YES / NO

2800 Torrey Pines Scenic Drive
La Jolla, CA 92037, USA

Black's Beach, located in San Diego, California, is one of the most famous and unique beaches in the area, known for its stunning natural beauty and its status as a popular clothing-optional beach. Situated near the Torrey Pines State Natural Reserve, this secluded beach is nestled between towering cliffs, offering visitors a serene and picturesque environment with stunning views of the Pacific Ocean. Access to the beach is somewhat challenging, which contributes to its quieter, more tranquil atmosphere compared to other beaches in San Diego.

The beach itself stretches for over a mile, with soft golden sand and gentle waves, making it a perfect spot for beachgoers who are looking for a peaceful place to relax, swim, or sunbathe. Black's Beach is unique in that it is one of the few officially designated clothing-optional beaches in the United States, which attracts a diverse group of people looking for an unhurried, natural beach experience. Visitors can enjoy the freedom of relaxing without the constraints of swimwear, while respecting others' personal space and preferences.

To reach Black's Beach, visitors must hike down steep, rugged cliffs, which provide breathtaking views of the coastline and the Pacific Ocean. The hike down from the Torrey Pines Gliderport is particularly popular and provides a scenic approach to the beach. The challenging descent and ascent make it less crowded, giving those who make the effort a more private and undisturbed beach experience. While the hike can be a bit strenuous, the reward is well worth it—once you reach the beach, you'll be greeted by stunning natural beauty and a peaceful, laid-back atmosphere.

One of the key features of Black's Beach is its sense of seclusion. Unlike other nearby beaches, it offers a sense of privacy due to its isolated location. The beach is often less crowded, which makes it a favorite for visitors who prefer a more tranquil environment to enjoy the outdoors. Surfers also frequent Black's Beach, as the waves can be ideal for those looking for more challenging surf conditions. The beach is known for having strong surf, making it suitable for experienced surfers, while others can enjoy the calmer waters closer to the shore.

In addition to its natural beauty and the opportunity for relaxation, Black's Beach is also a great spot for wildlife watchers. The surrounding cliffs and the nearby Torrey Pines State Natural Reserve are home to a variety of wildlife, including birds, lizards, and the rare Torrey Pine tree, which is one of the rarest pines in the world. The area is also a great place for hiking, offering various trails that lead through the reserve and provide spectacular views of the ocean and coastline.

For those who enjoy the sun and sand without the crowds, Black's Beach provides a peaceful, beautiful escape where visitors can immerse themselves in nature, enjoy stunning ocean views, and experience a sense of freedom in one of San Diego's most iconic beaches. Whether you're looking to relax, hike, surf, or just enjoy the unique atmosphere, Black's Beach is a must-visit destination in San Diego.

BOYDEN CAVERN

13

COUNTY: FRESNO

CITY: FRESNO

DATE VISITED: 〔 〕 WHO I WENT WITH:

RATING: ☆ ☆ ☆ ☆ ☆ WILL I RETURN? YES / NO

19 miles east of Grant Grove, Hwy 180, Kings Canyon CA
Sequoia and Kings Canyon National Park, CA 93257
559-565-3341

Boyden Cavern, located in the scenic Sierra Nevada Mountains within the Sequoia National Forest, is a hidden gem for nature enthusiasts and adventure seekers. Nestled near the small town of California Hot Springs, the cavern offers a fascinating underground experience that showcases the stunning natural formations of the region. As one of the most popular caves in the area, Boyden Cavern attracts visitors with its unique stalactites, stalagmites, and rich geological history, making it a must-see destination for those exploring the foothills of the Sierra Nevada.

The cavern was first discovered in 1930, and today, it serves as an educational and recreational site, where visitors can take guided tours through its winding passageways and awe-inspiring chambers. The tours provide a safe yet thrilling opportunity to explore the underground world, led by knowledgeable guides who share information about the cave's formation, history, and significance. Along the way, visitors can marvel at the impressive array of mineral formations, including dramatic stalactites (hanging from the ceiling) and stalagmites (rising from the floor), which have formed over thousands of years due to the slow process of mineral-rich water dripping from the cave's ceiling.

The cavern's natural beauty is complemented by the rich history of the area. Boyden Cavern is thought to have been used by Native American tribes for shelter, and it was later explored by settlers in the early 20th century. The cave's name is derived from John Boyden, a local who played a key role in its discovery. Today, the cavern is part of the larger Sequoia National Forest and serves as an important attraction for visitors seeking to experience the wonders of underground geology.

The tour itself is relatively easy to navigate, with a well-maintained path that leads through the cavern's various chambers. The walk is illuminated, allowing guests to fully appreciate the striking formations within the cave. The experience is both awe-inspiring and educational, as guides explain the natural processes that created the formations, how the cave continues to evolve, and the role that caves play in local ecosystems. Additionally, the cooler, subterranean climate of the cavern provides a refreshing respite during the hot summer months, making it a great option for outdoor enthusiasts looking to escape the heat.

Boyden Cavern is also located within a picturesque natural setting, surrounded by towering trees, rocky outcroppings, and wildlife that make the region a paradise for hikers and nature lovers. Visitors to the cavern often combine their trip with a hike in the nearby Sierra National Forest, where they can enjoy the stunning views and explore the diverse flora and fauna of the area.

For those planning a visit, the cavern is typically open seasonally, with tours available in the warmer months. The tours are family-friendly and suitable for all ages, although the cave's relatively narrow pathways and occasional uneven terrain mean that comfortable footwear is recommended. Boyden Cavern provides a unique opportunity to experience the wonders of the natural world, offering a rare glimpse into the geological history of California's Sierra Nevada region.

Whether you're interested in geology, history, or simply enjoying the beauty of the natural world, a visit to Boyden Cavern is a memorable experience that highlights the majestic underground landscapes of California. It's a perfect addition to any adventure in the Sierra Nevada foothills and a great way to connect with the stunning natural heritage of this remarkable region.

BRANDINI TOFFEE

(14)

DATE VISITED: **WHO I WENT WITH:**

RATING: ☆ ☆ ☆ ☆ ☆   **WILL I RETURN?** YES / NO

132 S Palm Canyon Dr, Palm Springs
Greater Palm Springs, CA 92262
877-327-2634

Brandini Toffee, located in the charming city of Palm Springs, California, offers a deliciously sweet experience for visitors seeking a taste of luxury handmade confections. Known for its rich, buttery toffee, Brandini Toffee has gained a reputation as one of the finest toffee producers in the country, combining traditional recipes with high-quality ingredients to create a treat that's both decadent and irresistible. Founded in 2006 by two lifelong friends, Brandini Toffee began as a passion project, quickly growing into a beloved brand that has become synonymous with premium toffee and other handcrafted sweets.

The company's signature product is their almond toffee, which is made with a blend of high-quality butter, sugar, and locally sourced almonds, all of which are carefully handcrafted in small batches. The toffee is then coated in premium chocolate and topped with more almonds for an extra crunch and flavor. The result is a rich, melt-in-your-mouth treat that has earned Brandini Toffee rave reviews from locals and visitors alike. Over the years, the company has expanded its offerings to include other delightful confections, such as chocolate-dipped toffee and toffee bark, each offering a unique twist on the classic toffee recipe.

Visitors to the Brandini Toffee shop in Palm Springs are treated to more than just a retail experience – it's a sensory journey that invites them to watch the toffee-making process firsthand. The shop features a cozy and inviting atmosphere, with large glass windows that allow guests to peek into the kitchen where the toffee is made. The team at Brandini Toffee takes pride in every batch, ensuring that each piece is made with care and attention to detail. The sweet aroma of freshly made toffee fills the air, making it impossible to resist trying a sample.

Brandini Toffee also offers a variety of packaged gifts, making it the perfect destination for anyone looking for a special treat to take home or to give as a gift. Their beautifully packaged toffee gift boxes, available in different sizes and configurations, are popular among visitors and locals alike. Whether it's a box of their classic toffee or an assortment of their signature creations, these gifts make for a thoughtful and indulgent present.

For those interested in the story behind the toffee, the Brandini Toffee factory in Palm Springs offers tours where guests can learn about the company's history, the toffee-making process, and the care that goes into crafting each batch. The tour provides an inside look at the brand's commitment to quality and craftsmanship, from the selection of ingredients to the final product.

As part of its dedication to the community, Brandini Toffee also works closely with local farmers to source the best almonds and other ingredients, ensuring that its products are both locally sustainable and of the highest quality. The company has made a name for itself not only for the exceptional taste of its toffee but also for its commitment to supporting local businesses and practices that benefit the community.

Whether you're a lifelong toffee lover or a first-time visitor to Palm Springs, Brandini Toffee provides an unforgettable experience. It's an ideal stop for anyone with a sweet tooth looking to indulge in one of California's finest handmade treats. The combination of delicious confections, warm hospitality, and a unique behind-the-scenes experience makes Brandini Toffee a must-visit destination for food lovers and travelers exploring the desert oasis of Palm Springs.

CABLE CAR MUSEUM

COUNTY: SAN FRANCISCO   **CITY:** SAN FRANCISCO

DATE VISITED: **WHO I WENT WITH:**

RATING: ☆ ☆ ☆ ☆ ☆   **WILL I RETURN?**   YES / NO

1201 Mason Street
San Francisco, CA 94108
415-474-1887

The Cable Car Museum, located in San Francisco, California, is a captivating destination that celebrates the history and mechanics of one of the city's most iconic forms of transportation. Nestled in the heart of the city, this unique museum offers visitors an immersive journey into the fascinating world of cable cars, providing an up-close look at the engineering marvels that have shaped San Francisco's urban identity since the late 19th century. A visit to the museum is a must for history enthusiasts, engineering aficionados, and anyone curious about the story behind these legendary vehicles.

The Cable Car Museum is housed in the same building that serves as the central powerhouse for San Francisco's cable car system. As a result, guests can witness the massive spinning wheels and winding machinery that drive the city's cable cars in real-time. This living exhibit provides a rare and thrilling opportunity to see the inner workings of the system that powers these historic streetcars, making it a unique combination of museum and operational hub.

The museum features an impressive collection of historical artifacts, including vintage cable cars that date back to the 1870s, photographs, tools, and other memorabilia. Visitors can explore the beautifully restored cable cars on display, such as the "Grip Car 8" and the "Trailer 54," gaining insight into the craftsmanship and ingenuity of the era. Informative exhibits detail the invention of the cable car system by Andrew Hallidie, its impact on San Francisco's development, and the efforts to preserve this beloved transportation network in the face of modernization.

One of the highlights of the museum is the Hallidie Ropeway Exhibit, which explains the ingenious cable-and-grip mechanism that allows the cars to traverse the city's steep hills with precision and reliability. This mechanism, a groundbreaking innovation of its time, remains a vital part of the system's operation today. Visitors can learn about the challenges faced by engineers in designing a transit solution for San Francisco's unique topography, as well as the social and economic factors that led to the creation of the cable car system.

The Cable Car Museum also delves into the cultural significance of these vehicles. Over the decades, cable cars have become a symbol of San Francisco, appearing in countless films, photographs, and works of art. The museum showcases their enduring legacy, from their practical role in transportation to their place as a cherished icon of the city's identity.

Admission to the Cable Car Museum is free, making it an accessible and enriching experience for visitors of all ages. The museum is conveniently located near Chinatown and North Beach, making it an excellent addition to a day of sightseeing in San Francisco. After exploring the exhibits, visitors can step outside and see working cable cars as they climb the city's famous hills, offering a deeper appreciation for the seamless blend of history and functionality that defines the system.

A visit to the Cable Car Museum is more than just a step back in time—it's a celebration of innovation, resilience, and the enduring charm of San Francisco. Whether you're a first-time visitor to the city or a long-time resident, the museum provides a fascinating glimpse into the heart of one of the most unique and enduring transit systems in the world.

CABRILLO NATIONAL MONUMENT

COUNTY: SAN DIEGO   **CITY:** SAN DIEGO

DATE VISITED: _____   **WHO I WENT WITH:** _____

RATING: ☆ ☆ ☆ ☆ ☆   **WILL I RETURN?** YES / NO

1800 Cabrillo Memorial Dr Point Loma Ecological Reserve
San Diego, CA 92106
619-523-4285

Cabrillo National Monument is a historical and natural landmark located at the southern tip of the Point Loma Peninsula in San Diego, California. This iconic monument commemorates the first European landing on the West Coast of the United States, made by Juan Rodríguez Cabrillo, a Portuguese explorer, on September 28, 1542. Cabrillo's arrival marked a significant moment in the history of exploration, as it was the first time that a European had set foot on the West Coast, shaping the course of California's history. The Cabrillo National Monument not only offers a deep dive into this crucial historical event but also provides visitors with stunning views of the coastline, wildlife, and the Pacific Ocean.

The Cabrillo Monument itself stands tall atop the Point Loma Peninsula, providing sweeping panoramic views of San Diego Bay, the Pacific Ocean, and the city of San Diego. The statue depicts Cabrillo in a traditional explorer's stance, symbolizing his arrival to the region. This commemorative monument honors his significant, though brief, exploration of the coast and his encounters with the indigenous people of the area. The National Park Service, which oversees the monument, provides various educational exhibits detailing Cabrillo's journey, the challenges he faced, and the impact of his exploration on the native populations and future European expeditions.

At the monument's base, visitors can explore a small visitor center that offers interactive displays, videos, and exhibits about Cabrillo's voyage, the history of the exploration, and the natural history of the area. The museum also highlights the interactions between Cabrillo's crew and the indigenous people they encountered during their time in what is now California. The center offers a comprehensive historical context to Cabrillo's legacy and provides information on the region's cultural heritage.

In addition to its historical significance, Cabrillo National Monument is also a haven for nature lovers. The surrounding Point Loma area features diverse landscapes, including tide pools, coastal bluffs, and lush vegetation. The Cabrillo Tide Pools are a major attraction, where visitors can explore the rich marine life that inhabits the rocky shores during low tide. These tide pools are home to a variety of sea creatures, including sea stars, crabs, anemones, and fish, offering a fascinating look at marine ecosystems. The monument's location also provides opportunities for birdwatching, with migratory birds frequently passing through the area.

Visitors can explore the Cabrillo National Monument through its network of walking trails, such as the Cabrillo Memorial Trail, which takes guests along the coastal bluffs, providing incredible views of the ocean and coastline while learning about the flora and fauna of the region. For those interested in learning more about the history and cultural significance of Cabrillo's exploration, the Cabrillo National Monument Visitor Center also offers programs and ranger-led tours that give deeper insight into the monument's history and natural beauty.

The Old Point Loma Lighthouse, located within the Cabrillo National Monument, is another important feature of the site. Built in 1855, this historic lighthouse is one of the oldest on the West Coast. Visitors can tour the lighthouse and its surrounding area to learn about its role in maritime navigation and the life of lighthouse keepers. The lighthouse provides another excellent vantage point for stunning views of the bay and ocean, making it a perfect spot for photography.

Cabrillo National Monument offers a blend of history, culture, and natural beauty, making it a fascinating destination for visitors of all ages. Whether you're interested in exploring the rich history of early European exploration or enjoying the natural landscapes and wildlife of the San Diego coast, Cabrillo National Monument provides an enriching experience that is both educational and scenic. It is a perfect place to gain insight into the history of California, the legacy of Juan Rodríguez Cabrillo, and the breathtaking coastal environment.

----

⑰ CHAMISAL VINEYARDS

COUNTY: SAN LUIS OBISPO | **CITY:** SAN LUIS OBISPO

DATE VISITED: | **WHO I WENT WITH:**

RATING: ☆ ☆ ☆ ☆ ☆ | **WILL I RETURN?** YES / NO

7525 Orcutt Rd
San Luis Obispo, CA 93401
805-541-9463

Chamisal Vineyards, located in the heart of California's Central Coast, is a celebrated winery known for producing exceptional wines in the Edna Valley, a region renowned for its cool climate and ideal conditions for growing high-quality Pinot Noir, Chardonnay, and other varietals. Situated just minutes from the coastal town of San Luis Obispo, Chamisal Vineyards offers visitors a serene and picturesque setting to enjoy world-class wines, beautiful landscapes, and a rich history of winemaking.

Founded in the early 1980s, Chamisal Vineyards was one of the first wineries in the Edna Valley, a region that has since become highly regarded for its unique terroir. The vineyard is nestled between the Santa Lucia Mountains and the Pacific Ocean, with cool ocean breezes and a diverse range of soil types that contribute to the distinctive flavors found in its wines. Chamisal Vineyards' commitment to sustainability and organic farming practices further enhances the quality and purity of the wines they produce.

Visitors to Chamisal Vineyards are treated to an immersive experience that blends wine tasting with breathtaking views of the valley and vineyards. The winery's tasting room is designed with modern elegance, offering both indoor and outdoor seating where guests can relax and enjoy their wine while overlooking the lush vineyards and rolling hills. The expansive patio provides a perfect spot to unwind and take in the beautiful surroundings, which include scenic views of the Edna Valley's natural beauty and the nearby Irish Hills.

The tasting experience at Chamisal Vineyards is a personalized journey through the winery's carefully crafted wine selection. The staff is knowledgeable and passionate about the wines they offer, guiding visitors through tastings of some of the winery's most popular varietals, including Pinot Noir, Chardonnay, and a selection of blends. The wines are known for their complexity, balance, and expression of the unique terroir of the region. Chamisal's winemaking philosophy focuses on minimal intervention, allowing the natural characteristics of the grapes to shine through in each bottle.

In addition to wine tasting, Chamisal Vineyards offers exclusive events, such as wine and food pairings, vineyard tours, and educational experiences. Guests can take guided tours of the vineyards, where they will learn about the cultivation of the grapevines, the winemaking process, and the importance of the local climate and soils in producing exceptional wines. The knowledgeable staff also shares insights into the history of the winery and the vision behind its commitment to sustainable practices.

Chamisal Vineyards also has a well-regarded wine club that allows members to enjoy regular shipments of their favorite wines, access to exclusive releases, and invitations to special events. The winery's commitment to producing high-quality wines has earned it recognition and accolades from wine enthusiasts and industry experts alike, solidifying its reputation as one of the premier wineries in the Central Coast.

For visitors looking to explore more of the surrounding area, Chamisal Vineyards is conveniently located near other top wineries in the Edna Valley and the nearby Paso Robles wine region, making it a great destination for wine tours. The proximity to San Luis Obispo also offers the opportunity to enjoy local attractions, restaurants, and the beautiful coastal scenery of the area.

Whether you're a seasoned wine connoisseur or a casual enthusiast, Chamisal Vineyards provides a welcoming and educational environment to explore the exceptional wines of the Central Coast. The combination of beautiful scenery, sustainable winemaking, and high-quality wines makes it a must-visit destination for anyone traveling to the region.

CHANNEL ISLANDS NATIONAL PARK

COUNTY: VENTURA   CITY: VENTURA

DATE VISITED: WHO I WENT WITH:

RATING: ☆ ☆ ☆ ☆ ☆   WILL I RETURN? YES / NO

1901 Spinnaker Drive
Ventura, CA 93001
805-658-5730

Channel Islands National Park, often called the "Galápagos of North America," is a pristine and remote destination off the southern coast of California. Comprising five rugged islands—Santa Cruz, Santa Rosa, Anacapa, San Miguel, and Santa Barbara—and the surrounding marine environment, this national park offers visitors a rare opportunity to experience unspoiled natural beauty and unique ecosystems. Each island is a world of its own, home to diverse wildlife, stunning landscapes, and a rich history.

The park is renowned for its extraordinary biodiversity, with over 2,000 species of plants and animals, many of which are found nowhere else on Earth. The islands' isolation has allowed endemic species like the Channel Island fox and the island scrub-jay to thrive. Marine life is equally abundant, with waters teeming with dolphins, sea lions, and migrating gray and blue whales. The kelp forests surrounding the islands form an underwater wonderland, attracting snorkelers and divers from around the world.

For outdoor enthusiasts, Channel Islands National Park is a paradise of recreational activities. Hiking is one of the most popular ways to explore the islands, with trails offering breathtaking vistas of the Pacific Ocean, dramatic sea cliffs, and wildflower-covered hillsides. Popular hikes include the Pelican Bay Trail on Santa Cruz Island and the Torrey Pines Trail on Santa Rosa Island, which leads to one of the few remaining groves of rare Torrey pine trees.

Kayaking is another favorite activity, allowing visitors to navigate through sea caves, archways, and rocky shorelines. Anacapa Island is famous for its picturesque Arch Rock and stunning coastal views, while Santa Cruz Island boasts the largest sea cave in the world, Painted Cave. The crystal-clear waters surrounding the islands are also perfect for snorkeling and diving, offering close encounters with vibrant marine life and spectacular underwater rock formations.

The islands are steeped in human history, from the earliest native Chumash inhabitants to European explorers and 19th-century ranchers. Visitors can explore remnants of the past, such as archaeological sites, old ranch buildings, and the Anacapa Island Lighthouse. Educational programs and guided tours provided by the National Park Service and partner organizations delve into the cultural and natural history of the islands, enriching the visitor experience.

Getting to Channel Islands National Park requires a sense of adventure, as there are no bridges or roads connecting the islands to the mainland. Visitors typically take a ferry operated by Island Packers from Ventura or Oxnard harbors, or arrive by private boat. There are no accommodations or restaurants on the islands, so day-trippers and campers must come prepared with food, water, and gear. Camping is available on all five islands, offering a unique chance to experience the tranquility of these remote landscapes under star-filled skies.

The park is open year-round, with each season offering its own unique highlights. Spring brings vibrant wildflower blooms and active wildlife, summer is ideal for kayaking and diving, autumn offers excellent whale-watching opportunities, and winter provides solitude and dramatic ocean vistas.

Whether you're a nature enthusiast, history buff, or adventurer, Channel Islands National Park promises a truly unforgettable experience. Its combination of raw natural beauty, abundant wildlife, and sense of seclusion makes it one of California's most cherished and unique national parks.

CLUB FUGAZI

19

DATE VISITED: WHO I WENT WITH:

RATING: ☆ ☆ ☆ ☆ ☆   WILL I RETURN?   YES / NO

678 Green St
San Francisco, CA 94133
415-273-0600

Club Fugazi, located in the heart of San Francisco's North Beach neighborhood, is an iconic venue known for its rich history, vibrant atmosphere, and eclectic performances. Established in 1912, Club Fugazi has long been a cultural hotspot, offering a unique blend of live entertainment, theater, and nightlife. It is perhaps best known as the home of "Beach Blanket Babylon", the longest-running musical revue in theatrical history, which entertained audiences for over four decades before its final performance in 2019. Club Fugazi's intimate setting, combined with its storied past, makes it a beloved landmark in San Francisco's cultural landscape.

The club's history is deeply intertwined with the entertainment scene in San Francisco, having hosted a wide variety of acts over the years, from jazz and burlesque to comedy and theater. Throughout its long existence, it has been a place where both locals and tourists gather to enjoy world-class performances in a setting that exudes old-world charm. With its vintage architecture and intimate atmosphere, the venue creates a close connection between performers and the audience, offering an experience that's both personal and memorable.

While "Beach Blanket Babylon" may have been its most famous production, Club Fugazi continues to be a celebrated venue for live performances and events. The club features a range of shows, from theatrical productions and comedy performances to live music and special events. The venue's versatility makes it an ideal location for a variety of entertainment, and it remains an integral part of the San Francisco cultural scene.

In addition to its performances, Club Fugazi also has a strong connection to the city's North Beach district, an area known for its vibrant history of art, culture, and nightlife. North Beach has been home to many influential figures in the arts, particularly during the Beat Generation era, and Club Fugazi's location allows visitors to immerse themselves in the rich cultural tapestry of the neighborhood. The area is also famous for its Italian heritage, and visitors to Club Fugazi can explore nearby cafes, restaurants, and landmarks that contribute to the unique charm of North Beach.

For those visiting San Francisco, a night at Club Fugazi offers a chance to experience the city's artistic and cultural history up close. The club's intimate setting allows for a truly memorable evening, where guests can enjoy the magic of live performance while surrounded by the club's historic ambiance. Whether you're attending a show, enjoying a drink at the bar, or simply taking in the atmosphere of this iconic venue, Club Fugazi remains one of San Francisco's most treasured cultural institutions.

Today, Club Fugazi continues to serve as a hub for creativity and performance, offering a glimpse into San Francisco's rich entertainment history while continuing to foster new artistic expressions. It stands as a testament to the city's vibrant cultural scene, a place where people come together to experience the arts in an unforgettable setting. Whether you're a local or a visitor, a trip to Club Fugazi is a unique way to experience the heart and soul of San Francisco's entertainment culture.

20

CONGRESS TRAIL

COUNTY: TULARE   **CITY:** VISALIA

DATE VISITED: **WHO I WENT WITH:**

RATING: ☆ ☆ ☆ ☆ ☆   **WILL I RETURN?**   YES / NO

47050 Generals Highway
Three Rivers, CA 93271
559-565-3341

The Congress Trail is one of the most beautiful and popular hiking trails located in the Sequoia National Park, California. Known for its breathtaking views and awe-inspiring giant sequoia trees, the trail offers an unforgettable experience for nature lovers and outdoor enthusiasts. The trail is a scenic, easy-to-moderate hike, making it suitable for visitors of all ages and skill levels. It is named after the towering trees along the path, which are often referred to as the "Congress of the Trees," a tribute to their majestic presence and the feeling of awe they inspire in those who walk among them.

The Congress Trail begins near the General Sherman Tree, the largest tree on Earth by volume, standing at over 275 feet tall and over 36 feet in diameter. The trail winds through the park's famous Giant Forest, where visitors can see some of the largest and oldest living trees in the world. The path is well-maintained and relatively flat, making it accessible for families, photographers, and anyone wanting to experience the grandeur of the sequoia trees up close. Along the way, hikers are treated to spectacular views of the towering giants, including the General Grant Tree, another massive sequoia in the area.

As you walk along the Congress Trail, you'll encounter a variety of awe-inspiring trees, each with its own unique characteristics. The giant sequoias in the park are known for their incredible size and age, with some trees believed to be over 3,000 years old. Their thick bark, which can be several feet deep in places, helps protect them from fire, insects, and harsh weather conditions, allowing these ancient trees to thrive for millennia. Along the trail, visitors will also find informative signs that provide details about the trees, wildlife, and ecosystem of the Giant Forest.

The Congress Trail is approximately 2 miles round-trip, making it an ideal choice for a half-day hike. The trail is especially popular during the summer and fall months when the weather is ideal for hiking, and the vibrant colors of autumn foliage provide an extra layer of beauty. The air is fresh and clean, and the peace and tranquility of the forest make it a perfect place for meditation or reflection.

For those who want to learn more about the natural wonders of the area, there are also ranger-led programs available, where knowledgeable guides share information about the history of the sequoias, the park's wildlife, and the ongoing efforts to preserve these ancient giants for future generations. The Congress Trail is an ideal starting point for exploring Sequoia National Park, as it provides a close-up view of the park's most famous trees while being easily accessible from the park's main attractions.

In addition to the natural beauty, the Congress Trail offers plenty of opportunities for wildlife viewing. Visitors might spot deer, squirrels, birds, and other creatures that call the Giant Forest home. The combination of towering trees, clear mountain air, and the surrounding wilderness creates a serene and magical atmosphere that draws visitors from around the world.

Whether you're a seasoned hiker or someone simply looking to enjoy the wonders of nature, the Congress Trail offers an accessible, scenic, and educational experience that showcases the majesty of Sequoia National Park and the remarkable trees that make it famous. Walking the trail allows visitors to connect with the natural world in a way that is both inspiring and humbling, leaving them with memories that will last a lifetime.

21

CORONADO ISLAND

COUNTY: SAN DIEGO   **CITY:** CORONADO

DATE VISITED: _____   **WHO I WENT WITH:** _____

RATING: ☆ ☆ ☆ ☆ ☆   **WILL I RETURN?**   YES / NO

Coronado Visitor Center
1100 Orange Ave
Coronado, CA 92118

Coronado Island is a picturesque resort destination located just across the bay from San Diego, California. Known for its beautiful beaches, historic landmarks, and charming small-town atmosphere, Coronado Island is a must-visit destination for tourists seeking a relaxing escape with stunning views and a variety of activities.

One of the most iconic features of Coronado is its world-famous Coronado Beach, which stretches for over a mile along the island's western shore. The beach is known for its sparkling white sand, which is made up of crushed seashells that give it a unique, glistening appearance in the sunlight. Coronado Beach is perfect for sunbathing, picnicking, or taking a leisurely walk along the shore. The gentle waves also make it an ideal spot for families to enjoy swimming, boogie boarding, and beach games. The beach is also home to the historic Hotel del Coronado, one of the most famous landmarks on the island and a National Historic Landmark. This grand Victorian hotel, often referred to as "The Del," has hosted numerous celebrities and dignitaries since it opened in 1888, and its iconic red turrets and stunning beachfront location make it a true architectural gem.

In addition to its beaches, Coronado Island offers visitors a range of outdoor activities. The Coronado Central Beach is ideal for walking, and the island has several scenic bike paths for those looking to explore the area on two wheels. The Silver Strand State Beach, located at the southern tip of the island, is a popular spot for camping, fishing, and birdwatching. This beach is also known for its stunning sunsets and views of the Pacific Ocean. For those looking to stay active, the Coronado Golf Course is one of the most beautiful courses in the region, offering views of the bay and the San Diego skyline.

Coronado is also a hub for history and culture. The Coronado Museum of History and Art is a great place to learn about the island's rich history, from its early days as a military outpost to its development into a vibrant residential and tourist community. The museum features exhibits on local history, art, and photography, making it a great stop for those looking to dive deeper into the culture of

Coronado. Visitors can also explore the island's charming downtown area, with its tree-lined streets, boutique shops, cafes, and restaurants. Orange Avenue, the main street in Coronado, is home to many of these local businesses, offering a friendly and relaxed atmosphere perfect for shopping and dining.

For families, Coronado Island offers plenty of fun activities for all ages. The Coronado Ferry Landing is a popular destination where visitors can enjoy shopping, dining, and taking in the views of the San Diego skyline. The ferry ride across the bay is a relaxing way to see the city from the water, and it connects Coronado to downtown San Diego, making it easy to explore both locations. For children, the Coronado Tidelands Park provides a playground, picnic areas, and stunning views of the water and the Coronado Bridge, making it an ideal spot for a family outing.

Nature enthusiasts can also enjoy exploring the island's beautiful parks, including Glorietta Bay Park and The Crown Room Garden at the Hotel del Coronado, which features beautiful landscaping and serene views. Birdwatchers will appreciate the variety of coastal birds that inhabit the area, especially along the bay and beaches.

Coronado also boasts some cultural events throughout the year. The Coronado Island Film Festival celebrates cinema, and the Coronado Arts Festival is a wonderful opportunity to experience local art and crafts. The island is also known for its Independence Day celebrations, which include a grand fireworks show over the bay.

Getting to Coronado Island is easy, as it is just a short drive from downtown San Diego or can be accessed via the Coronado Bridge, an iconic structure that spans the bay and connects the island to the city. Alternatively, visitors can take the ferry from downtown San Diego, providing a scenic and enjoyable route across the water.

Whether you're seeking a relaxing day on the beach, a walk through history, or an opportunity to explore local shops and restaurants, Coronado Island offers something for everyone. Its combination of natural beauty, historical landmarks, and small-town charm make it a standout destination in the San Diego area. Whether you're visiting for a day or staying for a week, Coronado Island promises an unforgettable experience.

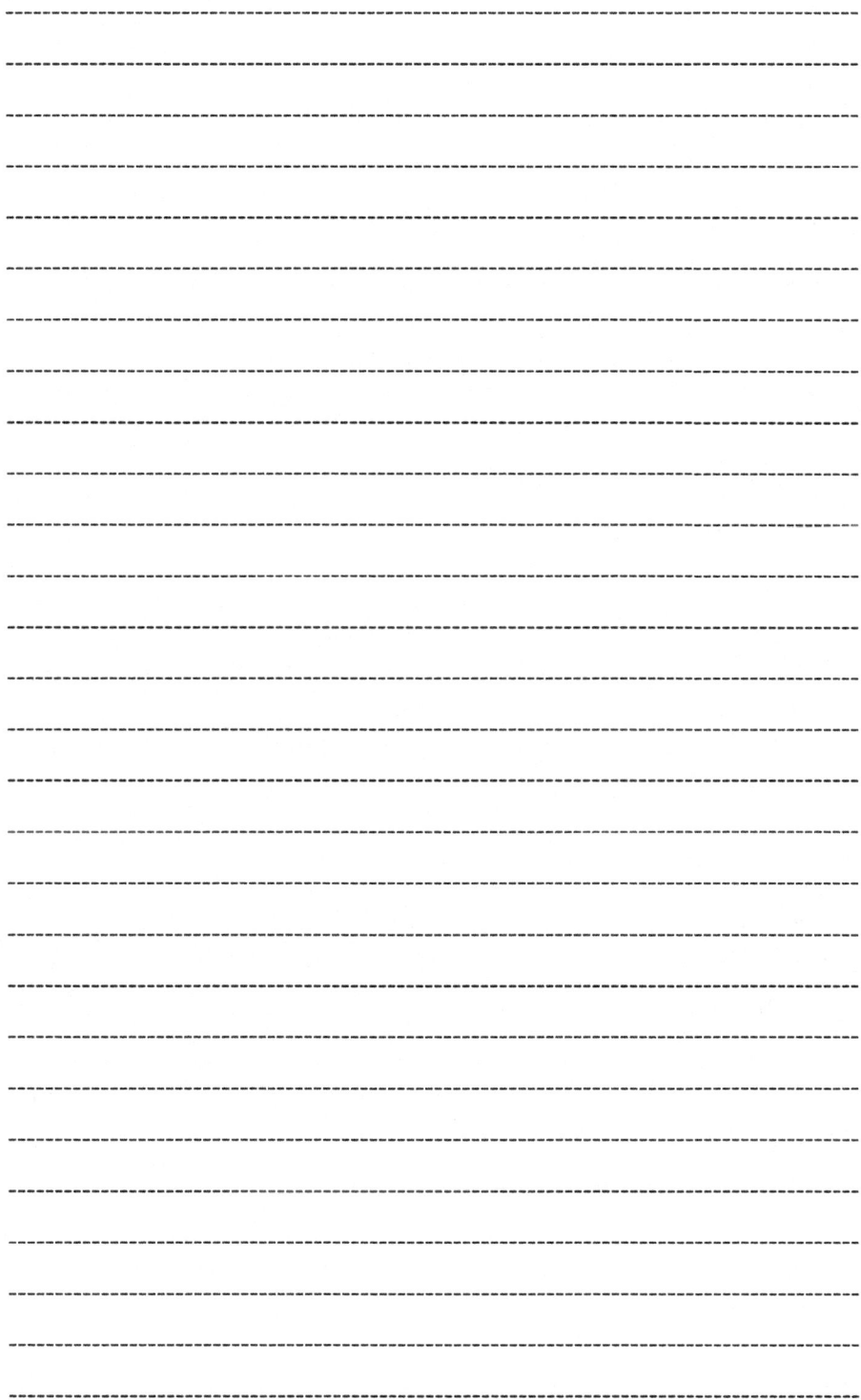

22 COURSEY GRAVES ESTATE WINERY

COUNTY: SONOMA   **CITY:** SANTA ROSA

DATE VISITED: **WHO I WENT WITH:**

RATING: ☆ ☆ ☆ ☆ ☆   **WILL I RETURN?** YES / NO

6860 Serenity Way
Santa Rosa, CA 95404
707-867-1888

Coursey Graves Estate Winery, located in the heart of Sonoma County, California, is a family-owned winery renowned for its exceptional wines and picturesque vineyard setting. Nestled in the Russian River Valley, one of the most celebrated wine-growing regions in the world, Coursey Graves is known for its commitment to producing small-lot, handcrafted wines that reflect the unique terroir of the region. The estate's stunning location, surrounded by rolling hills and lush vineyards, offers visitors an intimate and serene environment to explore and enjoy some of the best wines Sonoma has to offer.

Founded by husband-and-wife team Kevin Coursey and Danielle Graves, the winery focuses on creating wines that are both expressive and balanced, with an emphasis on sustainability and high-quality craftsmanship. The vineyard itself spans approximately 10 acres, and the winery produces a variety of wines, including Pinot Noir, Chardonnay, and other Bordeaux and Rhône varietals. With a combination of old-world techniques and modern innovation, Coursey Graves Estate Winery has quickly gained recognition for the purity and elegance of its wines, which are made with the finest hand-selected grapes grown on the estate.

The Russian River Valley is known for its cool climate, which provides the perfect growing conditions for Pinot Noir and Chardonnay. The valley's unique soils and microclimates contribute to the development of complex flavors and aromas in the grapes, resulting in wines that are nuanced and vibrant. At Coursey Graves Estate Winery, every bottle of wine reflects the dedication of the winemaking team and the care they take in each step of the process, from vine to bottle. The wines are crafted with minimal intervention, allowing the natural flavors of the fruit and the vineyard to shine through.

Visitors to Coursey Graves Estate Winery are welcomed to a beautiful and inviting tasting room, where they can sample the winery's wines and learn about the winemaking process. The tasting room is designed to be both elegant and comfortable, with floor-to-ceiling windows that offer breathtaking views of the vineyards and surrounding landscape. Guests can relax and savor a tasting flight of wines, each carefully chosen to showcase the winery's diverse offerings. The knowledgeable staff at Coursey Graves takes pride in sharing their expertise, offering insights into the characteristics of each wine and the unique features of the vineyard.

For those looking to make the experience even more special, the winery also offers private tours and tastings, providing a more in-depth look at the estate's winemaking practices and the history of the winery. During these tours, guests can walk through the vineyards, see the winemaking facilities, and learn about the sustainable farming practices that ensure the quality and health of the land. These personalized experiences are perfect for those looking to gain a deeper understanding of the artistry behind the wines and the dedication that goes into every bottle produced at Coursey Graves.

Coursey Graves Estate Winery also has a wine club that allows members to enjoy exclusive access to limited-production wines, special events, and private tastings. Wine club members receive regular shipments of the winery's best offerings, ensuring that they always have access to some of the finest wines produced in Sonoma County. The winery's commitment to quality and attention to detail has earned it a loyal following of wine lovers and collectors, making it a sought-after destination for those passionate about fine wine.

In addition to its world-class wines, Coursey Graves Estate Winery is located near other well-known wineries in the Sonoma Valley, making it a perfect stop for wine enthusiasts looking to explore the region's diverse offerings. The surrounding area is home to a wide range of wineries, each offering its own unique take on the winemaking process, and visitors to Coursey Graves can easily combine their visit with a wine tour of the region.

Whether you're a seasoned wine connoisseur or a casual enthusiast, Coursey Graves Estate Winery provides a welcoming and educational experience that showcases the beauty and quality of Sonoma County wines. The winery's combination of scenic views, expertly crafted wines, and personalized experiences make it a must-visit destination for anyone exploring the heart of California's wine country.

CRESCENT TRAIL RIDES

23

DATE VISITED: _____ WHO I WENT WITH: _____

RATING: ☆ ☆ ☆ ☆ ☆   WILL I RETURN?   YES / NO

Varies according to ride. No storefront
Crescent City, CA 95531
707-951-5407

Crescent Trail Rides, located in the beautiful Sierra Nevada foothills of California, offers an exceptional horseback riding experience that allows visitors to explore the stunning landscapes of the region. Whether you're an experienced rider or a beginner, Crescent Trail Rides provides guided trail rides suitable for all skill levels. Nestled near the charming town of Mariposa, which is just a short drive from the world-famous Yosemite National Park, Crescent Trail Rides offers a perfect escape into nature, allowing riders to experience the serenity and natural beauty of California's rugged countryside.

The company is known for its friendly and knowledgeable guides who lead guests through the picturesque landscapes of the Sierra Nevada. The trails wind through scenic hills, forests, and valleys, offering breathtaking views of the surrounding wilderness. As you ride along the peaceful trails, you'll have the opportunity to see a variety of wildlife, including deer, birds, and other native animals. The area is rich in history, and your guide will share insights into the region's cultural and natural history, making the ride both educational and enjoyable.

One of the highlights of Crescent Trail Rides is the opportunity to explore the vast open spaces of Mariposa County, known for its diverse ecosystems and dramatic terrain. The trails offer riders a chance to experience a variety of landscapes, from dense woodlands to open meadows, all while soaking in panoramic views of the nearby mountains. The peaceful environment allows for a unique connection with nature, as the sound of hooves on the trail is the only noise that interrupts the quiet of the wilderness.

The guided horseback rides are available in several lengths, from shorter one-hour rides to more extensive half-day adventures, allowing visitors to choose the experience that best fits their schedule and preferences. For those interested in a longer experience, Crescent Trail Rides offers custom rides that can be tailored to the needs of the group, making it an ideal activity for families, friends, or small groups. These rides provide ample opportunities to stop and take in the views, snap photos, and truly connect with the stunning natural surroundings.

In addition to the trail rides, Crescent Trail Rides also offers a variety of seasonal activities, including evening rides, which offer a magical experience as the sun sets behind the mountains and the sky fills with vibrant colors. The company's commitment to safety ensures that every ride is not only enjoyable but also secure, with experienced guides and well-trained horses that are suited to riders of all levels.

Crescent Trail Rides also caters to those looking for a more immersive experience by offering a selection of special events, including private rides for couples, birthday celebrations, and family outings. The peaceful and scenic setting of the Sierra foothills makes it the perfect backdrop for memorable occasions, and Crescent Trail Rides works with guests to create personalized experiences that make every ride unique.

Whether you're a seasoned rider or someone looking for a leisurely ride through beautiful landscapes, Crescent Trail Rides offers an unforgettable horseback riding experience in one of California's most scenic and tranquil regions. The combination of stunning scenery, well-maintained horses, and expert guides makes Crescent Trail Rides a must-visit destination for anyone seeking to experience the natural beauty of Mariposa County and the Sierra Nevada foothills. It's an ideal way to disconnect from the hustle and bustle of daily life and enjoy a peaceful ride through one of California's most beautiful and historic areas.

DEATH VALLEY NATIONAL PARK

COUNTY: INYO, SAN BERNARDINO   **CITY:** FURNACE CREEK

DATE VISITED: **WHO I WENT WITH:**

RATING: ☆ ☆ ☆ ☆ ☆   **WILL I RETURN?** YES / NO

The main road transecting Death Valley National Park from east to west is California Highway 190.On the east in Nevada, U.S. Route 95 parallels the park from north to south with connecting highways at Scotty's Junction (State Route 267), Beatty (State Route 374), and Lathrop Wells (State Route 373).

P.O. Box 579
Death Valley, CA 92328
760-786-3200

Death Valley National Park, located in eastern California and extending into Nevada, is a land of extremes and contrasts. It is the hottest, driest, and lowest national park in the United States, yet it offers a surprisingly diverse array of landscapes and attractions. Covering over 3.4 million acres, it is the largest national park in the contiguous United States and a haven for adventurers, photographers, and nature enthusiasts seeking the allure of the starkly beautiful desert.

The park's most famous feature is Badwater Basin, a vast salt flat that lies 282 feet below sea level, making it the lowest point in North America. The white-crusted salt formations stretch endlessly under a blazing sun, creating an otherworldly, surreal environment. Nearby, Devil's Golf Course offers another striking sight: a jagged expanse of crystallized salt formations, sculpted over millennia by wind and water.

Zabriskie Point is one of the park's most iconic viewpoints. Its golden-hued badlands glow at sunrise and sunset, providing stunning panoramas of eroded hills and desert landscapes. Another must-visit location is Dante's View, perched at over 5,000 feet above the valley floor, offering sweeping vistas of Death Valley and the Panamint Mountains.

The towering sand dunes of Mesquite Flat, near Stovepipe Wells, are a favorite for photographers and explorers. Their rippling patterns shift with the wind, creating an ever-changing landscape perfect for hiking and stargazing. For a more challenging adventure, the Eureka Dunes, among the tallest in North America, rise dramatically from the desert floor, offering unparalleled solitude and breathtaking views.

Artist's Palette, located along the scenic Artist's Drive, is a testament to the park's geologic diversity. Its vibrant, multicolored hills are caused by the oxidation of different metals, creating shades of green, pink, purple, and gold. Similarly, the layered rock formations in Golden Canyon showcase Death Valley's dynamic geology and provide excellent hiking opportunities.

Death Valley's history is as rich as its landscapes. Scotty's Castle, though currently undergoing restoration, tells the tale of the early 20th century with its Spanish-style architecture and intriguing backstory. The nearby Harmony Borax Works highlights the area's mining heritage, complete with preserved wagons used during the famous "20 Mule Team" era.

Despite its name, Death Valley is teeming with life. Springtime occasionally brings an ephemeral superbloom, when wildflowers carpet the desert floor in vivid colors, a rare and magical spectacle. Wildlife such as roadrunners, bighorn sheep, and kit foxes thrive in this seemingly inhospitable environment, demonstrating remarkable adaptability.

The park is also renowned for its dark skies, making it a top destination for stargazing and astrophotography. With minimal light pollution, visitors can witness a canopy of stars, planets, and even the Milky Way stretching across the night sky.

Death Valley is accessible year-round, but its seasons dramatically affect the experience. Winter and early spring are the most popular times to visit due to milder temperatures, while summer offers a chance to experience the region's legendary heat, with temperatures often exceeding 120°F.

Whether you're marveling at the vast salt flats, hiking through dramatic canyons, or gazing at the stars, Death Valley National Park offers an unparalleled journey into the extremes of nature. It's a destination that inspires awe and respect, inviting visitors to explore its raw beauty and untamed wilderness.

DISCOVERY WHALE WATCH

COUNTY: MONTEREY   **CITY:** MONTEREY

DATE VISITED: **WHO I WENT WITH:**

　　　RATING: ☆ ☆ ☆ ☆ ☆   **WILL I RETURN?** YES / NO

66 Fisherman's Wharf
Monterey, CA, 93940
831-372-7064

Discovery Whale Watch, located in Monterey, California, offers an extraordinary opportunity to witness the majestic marine life of the Monterey Bay National Marine Sanctuary, one of the richest marine ecosystems in the world. Whether you are a seasoned wildlife enthusiast or a first-time whale watcher, Discovery Whale Watch provides an unforgettable experience with their expert-guided tours and a chance to see a variety of whales, dolphins, sea lions, and other incredible marine animals in their natural habitat. The tour's location along the Pacific coastline makes it an ideal spot for whale watching, as the waters here are home to migrating whales, including gray whales, humpback whales, blue whales, and killer whales, depending on the time of year.

The tours offered by Discovery Whale Watch take visitors out on comfortable, well-equipped boats, where expert naturalists guide the journey, sharing insights about the animals, marine conservation, and the unique geography of Monterey Bay. The boat ride itself is an exciting part of the adventure, as you travel through waters rich with wildlife. Whether you're cruising along the coast in search of migrating whales or venturing further out into deeper waters, the tours are designed to maximize wildlife sightings and ensure a memorable experience for all guests.

The Monterey Bay is known for being one of the top whale-watching destinations in the world. Discovery Whale Watch's knowledgeable crew uses their expertise to locate and track the movements of the whales, ensuring that visitors have the best chance to witness these incredible creatures up close. Gray whale migration is one of the most anticipated events, with these animals traveling from their breeding grounds in Baja California to the feeding grounds in Alaska, making their annual migration a spectacular sight. Additionally, humpback whales and blue whales frequent the bay during the summer months, while orcas and dolphins are often spotted year-round.

In addition to whale sightings, Discovery Whale Watch guests may also encounter other incredible marine life, including playful sea otters, large groups of sea lions, and various species of dolphins, such as the common dolphin and bottlenose dolphin. The Monterey Bay waters are teeming with life, and the company offers a chance to explore and learn about this thriving ecosystem. The naturalists aboard provide an engaging and informative experience, discussing the biology, behaviors, and conservation efforts surrounding the different species encountered during the trip.

The tours typically last between 2 and 3 hours, depending on the route and the wildlife spotted. Discovery Whale Watch provides a safe and comfortable environment, with the boats designed to give everyone ample viewing opportunities. The boats are also equipped with modern amenities, including warm clothing and comfortable seating, to ensure a pleasant experience, even on chillier days at sea.

For those looking for an even more personalized experience, Discovery Whale Watch offers private charters, which allow for a more exclusive and tailored whale-watching adventure. These private tours are perfect for families, groups, or special occasions, providing an intimate setting for whale watching while allowing the naturalists to focus on the specific interests of the guests. The private charters also offer a unique opportunity for photography enthusiasts to capture the majestic marine life up close.

Discovery Whale Watch operates year-round, with the peak whale-watching season occurring from December to April, when the gray whale migration is at its height. However, whale sightings are not limited to these months, as the waters of Monterey Bay remain an active habitat for various whale species, dolphins, and other marine life throughout the year.

Whether you are a local resident or visiting the Monterey Peninsula, a trip with Discovery Whale Watch offers an unparalleled chance to experience the awe and wonder of the Pacific Ocean's marine wildlife. With knowledgeable guides, comfortable boats, and a commitment to conservation and education, it's a perfect outing for families, friends, or anyone wanting to immerse themselves in the natural beauty of California's coastal waters. Discovering whales and marine life in the stunning surroundings of Monterey Bay will undoubtedly be a highlight of your visit to California.

26

ESCAPOLOGY SAN DIEGO

COUNTY: SAN DIEGO   **CITY:** SAN DIEGO

DATE VISITED: **WHO I WENT WITH:**

RATING: ☆ ☆ ☆ ☆ ☆   **WILL I RETURN?**   YES / NO

3116 Mission Blvd
San Diego, CA 92109
858-412-5914

Escapology San Diego, located in the heart of San Diego, California, offers an exciting and immersive escape room experience that challenges participants to think critically, work together, and solve intricate puzzles under time pressure. Ideal for groups of friends, families, or corporate teams, Escapology is a premier destination for those seeking a fun and interactive adventure in San Diego. Known for its high-quality, thoughtfully designed rooms, Escapology San Diego offers a variety of themed escape scenarios that test problem-solving abilities, teamwork, and communication skills. Each escape room is uniquely crafted with detailed sets, high-tech features, and compelling narratives to create a truly immersive experience that will leave participants on the edge of their seats.

At Escapology San Diego, guests can choose from a selection of thrilling and engaging themed rooms, each offering a different storyline and set of challenges. Whether you're trying to break out of a prison cell, solving a mystery, or stopping a world-threatening disaster, there's a wide range of themes and difficulty levels to cater to both beginners and seasoned escape room enthusiasts. Some popular escape room options include "The Stolen", a suspense-filled heist scenario, and "Mansion Murder", where participants must uncover the mystery behind a chilling crime. The varying levels of difficulty mean that no matter your experience, there's an exciting and challenging adventure waiting for you.

Each escape room at Escapology San Diego is designed to engage participants with a series of clues, puzzles, and hidden objects, all of which must be uncovered and solved to escape before the clock runs out. The rooms are equipped with state-of-the-art technology and creative set designs that bring the themes to life, ensuring that every moment of the game is an immersive and interactive experience. Players are often surprised by the level of detail and creativity, making it a standout attraction in San Diego.

The escape rooms are ideal for a wide variety of occasions, from team-building events to birthday parties, family outings, or a unique group activity with friends. For those planning corporate outings, Escapology San Diego offers special packages that can be tailored for team-building exercises. These experiences focus on improving communication, leadership, and collaboration, all while having fun and working towards a common goal.

For those new to escape rooms, the friendly and professional staff at Escapology San Diego provides clear instructions and support throughout the experience, offering hints and guidance when necessary to ensure everyone has a good time. While the challenges are designed to be difficult, the goal is to make sure that all participants enjoy themselves and leave with a sense of accomplishment, whether or not they manage to escape in time.

Escapology San Diego is conveniently located in Mission Valley, a central area of San Diego with easy access to popular attractions, restaurants, and shops. After completing your escape room adventure, you can explore the nearby attractions, enjoy a meal at one of the area's great restaurants, or take in the stunning views of the San Diego Bay and surrounding coastline.

In addition to the traditional escape room experiences, Escapology San Diego also offers private events and group bookings, which are perfect for special occasions such as birthdays, corporate events, or social gatherings. The immersive nature of the escape rooms makes them an excellent choice for groups looking to bond and create memorable experiences while having fun.

Whether you're a first-timer or an escape room veteran, Escapology San Diego provides an exciting, challenging, and memorable experience in the heart of San Diego. The combination of engaging themes, high-quality design, and team-focused challenges ensures that it remains a top choice for anyone looking to experience the thrill of escaping a well-crafted scenario within an hour. If you're looking for an unforgettable experience that combines adventure, strategy, and entertainment, Escapology San Diego is a must-visit destination.

27

FANTASTIC RACE

COUNTY: LOS ANGELES   **CITY:** LOS ANGELES

DATE VISITED: **WHO I WENT WITH:**

        RATING: ☆ ☆ ☆ ☆ ☆   **WILL I RETURN?** YES / NO

1171 S Robertson Blvd
Los Angeles, CA 90035
818-942-3134

Fantastic Race, based in Southern California, offers a thrilling, interactive adventure that combines the excitement of a scavenger hunt with the challenges of a race, set against the backdrop of iconic city landmarks and hidden gems. Inspired by the popular concept of reality TV competition shows, Fantastic Race invites participants to team up and embark on a fun-filled journey through urban landscapes, solving puzzles, completing tasks, and racing against the clock in a bid to be crowned the winners. Whether you're a local resident or a visitor looking to explore a new city in a unique way, Fantastic Race offers an unforgettable experience full of adventure and camaraderie.

The race typically involves teams of participants who are given clues and challenges to solve at various locations around the city. These tasks are designed to test problem-solving skills, physical endurance, and teamwork, while also providing a deeper connection to the city's culture, history, and hidden secrets. Participants might find themselves deciphering cryptic clues, taking part in physical challenges, or visiting famous landmarks to gather information—all while competing against other teams for the fastest time.

What sets Fantastic Race apart from other scavenger hunts is its level of detail and creativity. The event organizers go to great lengths to ensure that the challenges are engaging and varied, creating an immersive experience that feels like a real race. Each city location is thoughtfully selected to offer participants an opportunity to discover unique spots they might not have otherwise visited, making it an ideal way to explore a city in a fun and exciting manner. The event is not just about speed—it's about engaging with the city, working together as a team, and making memories along the way.

Participants in Fantastic Race are typically equipped with a smartphone app or paper clues, depending on the specific race format, which they use to navigate through the city, mark completed challenges, and track their progress. The race's design encourages both locals and tourists to interact with the environment and learn about their surroundings in a way that's both educational and entertaining.

Each leg of the race brings a new challenge, ensuring that no two races are ever the same.

Fantastic Race can be enjoyed by all ages and skill levels, making it an excellent choice for families, friends, corporate teams, or tourists looking for a fun and interactive way to experience a new city. The race can be tailored to different group sizes and preferences, with the option for private or public events. Teams can compete for the fastest completion time, or simply enjoy the journey, knowing that the true reward is in the experience itself.

In addition to the thrill of the race itself, Fantastic Race promotes teamwork, communication, and problem-solving in a lighthearted and entertaining atmosphere. It's an activity that brings people together, whether they're working as a team to overcome obstacles or sharing laughs during the challenges. The sense of friendly competition adds an extra layer of excitement, while the opportunity to win prizes and bragging rights keeps the energy high throughout the event.

For those looking to add a unique twist to their next group outing, team-building event, or celebration, Fantastic Race offers a one-of-a-kind experience that is guaranteed to provide fun, adventure, and lasting memories. Whether you're navigating the streets of Los Angeles, San Diego, or other major cities in California, Fantastic Race delivers a thrilling and dynamic experience that brings the best of adventure and exploration to life.

28

FISCALINI RANCH PRESERVE

COUNTY: SAN LUIS	CITY: CAMBRIA

DATE VISITED:	WHO I WENT WITH:

RATING: ☆ ☆ ☆ ☆ ☆	WILL I RETURN? YES / NO

604 Main Street
Cambria, CA 93428
805-927-2856

Fiscalini Ranch Preserve, located in Cayucos, California, is a stunning natural preserve that offers visitors the opportunity to experience the beauty of the central coast's rugged coastline and diverse ecosystems. This 437-acre nature preserve, which is managed by the Land Conservancy of San Luis Obispo County, is a popular destination for nature lovers, outdoor enthusiasts, and anyone seeking to enjoy the natural splendor of California's Central Coast. With its expansive views, serene walking trails, and abundant wildlife, Fiscalini Ranch Preserve provides an ideal setting for hiking, birdwatching, photography, and simply enjoying the great outdoors.

One of the defining features of Fiscalini Ranch Preserve is its breathtaking scenery. The preserve encompasses a variety of landscapes, including rolling hills, coastal bluffs, grasslands, and a rich variety of plant and animal life. Visitors can enjoy sweeping vistas of the Pacific Ocean to the west, with stunning coastal views that stretch for miles, as well as panoramic views of the Cayucos area and surrounding agricultural lands. The coastal bluffs offer particularly spectacular views, making it a perfect spot for nature walks and photography.

The preserve is home to several miles of well-maintained trails, which are perfect for both casual walks and more strenuous hikes. The trails wind through the preserve's diverse habitats, allowing visitors to explore the various ecosystems that make up this beautiful area. Some of the most popular trails include the Bluff Trail, which offers striking views of the ocean and the rocky coastline, and the Canyon Trail, which takes hikers through shaded canyons and past lush vegetation. The trails are relatively easy to navigate, making them accessible for hikers of all skill levels, including families with children and individuals with limited mobility.

For those interested in wildlife, Fiscalini Ranch Preserve provides excellent opportunities for birdwatching and observing local wildlife. The preserve is home to a variety of birds, including hawks, kestrels, and songbirds, as well as other wildlife such as deer, foxes, and coyotes. The combination of coastal and inland habitats makes it an ideal location for spotting a wide range of species throughout the year. The preserve also supports a variety of plant species, with areas of wildflowers, native grasses, and coastal scrub, adding to the richness of the landscape.

Fiscalini Ranch Preserve is also an important part of the region's conservation efforts. The preserve was established to protect the area's natural resources and ensure that this beautiful stretch of land remains intact for future generations to enjoy. The Land Conservancy of San Luis Obispo County works to maintain and protect the preserve's habitats through sustainable management practices, ensuring that the preserve continues to thrive as an ecological sanctuary for both wildlife and visitors.

In addition to its natural beauty, Fiscalini Ranch Preserve is conveniently located near Cayucos, a charming coastal town with a small-town feel, making it an easy stop for those visiting the area. After exploring the preserve, visitors can head into Cayucos to enjoy the town's beautiful beaches, quaint shops, and restaurants that offer fresh seafood and local fare. The town's relaxed atmosphere makes it the perfect complement to a day spent in the peaceful surroundings of Fiscalini Ranch Preserve.

Fiscalini Ranch Preserve is open to the public year-round, with no admission fee, making it an accessible and affordable way to enjoy the natural beauty of the Central Coast. The preserve is also pet-friendly, allowing dogs on leashes, making it a great place for those traveling with their furry companions. Whether you're seeking a peaceful escape into nature, an opportunity to explore the coastal landscape, or simply a place to enjoy the outdoors, Fiscalini Ranch Preserve provides a perfect setting for relaxation and adventure. With its rich biodiversity, stunning coastal views, and well-maintained trails, it is a must-visit destination for anyone exploring the California Central Coast.

29

FISHERMAN'S WHARF

COUNTY: SAN FRANCISCO   **CITY:** SAN FRANCISCO

DATE VISITED: **WHO I WENT WITH:**

RATING: ☆ ☆ ☆ ☆ ☆   **WILL I RETURN?**   YES / NO

Jefferson Street Between Hyde and Powell Streets
San Francisco, CA 94133

Fisherman's Wharf, located in San Francisco, California, is a historic waterfront area that offers a vibrant blend of culture, history, and entertainment. Situated along the city's iconic Embarcadero, it is one of San Francisco's most popular and bustling tourist destinations. Known for its scenic views of the San Francisco Bay, historic piers, and lively atmosphere, Fisherman's Wharf offers something for everyone, from families to solo travelers, food lovers to history buffs. The area is home to a variety of attractions, including seafood restaurants, souvenir shops, museums, and historic ships, all set against the backdrop of the beautiful bay.

The area's history dates back to the early 19th century when it was the hub for the city's fishing industry. The name "Fisherman's Wharf" comes from the Italian-American fishermen who once populated the area and used the wharf as their base of operations. Over the years, it evolved into a lively district, where visitors could enjoy fresh seafood and watch the bustling activity of the harbor. Today, Fisherman's Wharf retains much of its historic charm while embracing modern entertainment and dining experiences.

One of the most iconic aspects of Fisherman's Wharf is its incredible selection of seafood. The area is renowned for its clam chowder, fresh Dungeness crab, and other delicious seafood dishes, with numerous seafood shacks and upscale restaurants offering an authentic taste of the bay. A must-try dish is the famous clam chowder served in a sourdough bread bowl, which can be enjoyed at one of the many casual eateries or outdoor stands along the wharf. The Boudin Bakery, one of the area's oldest establishments, is well-known for its sourdough bread and serves up fresh bread bowls filled with creamy chowder.

In addition to its culinary offerings, Fisherman's Wharf is home to a variety of attractions that highlight the city's maritime history. One of the most popular sites is Pier 39, a bustling shopping center that offers an array of shops, restaurants, and entertainment options. Visitors can enjoy street performers, live music, and even catch a glimpse of the famous sea lions that lounge on the docks nearby. The pier offers spectacular views of the Golden Gate Bridge and Alcatraz

Island, making it a great spot for sightseeing and photography.

Another must-see attraction at Fisherman's Wharf is the San Francisco Maritime National Historical Park. This collection of historic ships, including the Balclutha, a 19th-century square-rigged sailing ship, allows visitors to step back in time and learn about San Francisco's maritime history. The nearby Aquatic Park is also part of the park and provides a scenic place to relax by the water.

For those interested in exploring further, Fisherman's Wharf is the departure point for boat tours to Alcatraz Island, the notorious former prison located in the middle of the bay. Visitors can take a ferry from the wharf to tour the prison and learn about its fascinating history. Other boat tours from the wharf include harbor cruises, where guests can take in views of the city skyline, Golden Gate Bridge, and the bay's landmarks.

For a unique experience, visitors can also check out Madame Tussauds San Francisco at Pier 39, a famous wax museum that features lifelike figures of celebrities, sports stars, and historical figures. Similarly, the Ripley's Believe It or Not! museum offers a collection of oddities and curiosities, making it a fun stop for families and those looking for something quirky.

Fisherman's Wharf is not just about attractions and food—it also provides an excellent base to explore the rest of San Francisco. It is within walking distance to other famous destinations like Ghirardelli Square, North Beach, and Chinatown. The area is also well-served by public transportation, making it easy to get around the city and visit sites such as Golden Gate Park, the Palace of Fine Arts, and the Mission District.

For visitors with a love of history, the area's rich maritime heritage is preserved in places like the USS Pampanito, a World War II submarine that is now a museum at the wharf. Tourists can explore the inside of the submarine, gaining insight into life aboard a U.S. Navy vessel during wartime.

Whether you're looking to indulge in fresh seafood, take in scenic views of the bay, or learn about the city's history, Fisherman's Wharf offers a dynamic and unforgettable experience. Its combination of attractions, food, and culture makes it a must-visit destination for anyone traveling to San Francisco, offering a taste of the city's rich heritage and vibrant waterfront life.

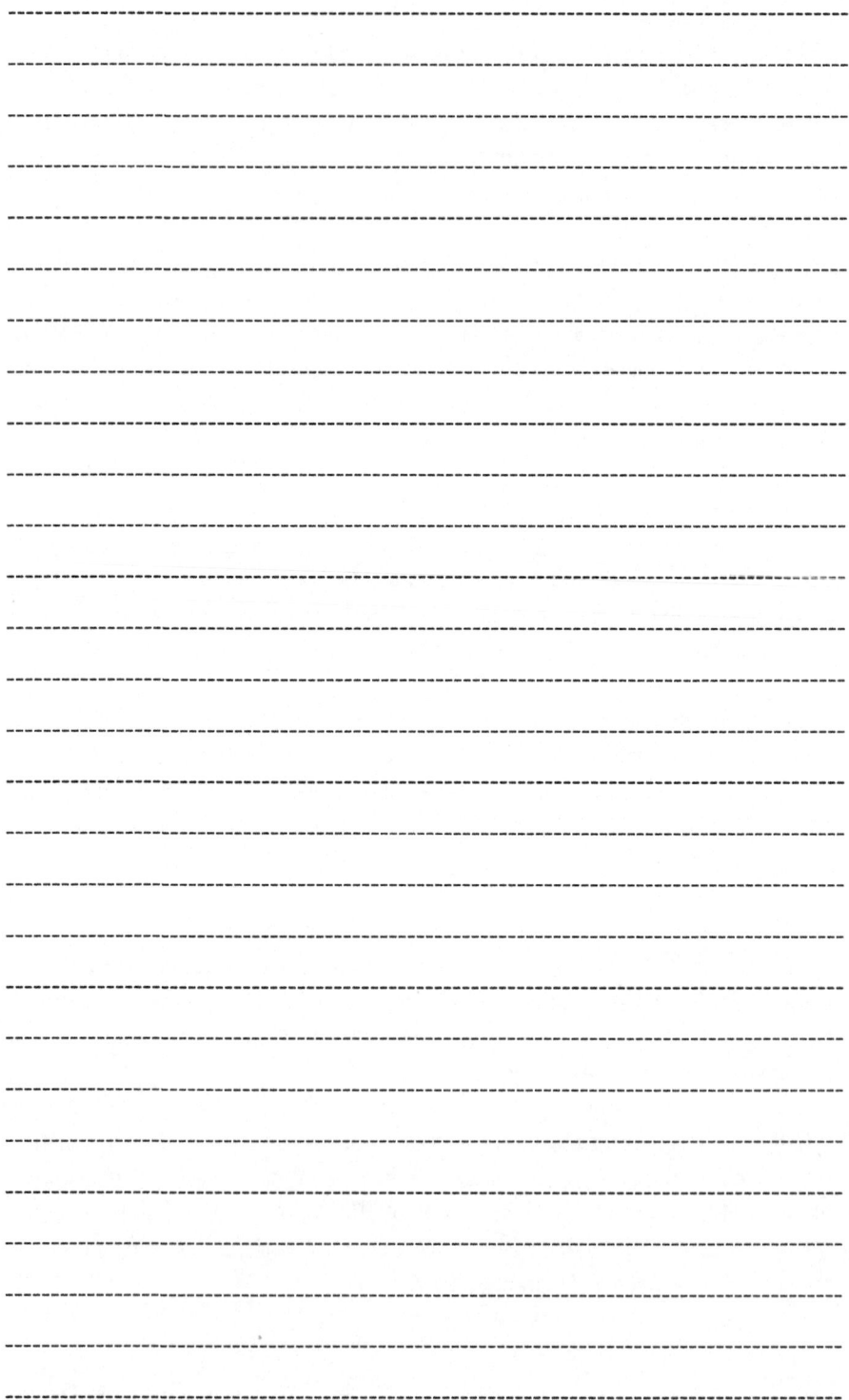

FORESTIERE UNDERGROUND GARDENS

(30)

COUNTY: FRESNO   CITY: FRESNO

DATE VISITED:	WHO I WENT WITH:

RATING: ☆ ☆ ☆ ☆ ☆   WILL I RETURN?   YES / NO

5021 W Shaw Ave
Fresno, CA 93722
559-271-0734

Forestiere Underground Gardens, located in Fresno, California, is a unique and fascinating attraction that offers visitors a glimpse into the vision and creativity of its creator, Basil Forestiere. Built over a period of 40 years, beginning in the early 1900s, the underground gardens are a series of hand-dug tunnels, courtyards, and rooms that were carved into the hardpan soil of the San Joaquin Valley. What makes the Forestiere Underground Gardens so special is not just their remarkable underground architecture, but also the lush, thriving gardens that flourish beneath the surface, a testament to Forestiere's ingenuity and determination. This hidden gem in the heart of California is one of the few subterranean gardens in the United States and has become a beloved landmark for those seeking something out of the ordinary.

The creation of Forestiere Underground Gardens began when Basil Forestiere, an Italian immigrant, arrived in California and was struck by the region's hot and dry climate. Hoping to grow fruit trees and create a cool, comfortable environment for himself, Forestiere began to dig into the hard soil beneath the surface of his property. Over the years, he carved out a network of tunnels and rooms, many of which are still standing today. These underground spaces were designed to be cool in the summer and warm in the winter, offering a perfect environment for growing a variety of plants, including fruit trees like oranges, lemons, grapefruits, and pomegranates. Forestiere used a combination of artistic design and practical farming techniques to create a subterranean oasis that allowed him to grow his crops and live comfortably.

As visitors take a guided tour through the gardens, they are led through a maze of cool, earthy passageways that lead to open-air courtyards, where trees and vines thrive. The tunnels and rooms are beautifully designed, with arches, skylights, and even a chapel-like space, giving the underground complex a sense of wonder and tranquility. The gardens themselves are filled with a variety of trees and plants, which have been carefully cultivated to take advantage of the unique underground conditions. Many of the plants, including fruit trees, flowering plants, and herbs, have thrived in this environment, growing in ways that are not typically seen in the above-ground world.

One of the highlights of the Forestiere Underground Gardens is the way in which the space is designed to optimize airflow and natural light. The tunnels were not just randomly dug but were planned in a way that would allow for airflow between the rooms, keeping the temperature stable and providing ventilation for the plants. The rooms were also strategically placed to take advantage of sunlight filtering in through skylights, allowing for natural light to nourish the plants without overwhelming the space with excessive heat. Visitors can see firsthand how Forestiere's design principles created a sustainable environment for both himself and his crops.

In addition to the underground garden spaces, the site also includes several above-ground features, such as the visitor center and a small museum that showcases the history and legacy of the Forestiere Underground Gardens. The museum includes artifacts, photographs, and personal items that tell the story of Forestiere's life and the creation of his extraordinary underground oasis. Visitors can learn about his early life, his decision to dig the tunnels, and how he managed to create a thriving garden in the harsh conditions of the San Joaquin Valley.

The Forestiere Underground Gardens are also a great place for photography, with their unusual and beautiful architecture and the vibrant greenery that grows beneath the earth. The gardens provide a peaceful and serene environment, making it an ideal location for a relaxing visit. The combination of nature, history, and architectural wonder makes the site an exceptional experience for visitors of all ages. Whether you're an architecture enthusiast, a lover of nature, or simply someone seeking a unique experience, the Forestiere Underground Gardens offers a one-of-a-kind adventure.

The gardens are open year-round, and tours are available for visitors, providing an educational and informative experience. Forestiere Underground Gardens is a family-friendly destination that allows guests to explore at their own pace while learning about this amazing underground world. The location is easily accessible from downtown Fresno, making it a great stop for those visiting the area or exploring the heart of California's Central Valley.

For those who appreciate history, creativity, and the natural world, Forestiere Underground Gardens is a must-visit attraction that offers a rare glimpse into an ingenious underground landscape. With its fascinating story, unique architecture, and lush gardens, it's no wonder that this extraordinary location has become a beloved part of Fresno's cultural and historical landscape. Whether you're visiting for the first time or returning to explore new corners of the garden, Forestiere Underground Gardens is sure to leave you with a sense of wonder and awe at the ingenuity and dedication of its creator.

31

GARY FARRELL WINERY

COUNTY: SONOMA   **CITY:** HEALDSBURG

DATE VISITED: **WHO I WENT WITH:**

RATING: ☆ ☆ ☆ ☆ ☆   **WILL I RETURN?** YES / NO

10701 Westside Rd
Healdsburg, CA 95448
707-473-2909

Gary Farrell Winery, located in the heart of Sonoma County, California, is a renowned destination for wine enthusiasts and those looking to experience the beauty and elegance of the Russian River Valley. Founded in 1982 by acclaimed winemaker Gary Farrell, the winery is known for producing high-quality Pinot Noir, Chardonnay, and other varietals that capture the essence of the region's terroir. The winery sits atop a hill, offering panoramic views of the surrounding vineyards and the lush, rolling landscape of Sonoma County, making it an ideal spot to enjoy world-class wine while taking in breathtaking scenery. With a reputation for crafting exceptional wines and its dedication to sustainable farming practices, Gary Farrell Winery has become a cornerstone of Sonoma's wine country, attracting visitors from around the globe.

Upon arriving at Gary Farrell Winery, guests are immediately struck by the picturesque setting, where modern architecture blends seamlessly with the natural beauty of the valley. The winery's stunning tasting room features large windows that allow guests to enjoy sweeping views of the vineyard-covered hills and the distant Russian River, creating a serene and inviting atmosphere. The elegant yet relaxed ambiance makes it a perfect place for wine lovers to unwind and appreciate the artistry behind each bottle of wine.

The tasting experience at Gary Farrell Winery is exceptional, with a variety of options to suit all preferences. Visitors can enjoy intimate, guided tastings led by knowledgeable staff members who are passionate about the winery's rich history and commitment to producing small-lot, handcrafted wines. The tasting menu features a selection of the winery's signature wines, including Pinot Noir and Chardonnay, which showcase the complex flavors and nuances of the region's diverse microclimates. The winery also offers exclusive and limited-edition wines, allowing guests to sample unique bottlings that are not available elsewhere.

One of the highlights of the tasting experience at Gary Farrell Winery is the opportunity to explore the winery's commitment to sustainable farming practices. The winery works with some of the best vineyard partners in the region, many of whom practice organic and sustainable farming methods. By utilizing these practices, Gary Farrell Winery ensures that its wines reflect the natural beauty of the land and the quality of the fruit grown in the region. Visitors can learn about the meticulous process of growing and harvesting the grapes, as well as the careful methods of fermentation and aging that contribute to the winery's award-winning wines.

For those looking to deepen their understanding of winemaking, Gary Farrell Winery offers educational tours that take guests behind the scenes to explore the winery's production facilities. During these tours, guests can learn about the steps involved in creating wine, from vineyard management and grape picking to fermentation and aging in French oak barrels. The tours provide a fascinating insight into the dedication and precision required to craft wines that capture the essence of the Russian River Valley's terroir.

In addition to its wines, Gary Farrell Winery is known for its hospitality and exceptional customer service. The staff takes pride in providing personalized experiences for guests, ensuring that each visit is memorable and enjoyable. Whether it's a private tasting, a group tour, or a special event, the winery offers a range of experiences to suit every visitor's needs.

For visitors who want to make their trip to the winery even more special, Gary Farrell Winery offers a range of events and experiences throughout the year. These include wine dinners, private tastings, and special occasions such as harvest celebrations, where guests can celebrate the bounty of the land and enjoy food pairings with the winery's exceptional wines. The winery's commitment to providing an unforgettable experience is evident in every detail, from the stunning views to the world-class wines.

Gary Farrell Winery is conveniently located near other prominent wineries in the Russian River Valley and Sonoma County, making it a great stop for those exploring California's wine country. Whether you are a seasoned wine connoisseur or new to the world of wine, a visit to Gary Farrell Winery offers a chance to experience some of the finest wines California has to offer while enjoying the beauty and tranquility of Sonoma's renowned wine-producing region.

With its breathtaking views, exceptional wines, and dedication to sustainable practices, Gary Farrell Winery provides an unforgettable wine country experience. Whether you're visiting for a casual tasting or a more immersive wine tour, the winery's hospitality and commitment to quality ensure that every guest leaves with a deeper appreciation for the art of winemaking and the incredible wines =

that define Sonoma County.

32

GLACIER POINT

COUNTY: MARIPOSA   **CITY:** MARIPOSA

DATE VISITED: **WHO I WENT WITH:**

RATING: ☆ ☆ ☆ ☆ ☆   **WILL I RETURN?** YES / NO

You can drive to Yosemite year-round and enter via Highways 41, 140, and 120 from the west. Tioga Pass Entrance (via Highway 120 from the east) is closed from approximately November through late May or June. Hetch Hetchy is open all year but may close intermittently due to snow. Please note that GPS units do not always provide accurate directions to or within Yosemite.
209-372-0200

Glacier Point, located in Yosemite National Park, California, is one of the park's most iconic and breathtaking viewpoints, offering panoramic views of some of the most stunning natural landscapes in the United States. Perched high above the Yosemite Valley, at an elevation of 7,214 feet (2,199 meters), Glacier Point provides visitors with sweeping vistas of Half Dome, the Yosemite Valley, Vernal Fall, Nevada Fall, and the vast wilderness of the Sierra Nevada mountain range. This dramatic viewpoint is a must-visit for nature lovers, photographers, and anyone seeking a truly awe-inspiring experience in one of America's most famous national parks.

The journey to Glacier Point offers spectacular scenery in itself. During the summer months, visitors can reach Glacier Point by car via the Glacier Point Road, a 16-mile drive from Yosemite Valley. The road is typically open from late May or early June until October, depending on snow conditions. As visitors ascend, they are treated to breathtaking views of the park's towering granite cliffs, lush meadows, and rushing rivers. For those looking for a more adventurous experience, there is also the option to hike to Glacier Point from the valley below, such as the Four-Mile Trail or the more challenging Panorama Trail, both of which offer stunning views along the way.

Once at Glacier Point, the views are simply unparalleled. From this vantage point, visitors can look down over the Yosemite Valley, one of the most famous glacial valleys in the world, where granite cliffs rise dramatically above the forested floor. The iconic Half Dome is the star of the show from Glacier Point, as it looms large in the distance, its distinctive shape standing out against the sky. Vernal Fall and Nevada Fall are also visible from this location, their waters tumbling down the cliffs in dramatic cascades, especially during the spring melt when the waterfalls are at their fullest.

One of the most popular activities at Glacier Point is simply taking in the view and marveling at the natural beauty of Yosemite. Visitors can stand at the edge of the viewpoint and gaze out over the expansive landscape, often feeling a sense of awe at the scale and grandeur of the wilderness. The clear, clean air and sweeping views make this a perfect spot for photography, with sunrise and sunset offering especially beautiful lighting conditions for capturing the scenery.

For those with a love for history and geology, Glacier Point also has a fascinating story to tell. The point was named by Lafayette Bunnell, one of the first non-Native American explorers of Yosemite, in honor of the glaciers that once carved the landscape of the valley below. Over time, Glacier Point has become a popular destination for park visitors, with its combination of beauty, history, and accessibility.

In addition to its views, Glacier Point is a fantastic spot for stargazing, especially on clear nights when the night sky is illuminated by thousands of stars. Due to its high elevation and relatively low levels of light pollution, Glacier Point offers some of the best stargazing opportunities in the park. In fact, Yosemite National Park as a whole is recognized as one of the best places in the U.S. for stargazing, and Glacier Point is a prime location to witness the night sky.

For those interested in guided experiences, the Yosemite Conservancy offers a variety of tours, including interpretive programs that delve into the history, geology, and natural features of the park. Visitors can learn more about the dramatic processes that shaped the valley and the surrounding mountains, as well as the flora and fauna that make the park so unique.

Glacier Point is also a popular spot for sunset viewing, as the sun sets behind the Sierra Nevada mountains, casting a golden glow over the landscape. Many visitors come specifically to witness this daily spectacle, which is nothing short of magical. Whether you're looking to take photographs, simply soak in the views, or enjoy a quiet moment of reflection, Glacier Point offers a peaceful and awe-inspiring atmosphere.

For those looking to explore further, Glacier Point serves as a gateway to other spectacular parts of Yosemite National Park, including the Yosemite High Sierra and the John Muir Trail, which begins in the valley and ends at Mount Whitney. The point is also within easy reach of other famous Yosemite landmarks, including El Capitan, Yosemite Falls, and the Mariposa Grove of Giant Sequoias.

Overall, Glacier Point is an essential part of any visit to Yosemite National Park. Whether you're there to experience the breathtaking views, hike the surrounding trails, or simply enjoy the tranquility of the mountains, Glacier Point provides an unforgettable experience that highlights the natural beauty of one of the world's most iconic national parks.

GOLDEN GATE BRIDGE

33

COUNTY: SAN FRANCISCO

CITY: SAN FRANCISCO

DATE VISITED:

WHO I WENT WITH:

RATING: ☆ ☆ ☆ ☆ ☆

WILL I RETURN?   YES / NO

Golden Gate Bridge Welcome Center
201 Fort Mason
San Francisco, CA 94123
415-921-5858

The Golden Gate Bridge, located in San Francisco, California, is one of the most recognizable and iconic landmarks in the world. Spanning the Golden Gate Strait, the entrance to the San Francisco Bay, the bridge connects the city of San Francisco with Marin County to the north. Completed in 1937, it was an engineering marvel of its time and remains one of the most photographed structures globally. With its striking International Orange color and elegant Art Deco design, the Golden Gate Bridge is a testament to both architectural ingenuity and the beauty of the surrounding natural landscape.

The Golden Gate Bridge stretches approximately 1.7 miles (2.7 kilometers) across the water, with its main span measuring 4,200 feet (1,280 meters). It was, at the time of its completion, the longest suspension bridge in the world, and it held that title until 1964. The bridge's design was the brainchild of Joseph Strauss, a bridge engineer, but it was architect Irving Morrow who is credited with the iconic color choice, which helps the bridge stand out against the often foggy San Francisco skies. The Golden Gate Bridge is not only a feat of engineering but also a work of art, with its graceful curves and sweeping lines.

Visitors to the Golden Gate Bridge can enjoy numerous ways to experience its grandeur. The Golden Gate Bridge Visitor Center, located on the San Francisco side, offers historical exhibits, interactive displays, and educational information about the bridge's construction, significance, and role in the development of the region. There are also plenty of spots around the area where visitors can capture stunning photographs of the bridge, especially from the Battery Spencer overlook in Marin Headlands, which provides a stunning view of the bridge with the San Francisco skyline in the background.

One of the most popular activities for visitors is walking or biking across the bridge. Pedestrians can stroll along the east sidewalk, which offers amazing views of the San Francisco Bay, Alcatraz Island, and the Marin Headlands to the north. On clear days, the views from the bridge are truly spectacular, with the fog often rolling in and out, creating a magical atmosphere. Cyclists can also use the bridge's paths to bike across, and many people take advantage of the opportunity to cycle through the bridge's beautiful surroundings, continuing into the Marin Headlands for scenic trails and ocean views.

For those who want a more immersive experience, guided tours are available, offering in-depth insights into the history of the bridge and its importance in connecting San Francisco to the rest of California. Some tours also include trips to Fort Point National Historic Site, located directly beneath the southern end of the bridge, which offers a unique perspective of the bridge from below. Here, visitors can learn about the fort's military history and its role in protecting the entrance to the bay during the Civil War.

The Golden Gate Bridge is also an important part of San Francisco's cultural and historical identity, serving as a symbol of innovation, resilience, and the spirit of the city. It has appeared in countless movies, TV shows, and commercials, cementing its status as one of the world's most recognized landmarks. It is also a vital transportation route, allowing vehicles to travel between San Francisco and Marin County, and helping to ease traffic congestion in the region.

In addition to its aesthetic and engineering value, the Golden Gate Bridge is also a center for environmental and conservation efforts. The bridge's location near the Golden Gate National Recreation Area means that it is surrounded by protected parks, beaches, and open spaces. These areas are home to a variety of wildlife and offer ample opportunities for hiking, birdwatching, and enjoying the beauty of the region.

Visitors to San Francisco can't miss the chance to see and experience the Golden Gate Bridge firsthand, whether they are simply admiring it from a distance or crossing it on foot or by bike. The bridge is a perfect blend of natural beauty and human achievement, embodying the spirit of innovation and creativity that has long been associated with the Bay Area. Whether you're taking a leisurely walk, enjoying a scenic bike ride, or simply marveling at the sight of the bridge from one of the many nearby vantage points, the Golden Gate Bridge offers an unforgettable experience that showcases both the beauty and the engineering excellence of California's most famous structure.

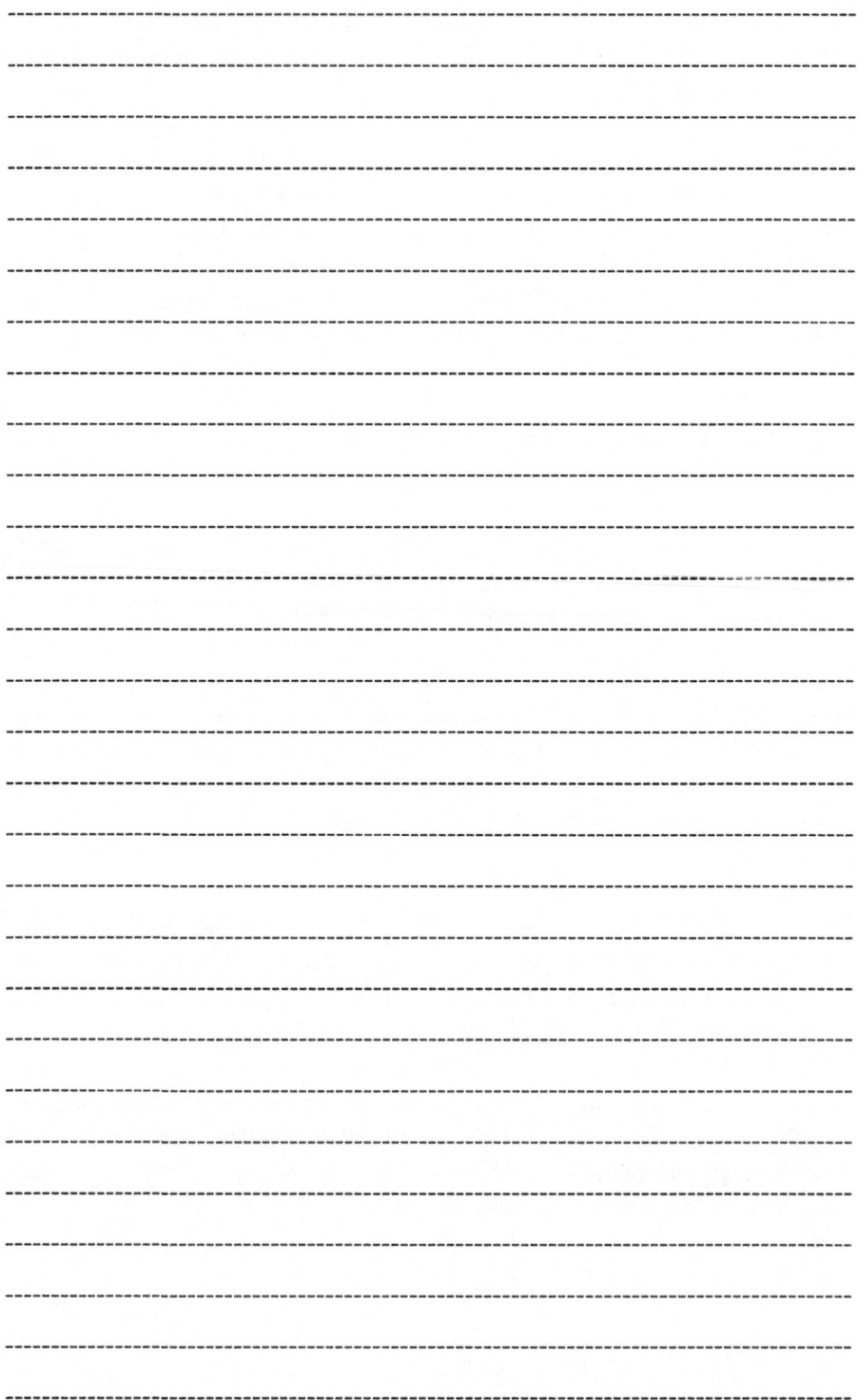

34

GOLDEN GATE PARK

COUNTY: SAN FRANCISCO   **CITY:** SAN FRANCISCO

DATE VISITED: **WHO I WENT WITH:**

RATING: ☆ ☆ ☆ ☆ ☆   **WILL I RETURN?** YES / NO

501 Stanyan St
San Francisco, CA 94117
415-831-2700

Golden Gate Park is an expansive urban park in San Francisco, California, spanning over 1,000 acres of beautifully landscaped gardens, recreational spaces, and cultural attractions. Often compared to New York City's Central Park, Golden Gate Park offers a diverse array of activities and experiences that make it a beloved destination for locals and visitors alike. With its rich history, stunning natural beauty, and array of landmarks, the park is a must-visit for anyone exploring the city.

Established in 1871, Golden Gate Park was designed to transform a stretch of sand dunes into a lush and vibrant green space. Under the vision of park superintendent William Hammond Hall and master gardener John McLaren, the park became a thriving oasis featuring over 7,000 plant species, sprawling meadows, serene lakes, and wooded groves. Today, the park attracts more than 24 million visitors annually, offering something for everyone.

One of the park's most iconic attractions is the de Young Museum, a premier fine arts museum that showcases American art from the 17th to the 21st centuries, as well as textiles and works from Africa, Oceania, and the Americas. Nearby is the California Academy of Sciences, a world-class natural history museum that houses an aquarium, planetarium, and a living rainforest under one roof. The academy is an educational treasure, appealing to families, science enthusiasts, and curious minds.

For those seeking tranquility, the Japanese Tea Garden provides a peaceful escape with its meticulously landscaped gardens, koi ponds, pagodas, and tea house. This historic garden is the oldest of its kind in the United States and offers a serene space for reflection and relaxation. Nearby, the San Francisco Botanical Garden showcases a diverse collection of plants from around the world, including rare and endangered species, all within beautifully themed gardens.

Golden Gate Park is also a hub for outdoor recreation. Visitors can rent paddle boats at Stow Lake, enjoy a leisurely walk through the Rhododendron Dell, or explore miles of trails perfect for biking and jogging. The park's open spaces, such as the Robin Williams Meadow and Hellman Hollow, are popular spots for picnics, outdoor yoga, and community events. Spreckels Lake is a favorite for model boat enthusiasts, while the Bison Paddock offers a glimpse of the park's resident bison herd, a unique and enduring feature.

Music and arts lovers will appreciate the Spreckels Temple of Music, an elegant bandshell that hosts concerts and performances. Seasonal events, such as the Outside Lands Music Festival and Hardly Strictly Bluegrass, transform the park into a vibrant cultural hotspot, drawing crowds from around the globe.

Golden Gate Park's many hidden gems include the Conservatory of Flowers, a Victorian-era greenhouse housing exotic plants and colorful floral displays, and the Windmills and Queen Wilhelmina Tulip Garden, where visitors can admire Dutch-inspired architecture and vibrant tulips in bloom.

The park is open year-round, and its beauty evolves with the seasons. Spring and summer bring colorful blooms and lively events, while autumn's golden hues and winter's crisp air offer a quieter charm. Admission to the park itself is free, though some attractions may have entry fees.

Easily accessible by public transportation, biking, or walking, Golden Gate Park is a place where natural beauty, cultural attractions, and recreational opportunities come together. Whether you're exploring world-class museums, enjoying a peaceful stroll, or attending a lively festival, Golden Gate Park captures the essence of San Francisco's vibrant spirit and is a destination that leaves a lasting impression.

35

GRACIANNA WINERY

COUNTY: SONOMA   **CITY:** HEALDSBURG

DATE VISITED: _____   **WHO I WENT WITH:** _____

              RATING: ☆ ☆ ☆ ☆ ☆   **WILL I RETURN?**   YES / NO

6914 Westside Road
Healdsburg, CA 95448
707-486-3771

Gracianna Winery, nestled in the heart of Sonoma County, California, is a family-owned winery that has earned a reputation for producing exceptional wines with a focus on Pinot Noir and Chardonnay. Located in the renowned Russian River Valley, a region known for its cool climate and fertile soils, the winery creates wines that truly capture the essence of the land. With its idyllic setting, exceptional wines, and commitment to sustainable practices, Gracianna Winery offers a memorable wine country experience for visitors seeking a taste of Sonoma's finest offerings.

The winery was founded by the Baldacci family, who named it after the matriarch of the family, Gracianna Baldacci, as a tribute to her unwavering spirit and passion for life. The winery's name reflects the family's dedication to creating wines that are as exceptional and enduring as the woman it honors. Gracianna Winery produces a small, hand-crafted selection of wines, ensuring that each bottle is a reflection of the family's commitment to quality and craftsmanship.

Upon visiting Gracianna Winery, guests are immediately captivated by the breathtaking views of the surrounding vineyards and rolling hills. The winery is situated on a hilltop, offering stunning vistas of the Russian River Valley and the Sonoma Coast, making it an ideal location to enjoy a glass of wine while taking in the natural beauty of the region. The tasting room itself is elegant yet welcoming, featuring floor-to-ceiling windows that allow visitors to admire the spectacular landscape while enjoying their wine.

The wine-tasting experience at Gracianna Winery is both intimate and educational. Guests can indulge in a variety of tastings, with options to sample the winery's signature Pinot Noir, Chardonnay, and limited-edition wines. Each wine is carefully selected to showcase the unique terroir of the Russian River Valley, where cool morning fog and warm afternoons create the perfect conditions for growing exceptional grapes. The knowledgeable and friendly staff at Gracianna Winery is passionate about sharing the story behind the wines and the winery's dedication to sustainable farming practices, providing guests with a deeper understanding of the art of winemaking.

In addition to its wine offerings, Gracianna Winery is committed to sustainable and environmentally conscious farming practices. The winery employs organic and biodynamic techniques, ensuring that its vineyards remain healthy and fertile for future generations. This commitment to sustainability is reflected in the quality of the wines, as the careful attention to the land results in grapes that are rich in flavor and character. Gracianna Winery also focuses on water conservation, energy efficiency, and soil health, further underscoring its dedication to preserving the natural beauty of the region.

For those who wish to experience the winery beyond the tasting room, Gracianna Winery offers a range of exclusive tours and experiences. Guests can take guided tours of the vineyard, learning about the sustainable farming practices that make the wines so special. The winery also offers private tastings and events, perfect for groups or special occasions, where visitors can enjoy an intimate, personalized experience with some of Sonoma's finest wines.

In addition to its stunning location and exceptional wines, Gracianna Winery is known for its warm and welcoming atmosphere. The family-owned nature of the winery means that visitors are treated like guests, with personalized service and a genuine commitment to making every experience memorable. Whether enjoying a casual tasting or a more immersive tour, visitors to Gracianna Winery can expect a relaxed and inviting environment where the focus is on creating lasting memories and enjoying the beauty of Sonoma County.

As part of the Russian River Valley wine region, Gracianna Winery is ideally situated among some of the best vineyards in the area. The winery is surrounded by other top-tier wineries, making it a great stop for anyone exploring Sonoma's wine country. Whether you are a seasoned wine connoisseur or new to the world of wine, Gracianna Winery offers a unique and unforgettable experience that showcases the very best of what Sonoma County has to offer.

With its stunning views, world-class wines, and dedication to sustainability, Gracianna Winery is a must-visit destination for anyone exploring Sonoma County. Whether you are tasting wine in the elegant tasting room, walking among the vineyards, or learning about the sustainable practices that make this winery so special, a visit to Gracianna Winery offers a unique opportunity to experience the beauty and craftsmanship of one of Sonoma's premier wineries.

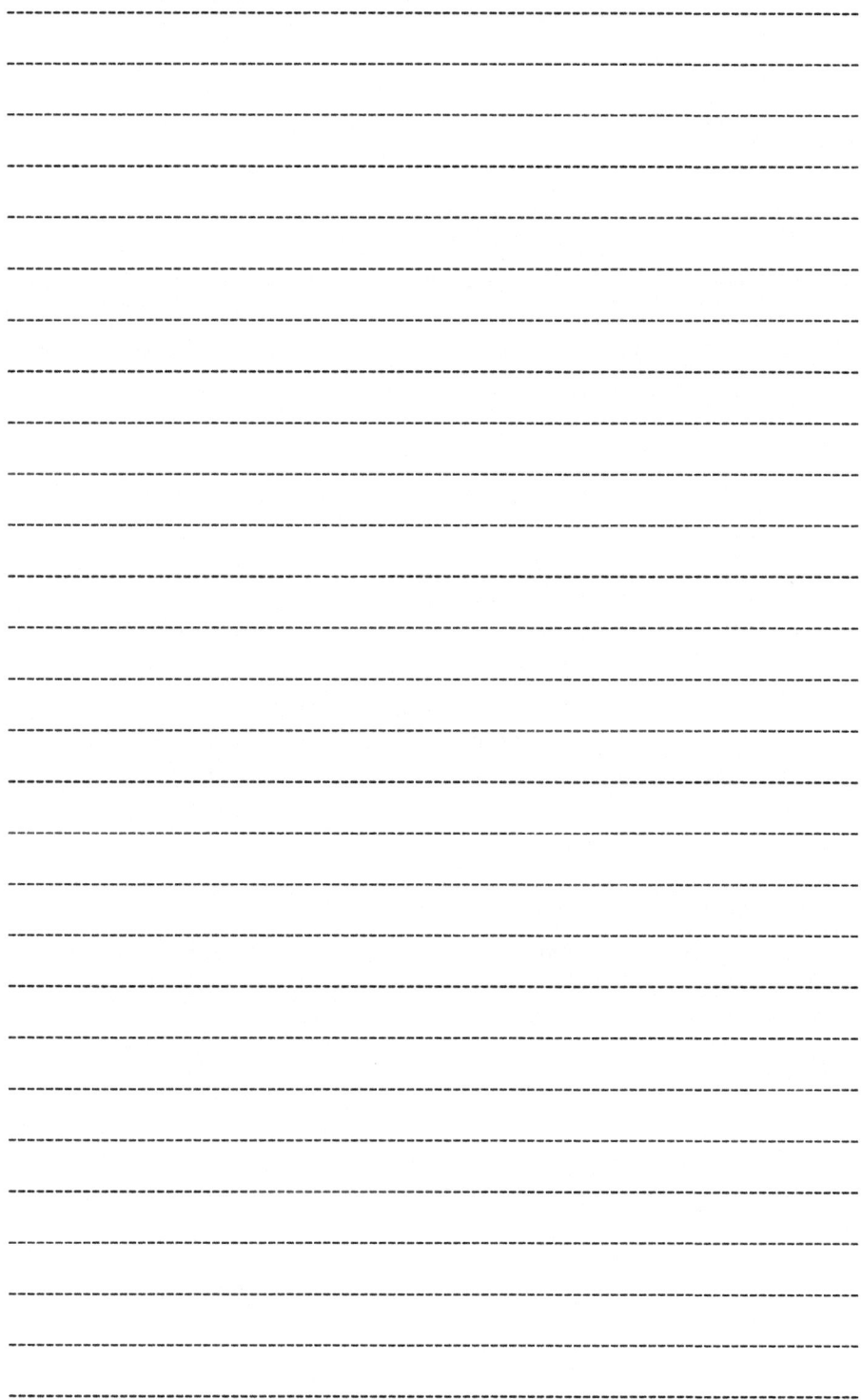

GRIFFITH OBSERVATORY

COUNTY: LOS ANGELES   **CITY:** LOS ANGELES

DATE VISITED: **WHO I WENT WITH:**

RATING: ☆ ☆ ☆ ☆ ☆   **WILL I RETURN?**   YES / NO

2800 E. Observatory Rd.
Los Angeles, CA 90027
213-473-0800

Griffith Observatory, located in Los Angeles, California, is one of the most iconic landmarks in the city and a popular destination for both locals and visitors. Perched on the south-facing slope of Mount Hollywood in Griffith Park, the observatory offers spectacular views of the city, including a sweeping panorama of downtown Los Angeles, the Hollywood Sign, and the Pacific Ocean on clear days. Established in 1935, Griffith Observatory is not only a major astronomical observatory but also a beloved public space where visitors can engage with science, explore the wonders of the universe, and enjoy breathtaking vistas.

One of the most notable features of Griffith Observatory is its rich history and the role it has played in the development of public astronomy. The observatory was designed by architect James Dean and opened to the public as a space where people could come to learn about the stars, planets, and the cosmos. The observatory is home to a variety of scientific exhibits, including models of the solar system, interactive displays, and detailed explanations of astronomical phenomena. It also boasts the Samuel Oschin Planetarium, which features state-of-the-art digital shows that transport visitors on an immersive journey through space, showcasing the wonders of the universe.

The observatory's main building houses the iconic Zeiss Telescope, a 12-inch refracting telescope that has been in use since the observatory's opening. This telescope, along with others on the property, is used for public star parties and special astronomy events, where visitors can peer through the lenses and see planets, stars, and other celestial bodies up close. The observatory also hosts numerous educational programs and public events throughout the year, including lectures, workshops, and stargazing nights, making it a hub for science enthusiasts of all ages.

In addition to its scientific offerings, Griffith Observatory is a fantastic place to visit simply for the views. The observatory is situated at an elevation of 1,134 feet (345 meters), providing an unobstructed view of Los Angeles and the surrounding landscape. From the observation deck, visitors can see the vast expanse of the city stretching out to the horizon, and on clear days, the Pacific Ocean is visible in the distance. The Hollywood Sign is also visible from the observatory, making it a popular spot for iconic photographs. The area surrounding the observatory is part of Griffith Park, one of the largest urban parks in the United States, and offers numerous hiking trails, picnic areas, and opportunities to explore the natural beauty of the region.

The observatory is also a cultural landmark, appearing in several films, television shows, and books over the years. Its most famous appearance was in the 1955 classic film "Rebel Without a Cause", starring James Dean, which helped cement its place in popular culture. Today, Griffith Observatory remains a beloved spot for tourists, families, and stargazing enthusiasts, offering a perfect mix of science, history, and natural beauty.

Griffith Observatory is also free to the public, making it an accessible destination for all visitors. While there is a fee for planetarium shows and special exhibits, the observatory's grounds, exhibits, and views can be enjoyed without any cost, which adds to its appeal as a must-see destination in Los Angeles. The observatory is open every day except Mondays, and it stays open late on certain days, allowing visitors to experience the magic of the night sky. The combination of accessible astronomy education, engaging exhibits, and stunning views makes Griffith Observatory one of the most popular and beloved attractions in Los Angeles.

Whether you are a seasoned astronomy enthusiast or simply someone looking to take in the incredible views of the city, Griffith Observatory offers an unforgettable experience. It is a place where science, history, and the natural beauty of Los Angeles come together, creating a unique and enriching experience for all who visit.

----

37 **HUMBOLDT REDWOODS STATE PARK**

COUNTY: HUMBOLDT   CITY: GARBERVILLE

DATE VISITED: WHO I WENT WITH:

RATING: ☆ ☆ ☆ ☆ ☆   WILL I RETURN?   YES / NO

Avenue of the Giants
Weott, CA 95571
707-946-2409

Humboldt Redwoods State Park, located in Humboldt County, California, is a stunning natural gem that offers visitors a chance to experience the awe-inspiring beauty of ancient redwood forests. Known for its towering trees and diverse ecosystems, the park is home to some of the tallest and oldest trees in the world. Spanning over 53,000 acres, Humboldt Redwoods State Park preserves a significant portion of the Avenue of the Giants, a famous scenic highway that runs through the heart of the park and provides access to the towering redwoods.

The highlight of Humboldt Redwoods State Park is the incredible collection of Coast Redwoods (Sequoia sempervirens), some of which are over 2,000 years old and reach heights of over 350 feet. These ancient trees, the tallest living organisms on Earth, create an atmosphere of wonder and tranquility as they rise above the forest floor, casting long shadows and filtering sunlight through their dense canopy. Visitors often describe walking among the redwoods as a humbling and peaceful experience, with the towering trees creating a serene and almost magical environment.

One of the best ways to explore Humboldt Redwoods State Park is through the Avenue of the Giants, a scenic drive that winds through the heart of the park, providing breathtaking views of the massive trees. The route is ideal for visitors who want to experience the grandeur of the redwoods from the comfort of their car, with plenty of pull-outs along the way for photo opportunities. There are also several hiking trails that allow visitors to immerse themselves even deeper in the beauty of the forest, including easy walks and more challenging treks. Popular trails include the Founders Grove, which showcases some of the park's largest and most impressive trees, and the Drury-Chaney Loop, a trail that leads to a series of awe-inspiring giants.

In addition to the redwoods, Humboldt Redwoods State Park is home to a wide variety of wildlife and plant species. The park's diverse ecosystems, including riparian zones, wetlands, and grasslands, provide habitats for animals such as black bears, deer, squirrels, and numerous bird species. Visitors may also spot mushrooms, ferns, and wildflowers in the spring and summer months, adding to the vibrant colors of the park's landscape. For birdwatchers and nature lovers, the park offers a rich diversity of wildlife, making it an excellent destination for outdoor enthusiasts of all kinds.

The park offers a variety of recreational opportunities for visitors. In addition to hiking, the park is a popular destination for camping, with several campgrounds available for both tent camping and RVs. Humboldt Redwoods State Park's Bull Creek Flats Campground and Jedediah Smith Campground provide visitors with the chance to camp under the canopy of ancient redwoods, offering an immersive experience in nature. Many of the campgrounds are located near trailheads, making it easy to explore the park on foot, and several also provide access to the nearby Eel River, where visitors can enjoy activities such as swimming, fishing, and kayaking.

For those interested in learning more about the history and ecology of the park, the Visitor Center at Humboldt Redwoods State Park provides educational exhibits about the redwoods, the history of the area, and the conservation efforts that have helped protect this remarkable landscape. The center also offers maps, brochures, and information on current park conditions, making it a great starting point for any visit.

Humboldt Redwoods State Park is not just a destination for nature lovers, but also for those interested in preserving natural spaces for future generations. The park is part of the California State Parks system and plays an important role in the conservation of the redwood ecosystem. Efforts to protect the park's ancient trees began in the early 20th century, and today it stands as a testament to the power of conservation. The park's commitment to maintaining the beauty and integrity of the forest allows future generations to experience the same awe and wonder that visitors feel today.

Whether you're looking to explore the ancient redwood groves, hike through diverse ecosystems, or simply relax and enjoy the serenity of one of the world's most spectacular natural environments, Humboldt Redwoods State Park is a must-visit destination in Northern California. Its combination of towering trees, abundant wildlife, and rich history makes it a unique and unforgettable experience for all who venture into its depths.

INDIAN CANYONS

COUNTY: RIVERSIDE   **CITY:** PALM SPRINGS

DATE VISITED: **WHO I WENT WITH:**

RATING: ☆ ☆ ☆ ☆ ☆   **WILL I RETURN?** YES / NO

38520 S Palm Canyon Dr, Palm Springs
Greater Palm Springs, CA 92264

Indian Canyons, located near Palm Springs in Riverside County, California, is a stunning and historically rich natural area known for its scenic beauty, cultural significance, and outdoor recreational opportunities. The canyons, which include Palm Canyon, Andreas Canyon, and Murray Canyon, are nestled in the rugged terrain of the San Jacinto Mountains and are home to an abundance of wildlife, unique plant species, and towering palm trees that give the area its distinct appearance. For visitors seeking a combination of natural wonders and cultural history, Indian Canyons offers a unique and captivating experience.

The area is owned and managed by the Agua Caliente Band of Cahuilla Indians, who have lived in the region for thousands of years. The canyons are an important part of the tribe's history and culture, and they continue to be a sacred site for the Cahuilla people. Indian Canyons served as an essential area for the Cahuilla tribe, who utilized the land for food, shelter, and spiritual purposes. The canyons are dotted with evidence of this ancient way of life, including remnants of traditional rock shelters, mortars, and other artifacts that speak to the deep connection between the Cahuilla people and the land.

Palm Canyon, the largest and most famous of the canyons, is home to a striking fan palm oasis, one of the largest naturally occurring palm oases in the United States. The towering palms line the canyon's floor, creating a lush and inviting environment that contrasts with the surrounding desert landscape. Visitors to Palm Canyon can enjoy hiking trails that wind through the oasis, offering breathtaking views of the palm trees, the surrounding mountains, and the desert below. The Palm Canyon Trail is a popular choice for hikers, leading visitors through the heart of the oasis and providing an opportunity to experience the beauty and tranquility of this unique desert ecosystem. Along the trail, hikers may encounter wildlife such as birds, lizards, and the occasional desert bighorn sheep. The lush palm groves provide shade and a cool retreat from the hot desert sun, making the hike an especially refreshing experience.

In addition to Palm Canyon, Andreas Canyon offers a more intimate and tranquil hiking experience. The Andreas Canyon Trail is a shorter, less strenuous trail that takes visitors through a beautiful narrow gorge lined with palm trees and other desert vegetation. The trail follows a stream that runs through the canyon, creating an oasis-like environment filled with lush greenery. Andreas Canyon is also home to several unique geological features, including rock formations and waterfalls that add to its charm.

For those seeking a more adventurous experience, Murray Canyon offers a slightly more challenging trail, known as the Murray Canyon Trail. This hike takes visitors through a diverse landscape that includes palm oases, rocky cliffs, and desert brush. The trail follows a path that leads to a secluded waterfall, which is particularly refreshing during the warmer months. The Murray Canyon Trail is also a great spot for birdwatching, as the diverse ecosystem attracts a variety of bird species, including migratory birds and resident species such as quail and hawks.

In addition to hiking, Indian Canyons offers other outdoor activities, including picnicking and wildlife viewing. Several picnic areas are scattered throughout the canyons, offering visitors a chance to relax and enjoy the natural beauty of the surroundings. The area is also an excellent spot for photographers, as the unique combination of desert landscapes, lush oases, and towering mountains provides plenty of opportunities for stunning photos.

The cultural significance of Indian Canyons is evident throughout the area, with interpretive signs and guided tours available to help visitors learn about the history and traditions of the Cahuilla tribe. The tribe's connection to the land is deeply rooted in the canyons, and visitors are encouraged to respect the cultural and spiritual importance of the area. The Agua Caliente Band of Cahuilla Indians operates a visitor center at the entrance to the canyons, where guests can learn more about the tribe's history and the significance of the canyons in their cultural practices. The visitor center also offers a small gift shop featuring Native American crafts and artwork, providing visitors with a unique opportunity to take home a piece of the region's rich cultural heritage.

Indian Canyons is open year-round, and visitors are encouraged to explore the area at their own pace. The park is typically open from morning until late afternoon, with extended hours during peak tourist seasons. There is an entrance fee for visitors, which helps fund the ongoing preservation and maintenance of the area. The canyons are easily accessible from Palm Springs, located just a short drive away, making it a convenient destination for those staying in the area.

Whether you are interested in hiking, wildlife watching, or learning about the rich cultural history of the Cahuilla tribe, Indian Canyons offers something for everyone. The combination of natural beauty, outdoor recreation, and cultural significance makes it one of the most unique and memorable destinations in the Palm Springs area. For those seeking a deeper connection to the desert landscape and its indigenous people, a visit to Indian Canyons provides an unforgettable experience.

㊲ JEDEDIAH SMITH REDWOODS STATE PARK

COUNTY: DEL NORTE   **CITY:** CRESCENT CITY

DATE VISITED: **WHO I WENT WITH:**

RATING: ☆ ☆ ☆ ☆ ☆   **WILL I RETURN?** YES / NO

1440 Highway 199
Crescent City, CA 95531
707-464-6101

Jedediah Smith Redwoods State Park, located in Del Norte County, California, is a stunning natural haven that is part of the larger Redwood National and State Parks. Situated near the Smith River, this park offers visitors the opportunity to experience some of the tallest and most ancient trees in the world, the Coast Redwoods. These magnificent trees, some of which are over 2,000 years old and rise to heights of over 350 feet, create an awe-inspiring environment that attracts nature lovers, hikers, and photographers from all over the world. Named after Jedediah Smith, an early explorer of the Pacific Coast, the park is known for its incredible beauty, tranquility, and the chance to explore one of the most unique ecosystems on the planet.

The centerpiece of Jedediah Smith Redwoods State Park is its ancient redwood forests, which are some of the best-preserved in California. Visitors are immediately struck by the sheer size and grandeur of the towering trees, which seem to stretch endlessly upward, their trunks thick and gnarled with age. Walking through the park's lush, fern-filled groves, you feel as if you've stepped into another world, where time slows down, and the forest whispers with the sound of rustling leaves and distant birdcalls. The park offers a number of scenic hiking trails that allow visitors to immerse themselves in the beauty of the redwoods. These trails range in difficulty from easy, wheelchair-accessible routes to more strenuous hikes for those seeking a deeper exploration of the park.

One of the most popular trails in the park is the Stout Grove Trail, an easy-to-moderate hike that takes visitors through a picturesque grove of ancient redwoods. The trail is a short, 0.5-mile loop that winds through towering trees and offers plenty of opportunities for photography and quiet reflection. Another popular trail is the Jedediah Smith Campground Loop, which takes visitors through a mix of forested areas and along the banks of the Smith River, offering stunning views of both the towering redwoods and the pristine water below. For those who prefer a longer hike, the Nickerson Ranch Trail offers a more challenging adventure with even more breathtaking views of the park's forests and wildlife.

In addition to hiking, Jedediah Smith Redwoods State Park offers opportunities for other outdoor activities, including wildlife viewing, birdwatching, and camping. The park is home to a diverse range of animals, including black bears, elk, deer, and river otters, as well as numerous species of birds. Birdwatchers can spot everything from woodpeckers to owls, especially in the early mornings or at dusk when the forest is most active. For those who enjoy camping, the Jedediah Smith Campground offers a beautiful, peaceful setting to spend the night under the towering trees. The campground is equipped with both tent and RV sites and provides easy access to the park's hiking trails and the Smith River, which is known for its crystal-clear waters and opportunities for fishing, swimming, and canoeing.

One of the unique features of Jedediah Smith Redwoods State Park is its proximity to the Smith River, which is the last undammed river in California. The river's clear, cool waters meander through the park, offering visitors a chance to explore the pristine wilderness surrounding it. The river is home to salmon, steelhead, and trout, making it a popular spot for fishing enthusiasts. Kayaking and canoeing along the river are also popular activities, as the calm waters provide a serene way to take in the beauty of the park from a different perspective. The surrounding forested hills and lush vegetation add to the picturesque setting, making this a perfect location for outdoor adventures.

The visitor center at Jedediah Smith Redwoods State Park provides useful information about the park's history, ecology, and conservation efforts. Visitors can learn about the important role the redwoods play in the local ecosystem, as well as the history of the region and the efforts made to preserve these incredible trees. The center also offers maps, brochures, and educational programs for those interested in learning more about the park's natural wonders. The park rangers are knowledgeable and passionate about the area, and they offer programs and guided tours to enhance visitors' understanding of the park's rich biodiversity.

In addition to its natural beauty, Jedediah Smith Redwoods State Park is a part of the Redwood National and State Parks, which have been designated as a UNESCO World Heritage Site due to their outstanding universal value. The park is also a part of the Redwood National Park complex, which includes several other state parks, national parks, and protected areas along the North Coast of California. Together, these areas help to preserve the last remaining ancient redwood forests and provide important habitats for a wide range of wildlife.

Whether you're visiting for a day hike, a peaceful camping trip, or simply to marvel at the towering trees, Jedediah Smith Redwoods State Park offers an unforgettable experience in one of the world's most extraordinary natural environments. With its breathtaking scenery, diverse ecosystems, and abundant wildlife, the park provides a rare opportunity to connect with nature and experience the majesty of the redwoods firsthand.

JOSHUA TREE NATIONAL PARK

40

COUNTY: SAN BERNARDINO   CITY: TWENTYNINE PALMS

DATE VISITED: _____ WHO I WENT WITH: _____

RATING: ☆ ☆ ☆ ☆ ☆   WILL I RETURN?   YES / NO

74485 National Park Drive
Twentynine Palms, CA 92277
760-367-5500

Joshua Tree National Park, located in Southern California where the Mojave and Colorado deserts converge, is a captivating landscape of rugged beauty and surreal contrasts. Spanning over 790,000 acres, the park is renowned for its namesake Joshua trees, dramatic rock formations, and vibrant desert ecosystems. This natural wonderland attracts climbers, hikers, stargazers, and nature lovers alike, offering countless opportunities for adventure and reflection.

The park's most iconic feature, the Joshua tree, is actually a type of yucca plant with twisted, spiky branches that give it an otherworldly appearance. These unique trees thrive in the Mojave Desert, which occupies the western part of the park. The eastern portion, dominated by the lower-elevation Colorado Desert, features creosote bushes, ocotillo, and cholla cactus gardens that add variety to the park's scenery. The Cholla Cactus Garden, in particular, is a mesmerizing spot to witness the golden glow of these cacti during sunrise or sunset.

One of the park's most celebrated attractions is its rock formations, which draw climbers and photographers from around the world. Massive granite boulders and monzogranite domes, weathered into unique shapes, create a playground for climbers and boulderers of all skill levels. Hidden Valley, a sheltered area surrounded by these formations, is a favorite for both climbers and hikers. Nearby, Skull Rock, named for its resemblance to a human skull, is a fascinating stop along the main park road.

For hikers, Joshua Tree National Park offers a variety of trails ranging from short nature walks to challenging treks. Barker Dam Trail, a 1.1-mile loop, leads visitors to a historic reservoir and often provides glimpses of desert wildlife. The Ryan Mountain Trail is a more strenuous hike, ascending 1,070 feet to a summit with panoramic views of the park's stunning desert landscape. For a more secluded experience, the Lost Palms Oasis Trail takes visitors to a lush grove of native California fan palms.

The park is also a haven for stargazers, thanks to its designation as an

International Dark Sky Park. Free from city light pollution, the night skies above Joshua Tree are breathtaking, revealing countless stars, planets, and the shimmering band of the Milky Way. Stargazing events and photography workshops are popular ways to immerse oneself in the celestial beauty.

Wildlife enthusiasts will find the park teeming with life, especially during the cooler months. Desert tortoises, jackrabbits, bighorn sheep, and a variety of bird species are just some of the creatures that call Joshua Tree home. Springtime occasionally brings vibrant wildflower blooms, adding bursts of color to the arid terrain.

The park is rich in cultural history as well. Native American tribes, such as the Cahuilla, left behind petroglyphs and other artifacts, highlighting their deep connection to the land. Later settlers and miners also left their mark, with sites like the Keys Ranch and remnants of old gold mining operations offering a glimpse into the area's past.

Joshua Tree National Park is accessible year-round, but the best times to visit are fall, winter, and spring when temperatures are more moderate. Summers can be extremely hot, but early mornings and evenings remain pleasant. Visitors are advised to come prepared with plenty of water, sunscreen, and sturdy footwear to navigate the rugged terrain.

Whether you're scaling its iconic rock formations, wandering among its peculiar Joshua trees, or marveling at its star-filled skies, Joshua Tree National Park offers a truly unique and unforgettable experience. Its dramatic beauty and serene atmosphere make it one of California's most beloved natural destinations.

LA JOLLA COVE

41

COUNTY: SAN DIEGO   **CITY:** SAN DIEGO (LA JOLLA)

DATE VISITED: **WHO I WENT WITH:**

RATING: ☆ ☆ ☆ ☆ ☆   **WILL I RETURN?** YES / NO

1100 Coast Blvd
La Jolla, San Diego, CA 92037

La Jolla Cove, located in the coastal community of La Jolla, California, is one of the most beautiful and iconic spots in San Diego. Famous for its breathtaking natural beauty, this small, picturesque cove offers pristine beaches, clear turquoise waters, and stunning cliffs, making it a popular destination for tourists and locals alike. Nestled between towering cliffs, La Jolla Cove is part of the larger La Jolla Underwater Park, a protected marine reserve, and serves as a sanctuary for various marine life species, offering visitors an unparalleled opportunity to connect with nature.

The cove's tranquil waters are ideal for a variety of water activities, including snorkeling, scuba diving, swimming, and kayaking. Thanks to the protection offered by the surrounding cliffs, the waters at La Jolla Cove are relatively calm, providing an excellent environment for those looking to explore the underwater world. The La Jolla Underwater Park, which extends along the coastline, is home to an abundance of sea life, including kelp forests, sea lions, garibaldi fish, and even the occasional sea turtle. Snorkelers and divers are often treated to spectacular views of colorful marine species, making it a prime destination for underwater enthusiasts. The visibility in the cove is generally excellent, making it a favorite for both beginner and experienced divers.

One of the most famous residents of La Jolla Cove is the California sea lion. These playful marine mammals often haul out on the rocks around the cove and can be seen basking in the sun or swimming in the water. Visitors to La Jolla Cove can enjoy watching these fascinating creatures, but it's important to remember that they are wild animals and should be admired from a distance. The presence of sea lions adds a special charm to the cove, contributing to its reputation as a must-see wildlife and nature destination.

For those who prefer to stay on land, La Jolla Cove offers a stunning setting for a leisurely walk or a relaxing day at the beach. The cove is framed by dramatic cliffs, and the surrounding La Jolla Coast Walk Trail provides a scenic path along the coast, offering spectacular views of the ocean, the rugged coastline, and the neighboring beaches. The trail is relatively easy, making it accessible for visitors of all ages and abilities. The area is also perfect for picnicking, with several nearby grassy areas where visitors can enjoy a meal while taking in the beautiful surroundings.

Adjacent to La Jolla Cove is Ellen Browning Scripps Park, a large, well-maintained green space where people often gather for outdoor activities, events, and socializing. The park is an ideal spot for a family picnic or a relaxing afternoon, with the sounds of the ocean in the background and views of the cliffs and coastline. The park is also home to several benches, offering ample seating to take in the stunning views of the Pacific Ocean. The combination of the park and the cove makes this area one of the most picturesque locations in all of San Diego.

For visitors interested in the local culture, La Jolla Cove is located just a short distance from the La Jolla Village area, which is filled with boutique shops, art galleries, restaurants, and cafes. After spending time at the cove, visitors can enjoy a leisurely stroll through the village, sampling delicious cuisine, browsing unique shops, or enjoying one of the many art exhibitions. The area is known for its upscale, yet relaxed atmosphere, making it a perfect spot to unwind after a day of outdoor activities.

La Jolla Cove is not just a beautiful place to visit—it's also a historical and cultural gem. The cove has been a popular destination for decades, attracting artists, nature lovers, and adventurers from all over the world. Its combination of natural beauty, recreational opportunities, and proximity to the vibrant La Jolla community makes it a must-see for anyone visiting San Diego. Whether you're snorkeling in its clear waters, enjoying a peaceful walk along the cliffs, or simply taking in the stunning views, La Jolla Cove provides an unforgettable experience for every visitor.

LA JOLLA SEA CAVE KAYAKS

42

COUNTY: SAN DIEGO   **CITY:** SAN DIEGO (LA JOLLA)

DATE VISITED: **WHO I WENT WITH:**

RATING: ☆ ☆ ☆ ☆ ☆   **WILL I RETURN?** YES / NO

2164 Avenida de la Playa
La Jolla, CA 92037
858-454-0111

La Jolla Sea Cave Kayaks, located in the coastal community of La Jolla, California, offers an unforgettable adventure for those seeking to explore the beauty of the Pacific Ocean from the water. Known for its stunning sea caves, clear waters, and abundant marine life, La Jolla Sea Cave Kayaks provides guided kayak tours that allow visitors to get up close and personal with the area's natural wonders. The sea caves, nestled along the rugged coastline of La Jolla Cove, are one of the most unique features of the area, and the kayak tours offer the perfect opportunity to explore them in a fun and exciting way.

The main draw of La Jolla Sea Cave Kayaks is the chance to paddle through the iconic La Jolla sea caves, which are only accessible by boat or kayak. These natural wonders, carved into the cliffs over thousands of years by the constant pounding of the ocean, are truly spectacular. Visitors will experience the thrill of entering these mysterious caves, paddling through their narrow passages, and marveling at the cool, dark interiors that open up to reveal stunning views of the ocean. The sea caves vary in size, some large enough to allow a group of kayakers to enter, while others are smaller and more intimate. The highlight of the tour is often the moment when kayakers glide through the caves and emerge into the bright, open ocean, surrounded by the breathtaking coastline.

The kayaks used at La Jolla Sea Cave Kayaks are designed for stability and ease of use, making them accessible to people of all skill levels. Whether you're an experienced kayaker or a beginner, the guides ensure that you feel comfortable and safe while navigating the waters. The kayaks are tandem, so you can share the experience with a partner or friend, paddling together as you explore the caves and coastline. The guided tours are perfect for families, groups, and solo travelers alike, and they provide a fantastic way to enjoy the scenic beauty of La Jolla while learning about the history and ecology of the area.

In addition to the sea caves, La Jolla Sea Cave Kayaks tours provide the opportunity to encounter a variety of marine life. La Jolla Cove and the surrounding waters are part of the La Jolla Underwater Park, a protected marine reserve that is home to an incredible array of sea creatures. While kayaking, you might spot playful sea lions, dolphins, and sea turtles, as well as schools of colorful fish swimming beneath the crystal-clear waters. The area is also home to kelp forests, which provide important habitats for many marine species. The tours offer a chance to learn about the ecology of the region, with guides sharing fascinating facts about the animals and plants that call this part of the ocean home.

La Jolla Sea Cave Kayaks also provides snorkeling opportunities as part of their tours. For those interested in exploring the underwater world, the tours offer stops where participants can snorkel and experience the beauty of the ocean up close. The warm waters of La Jolla Cove are ideal for snorkeling, and visitors can enjoy a peaceful swim among the kelp forests and the diverse marine life that thrives in the area.

For those looking to add a little extra excitement to their adventure, La Jolla Sea Cave Kayaks also offers sunset kayak tours. These evening tours are perfect for those wanting to experience the tranquility and beauty of the ocean as the sun sets over the Pacific. Paddling along the coastline during sunset provides a magical atmosphere, with the changing colors of the sky reflecting off the water and the cliffs illuminated by the soft golden light. It's an unforgettable experience that adds an extra layer of beauty to an already incredible adventure.

Whether you're looking for a relaxing day on the water or an adventurous exploration of the La Jolla coastline, La Jolla Sea Cave Kayaks offers something for everyone. With its combination of sea cave exploration, marine wildlife sightings, and the opportunity to enjoy the stunning natural beauty of the region, it's no wonder that La Jolla Sea Cave Kayaks has become a must-do activity for visitors to San Diego. The knowledgeable guides, safe equipment, and spectacular scenery make it an experience that will be remembered for years to come.

43

LANDS END

COUNTY: SAN FRANCISCO   **CITY:** SAN FRANCISCO

DATE VISITED: **WHO I WENT WITH:**

RATING: ☆ ☆ ☆ ☆ ☆   **WILL I RETURN?** YES / NO

El Camino del Mar
San Francisco, CA 94121

Lands End, located in San Francisco, California, is a rugged and scenic coastal area known for its breathtaking views, historical landmarks, and natural beauty. Situated at the northwestern tip of the city, Lands End is part of the Golden Gate National Recreation Area and offers visitors a unique combination of history, nature, and stunning vistas. The area is a popular destination for both locals and tourists, offering a variety of outdoor activities, picturesque landscapes, and glimpses of San Francisco's rich cultural heritage.

One of the highlights of Lands End is its hiking trails, which wind along the coastline and offer spectacular views of the Pacific Ocean and the Golden Gate Bridge. The Lands End Trail is the main hiking route, providing an easy to moderate walk that leads visitors through coastal scrub, cypress trees, and wildflowers, with panoramic views of the ocean and the rugged cliffs below. Along the trail, there are several scenic viewpoints where visitors can pause and take in the sweeping vistas of the coastline and nearby landmarks. One of the most famous viewpoints along the trail is the Lands End Lookout, which provides a clear view of the Golden Gate Bridge, the Marin Headlands, and the entrance to San Francisco Bay.

Lands End is also home to Sutro Baths, a historic site that was once a grand swimming pool complex in the late 19th century. Built by Adolph Sutro, a wealthy businessman and former mayor of San Francisco, the Sutro Baths were once the largest indoor swimming pool complex in the world. Today, visitors can explore the ruins of the baths, which sit on the edge of the cliffs overlooking the Pacific Ocean. The remains of the baths, along with the nearby Sutro Heights Park, provide a glimpse into the area's rich history and offer an atmospheric setting for photography and exploration. The site is a popular spot for both history buffs and nature lovers, as it combines a fascinating historical narrative with stunning natural surroundings.

For those interested in wildlife, Lands End offers excellent opportunities for birdwatching, with numerous species of birds inhabiting the area. The coastline is also home to marine life, including seals and sea lions, which can often be spotted basking on the rocks or swimming in the waters below. The area's coastal cliffs and tidal pools provide an ideal habitat for a variety of marine creatures, and visitors can explore the shore to discover starfish, crabs, and other fascinating marine life.

The area around Lands End also features a number of landmarks, including the Sutro Tower, a television and radio tower that rises above the hills and provides a distinctive backdrop to the area's landscapes. The tower offers a striking contrast to the natural beauty of the surrounding coastline, and it is an iconic part of the San Francisco skyline.

Another notable feature of Lands End is China Beach, a small, secluded beach located near the Golden Gate Bridge. This peaceful spot offers a quiet place to relax, enjoy the views, and take in the surrounding beauty. The beach is a favorite among locals, who come here to enjoy picnics, sunbathe, and take in the spectacular views of the bridge and the bay. The beach is also home to a memorial for those who served in World War II, adding a somber and reflective element to the serene atmosphere.

For visitors looking for a more educational experience, Lands End is home to the Lands End Lookout Visitor Center, which provides information about the area's history, ecology, and wildlife. The visitor center features exhibits, maps, and displays that help visitors understand the cultural and natural significance of the area. It is a great starting point for anyone looking to learn more about the history and ecology of Lands End before venturing out on the trails.

In addition to its natural beauty and historical sites, Lands End is a great place for photography. The combination of dramatic coastal cliffs, the Golden Gate Bridge in the distance, and the varied landscapes makes it an ideal spot for capturing iconic images of San Francisco's coastline. Whether you're photographing the rugged cliffs, the ruins of the Sutro Baths, or the stunning views of the bay, Lands End offers countless opportunities for stunning photography.

Lands End is easily accessible from various parts of San Francisco, making it a popular destination for both tourists and residents. The area is well-served by public transportation, and parking is available for those who choose to drive. Whether you're interested in hiking, exploring history, enjoying a peaceful beach, or simply taking in the views, Lands End is a must-see destination that offers something for everyone. With its stunning natural beauty, fascinating history, and peaceful atmosphere, it's no wonder that Lands End is one of San Francisco's most treasured gems.

44

LASSEN VOLCANIC NATIONAL PARK

COUNTY: TEHAMA   CITY: MINERAL

DATE VISITED: WHO I WENT WITH:

RATING: ☆ ☆ ☆ ☆ ☆   WILL I RETURN?   YES / NO

38050 Highway 36 East
Park Headquarters
Mineral, CA 96063
530-595-4480

Lassen Volcanic National Park, located in northeastern California, is a striking natural wonderland where the forces of fire and water have shaped a dramatic and diverse landscape. Spanning over 166 square miles, the park is renowned for its geothermal features, pristine alpine lakes, lush forests, and volcanic peaks. It offers visitors an unparalleled opportunity to explore one of the most geologically active regions in the United States while experiencing its serene natural beauty.

At the heart of the park is Lassen Peak, a massive plug dome volcano that last erupted between 1914 and 1921. Standing at 10,457 feet, it is one of the largest plug dome volcanoes in the world and serves as a symbol of the park's volcanic heritage. Adventurous visitors can hike the Lassen Peak Trail, a 5-mile round trip that ascends over 2,000 feet to the summit, offering breathtaking panoramic views of the surrounding landscape and a close-up look at the rugged volcanic terrain.

The park's geothermal features are a fascinating highlight, showcasing the ongoing activity beneath the surface. Bumpass Hell, the largest hydrothermal area in the park, features bubbling mud pots, steaming fumaroles, and vibrant pools of boiling water. The 3-mile Bumpass Hell Trail takes visitors through this surreal landscape, where the earth hisses, bubbles, and steams in vivid shades of yellow, orange, and green. Other geothermal areas include Sulphur Works, located near the park's southern entrance, and Devil's Kitchen, which offers an equally captivating look at the power of geothermal energy.

Water plays an equally prominent role in shaping the park's scenery. Numerous lakes, ranging from sparkling alpine gems to serene forest-lined waters, dot the landscape. Manzanita Lake, located near the park's northwest entrance, is a favorite spot for kayaking, fishing, and photography, with Lassen Peak reflecting in its calm waters. Summit Lake and Butte Lake offer opportunities for swimming and picnicking, while Boiling Springs Lake captivates visitors with its steaming surface and vivid mineral colors.

Hikers will find a wide range of trails, from easy strolls to challenging backcountry treks. The King's Creek Falls Trail leads to a stunning cascade surrounded by lush greenery, while the Cinder Cone Trail provides a unique opportunity to climb an ancient volcanic cone for spectacular views of the park's painted dunes and lava beds. For those seeking solitude, the park's wilderness areas offer miles of remote trails through pristine forests and meadows.

Lassen Volcanic National Park is also a haven for wildlife, with habitats ranging from dense coniferous forests to high-altitude meadows. Visitors might encounter black bears, mule deer, bobcats, and an array of bird species. In the spring and summer, wildflowers blanket the meadows, adding bursts of color to the landscape. The park's dark night skies, free from light pollution, make it an ideal destination for stargazing and astronomy enthusiasts.

The park's rich geological and cultural history adds another layer of fascination. Lassen's volcanic origins date back millions of years, and the park encompasses all four types of volcanoes: shield, plug dome, cinder cone, and stratovolcano. Native American tribes, such as the Atsugewi and Yana, have long held the region as sacred, and evidence of their presence can still be found. Early settlers and scientists who studied the area have contributed to our understanding of volcanology and conservation.

Lassen Volcanic National Park is open year-round, though the best time to visit is during the warmer months when the roads and trails are free of snow. Winter brings a quieter charm, with opportunities for snowshoeing, cross-country skiing, and exploring the snowy landscapes. Visitors should come prepared for rapidly changing weather conditions, particularly in higher elevations.

Whether you're marveling at the geothermal wonders, hiking among volcanic peaks, or enjoying the tranquility of its alpine lakes, Lassen Volcanic National Park offers a unique and unforgettable experience. It is a true testament to the power and beauty of nature's forces, making it a must-visit destination for anyone seeking adventure and inspiration in California's great outdoors.

45

LOMBARD STREET

COUNTY: SAN FRANCISCO   **CITY:** SAN FRANCISCO

DATE VISITED: **WHO I WENT WITH:**

RATING: ☆ ☆ ☆ ☆ ☆   **WILL I RETURN?** YES / NO

Between Hyde St & Leavenworth St
San Francisco, CA 94109

Lombard Street, located in San Francisco, California, is one of the most famous streets in the world, often referred to as the "crookedest street." Known for its unique and winding design, this iconic street is a popular tourist attraction that showcases the charm of San Francisco's hilly terrain. Stretching from Leavenworth Street to The Embarcadero, Lombard Street is famous for its series of eight steep, hairpin turns that zigzag down a hill, offering one of the most picturesque and unusual driving experiences in the United States.

The street's distinctive design was originally created in 1922 to reduce the steepness of the hill, which was too sharp for vehicles to ascend safely. The winding pattern of Lombard Street was the solution, making it easier for drivers to navigate the hill while providing a visually striking landscape. The combination of lush gardens, colorful flowers, and the dramatic twists and turns of the street has made it a popular spot for visitors to capture photos and take in the scenery. The street is beautifully landscaped with vibrant flowers and plants, including hydrangeas, begonias, and azaleas, which add to its allure, particularly in spring and summer when the blooms are in full display.

Driving down Lombard Street is a thrilling experience for many tourists. As you navigate its steep, narrow path, you are treated to panoramic views of San Francisco's downtown skyline, the Bay Area, and the Golden Gate Bridge in the distance. The eight curves of the street are not only an architectural marvel but also provide a unique perspective on the city's hilly terrain. Many visitors also choose to walk down the street to enjoy its charm at a slower pace, making it a great spot for a leisurely stroll while taking in the breathtaking views and intricate design of the street. On busy days, expect a line of cars waiting to drive down the street, as it has become a must-see attraction in the city.

Beyond its famous winding curves, Lombard Street is also notable for its historical significance. It runs through Russian Hill, one of San Francisco's most desirable and picturesque neighborhoods. Along the street, you will find beautiful Victorian and Edwardian homes, adding to the street's historical and architectural appeal. It is an excellent example of how urban planning in San Francisco has embraced the natural landscape, utilizing the steep hills to create visually stunning streets that are both functional and beautiful.

The street's popularity also comes from its proximity to other famous San Francisco landmarks. Just a short distance from Lombard Street, visitors can explore attractions like Coit Tower, Pier 39, and the Fisherman's Wharf area, all offering additional opportunities to experience the beauty and culture of the city. The nearby Telegraph Hill provides another stunning viewpoint of the city, and visitors can enjoy breathtaking vistas of the San Francisco Bay.

For those visiting Lombard Street, the best time to visit is early in the morning or during weekdays to avoid the crowds, as the street can become quite busy, especially on weekends. The area around Lombard Street offers several nearby parking options for those who wish to drive and explore, although public transportation and walking are also popular methods of getting around in San Francisco.

In conclusion, Lombard Street in San Francisco is not only a remarkable feat of urban design but also a symbol of the city's distinctive charm. Its winding curves, vibrant flowers, and stunning views make it a must-see destination for anyone visiting San Francisco. Whether you're driving, walking, or simply admiring the view from a nearby hilltop, Lombard Street offers a unique and memorable experience that captures the essence of San Francisco's beauty and creativity.

46

MANHATTAN BEACH

COUNTY: LOS ANGELES   **CITY:** MANHATTAN BEACH

DATE VISITED: **WHO I WENT WITH:**

RATING: ☆ ☆ ☆ ☆ ☆   **WILL I RETURN?** YES / NO

Manhattan Beach Pier
2 Manhattan Beach Blvd
Manhattan Beach, CA 90266

Manhattan Beach is a vibrant coastal city located in the western part of Los Angeles County, California. Renowned for its pristine beaches, upscale living, and lively atmosphere, Manhattan Beach offers a perfect blend of relaxation, recreation, and refined charm. It is a popular destination for both locals and visitors, making it one of the most coveted beach cities in Southern California.

The heart of Manhattan Beach is its beachfront, where visitors can enjoy the iconic Pacific Ocean views, soft golden sand, and the laid-back coastal lifestyle. The Manhattan Beach Pier, extending 928 feet into the ocean, is one of the city's most recognizable landmarks. At the end of the pier, visitors can find the Roundhouse Aquarium, a small but educational spot featuring marine life exhibits, tide pools, and interactive displays. The pier also offers stunning views of the coastline and is a popular location for fishing, strolling, and watching breathtaking sunsets. The beachfront boardwalk along the sand is perfect for a leisurely walk or bike ride, offering a fantastic way to soak in the coastal scenery.

The beach itself is ideal for a range of activities, from sunbathing and beach volleyball to surfing and swimming. Manhattan Beach is famous for its world-class surf breaks, drawing surfers from around the globe. The area is also known for its wide sandy shores, which provide ample space for beachgoers to spread out and enjoy the sun. The volleyball courts on the beach are particularly popular, as Manhattan Beach is considered the birthplace of beach volleyball, with numerous professional tournaments held here each year.

In addition to its beautiful beach, Manhattan Beach boasts a lively downtown area with a mix of high-end boutiques, trendy restaurants, and cafes. The main thoroughfare, Manhattan Beach Boulevard, is lined with chic shops, offering everything from fashion and jewelry to surf gear and home décor. The city's dining scene is equally impressive, with a variety of restaurants offering diverse cuisines. From casual beachside eateries to upscale dining with ocean views, Manhattan Beach has something to satisfy every palate. Seafood is a highlight, with several local restaurants serving fresh catches of the day, often paired with stunning ocean views.

For those interested in outdoor recreation, Manhattan Beach provides numerous opportunities for sports and fitness activities. The city has several parks and recreational areas, including the Polliwog Park, which features walking trails, picnic areas, and a lake with ducks and geese. Sand Dune Park, with its steep sand dunes, is a popular spot for a challenging workout, as locals frequently climb the dunes for exercise. The Manhattan Beach Greenbelt, a stretch of lush greenery running through the city, offers walking and biking paths that connect different parts of the community.

Manhattan Beach also offers a variety of events throughout the year. The Manhattan Beach Open, a professional beach volleyball tournament, is one of the most famous and highly anticipated events, attracting top athletes and spectators from around the world. Additionally, the city hosts a summer concert series, outdoor movie nights, and seasonal festivals, making it a dynamic place to visit year-round.

The city is also home to historic landmarks such as the Manhattan Beach Historical Society, which provides a glimpse into the area's past, from its origins as a small seaside community to its present status as one of Los Angeles' most desirable neighborhoods. Visitors can learn about the city's history, its development, and its unique role in the rise of beach culture.

With its stunning coastline, welcoming community, and variety of activities, Manhattan Beach offers a quintessential Southern California experience. Whether you're looking to relax by the ocean, engage in outdoor sports, or enjoy delicious food and shopping, this coastal gem has it all. The laid-back yet sophisticated vibe of Manhattan Beach makes it an ideal destination for families, couples, and solo travelers alike, offering a perfect mix of beachside relaxation and city excitement.

----

47 · MARIPOSA GROVE OF GIANT SEQUOIAS

COUNTY: MARIPOSA	CITY: MARIPOSA

DATE VISITED:	WHO I WENT WITH:

RATING: ☆ ☆ ☆ ☆ ☆	WILL I RETURN? YES / NO

Mariposa Grove Road
Yosemite National Park, CA 95389
209-372-0200

The Mariposa Grove of Giant Sequoias is a must-see natural wonder located in Yosemite National Park in California's Sierra Nevada Mountains. Known for its towering and ancient sequoia trees, the Mariposa Grove offers visitors a chance to witness one of the world's largest and oldest living organisms. This grove is home to over 500 mature giant sequoias, including some of the largest trees on Earth, making it a breathtaking destination for nature lovers and those eager to experience the grandeur of these monumental trees.

The giant sequoias in Mariposa Grove are famous for their incredible size, with some towering over 300 feet (91 meters) tall and having trunks that measure more than 30 feet (9 meters) in diameter. The Grizzly Giant, one of the most famous trees in the grove, is estimated to be over 2,700 years old, while the California Tunnel Tree, which was hollowed out to create a tunnel for cars in the 19th century, offers an incredible photo opportunity as visitors can walk through its massive trunk. These ancient trees are considered some of the oldest living organisms on the planet, with many of them dating back thousands of years.

Visitors to Mariposa Grove can explore its scenic trails, offering a variety of paths that cater to different levels of hiking expertise. The Grizzly Giant Loop Trail is a popular, relatively easy route that loops through the grove, giving visitors the chance to view some of the largest and oldest trees, including the Grizzly Giant and California Tunnel Tree. For those looking for a more extensive hike, the Mariposa Grove Trail offers a longer journey that leads deeper into the grove, with spectacular views and opportunities to see more of the park's diverse flora and fauna.

In addition to its stunning trees, the Mariposa Grove is part of a larger ecosystem that provides a home to a variety of wildlife, including birds, deer, squirrels, and other forest creatures. The cool, shaded environment of the grove offers a peaceful retreat, especially during the hot summer months, when the towering trees provide welcome relief from the heat. The surrounding landscape is equally beautiful, with sweeping views of Yosemite's mountainous terrain, making

Mariposa Grove a perfect spot for photography and wildlife observation.

The grove's visitor center provides informative exhibits about the history of the giant sequoias, their ecology, and conservation efforts. Here, visitors can learn about the efforts to preserve the trees, as well as the cultural significance of the grove to the indigenous tribes that have lived in the Yosemite region for thousands of years. The Mariposa Grove was designated a protected area in 1864, and its preservation has been vital in maintaining this natural treasure for future generations.

Getting to Mariposa Grove involves traveling to Yosemite National Park and taking a shuttle bus from the Yosemite South Entrance during most of the year. This shuttle service helps minimize environmental impact and parking congestion in the area, especially during peak tourist seasons. The Mariposa Grove Road is typically closed in the winter due to snow, but during the warmer months, it is accessible by shuttle or on foot for those seeking a more strenuous hike.

A visit to Mariposa Grove offers an unforgettable experience, where visitors can walk among giants and immerse themselves in one of the most iconic landscapes in the world. Whether you're hiking among the sequoias, photographing the natural beauty, or simply taking in the peaceful surroundings, Mariposa Grove is an awe-inspiring destination that showcases the power and majesty of nature at its finest. It's a testament to the incredible resilience of the giant sequoias and a perfect place for anyone seeking a deeper connection to the natural world.

48

MARVYN'S MAGIC THEATER

COUNTY: RIVERSIDE   **CITY:** LA QUINTA

DATE VISITED: **WHO I WENT WITH:**

RATING: ☆ ☆ ☆ ☆ ☆   **WILL I RETURN?** YES / NO

46630 Washington St, La Quinta
Greater Palm Springs, CA 92253
833-627-8967

Marvyn's Magic Theater, located in Palm Springs, California, is a must-visit destination for anyone seeking a fun and enchanting experience. This intimate, family-friendly venue is known for its mesmerizing magic shows that combine comedy, illusion, and sleight of hand in a captivating performance. Owned and operated by Marvyn, a talented magician with years of experience, the theater offers a unique and personal magic show experience that has made it one of the top entertainment spots in Palm Springs.

At Marvyn's Magic Theater, visitors are treated to close-up magic and spectacular illusions that will leave them spellbound. The intimate setting of the theater ensures that the audience is up close to the action, making the magic feel personal and engaging. Marvyn's performances include a combination of classic tricks, mind-bending illusions, and interactive magic that involves audience participation. Whether it's pulling a rabbit out of a hat, making objects disappear, or performing incredible card tricks, the show keeps the audience on the edge of their seats, wondering how the tricks are done.

One of the highlights of Marvyn's Magic Theater is its personal touch. Unlike large-scale performances where the audience is distant from the action, Marvyn's Magic Theater allows for an up-close experience that creates a sense of wonder and connection. Marvyn often involves guests in the magic, inviting them to participate in tricks and illusions, making each show feel special and memorable. His charm, wit, and energy create an atmosphere where both children and adults are equally entertained.

The theater itself is small, ensuring that every seat offers a great view of the stage, providing an intimate and engaging experience. It's perfect for those who want to enjoy high-quality magic without the distraction of a massive audience. This personal atmosphere makes the theater stand out from other entertainment options in Palm Springs and has earned it a loyal following of both locals and tourists. Whether you're a first-time visitor or a seasoned magic enthusiast, Marvyn's Magic Theater offers a unique, unforgettable experience.

For visitors to Palm Springs, Marvyn's Magic Theater offers a perfect evening of entertainment for families, couples, or friends. It's a great way to enjoy some of the world's best magic while experiencing the warm hospitality and creativity of Palm Springs. The theater also provides a relaxing atmosphere with refreshments available, making it an ideal choice for a fun night out.

Overall, Marvyn's Magic Theater offers a magical experience that is as entertaining as it is impressive. Whether you're looking to be amazed by jaw-dropping illusions, share laughs with a talented magician, or simply enjoy a fun and unique evening, Marvyn's Magic Theater is the place to be in Palm Springs. Its intimate setting, incredible magic, and engaging performances make it a standout attraction for anyone visiting the area.

49

MCWAY FALLS

COUNTY: MONTEREY, SAN LUIS OBISPO   **CITY:** BIG SUR

DATE VISITED: **WHO I WENT WITH:**

RATING: ☆ ☆ ☆ ☆ ☆   **WILL I RETURN?** YES / NO

Julia Pfeiffer Burns State Park
Big Sur, CA 93920
831-667-1112

McWay Falls, located in Julia Pfeiffer Burns State Park in Big Sur, California, is one of the most iconic and picturesque natural landmarks along the Central Coast. The falls are a breathtaking 80-foot waterfall that plunges directly into the Pacific Ocean, creating a stunning visual spectacle. This unique waterfall is notable for its striking beauty and for being one of the few waterfalls in California that falls directly into the ocean, making it an unforgettable sight for visitors.

The falls are surrounded by lush vegetation, with vibrant green cliffs framing the waterfall and its serene cove. McWay Falls is especially renowned for its pristine, untouched landscape, which is accessible via a short, easy trail within the state park. The short hike to the falls is a popular route for visitors, offering spectacular viewpoints of the waterfall and the surrounding coastal scenery. The trail leads to an overlook, where visitors can admire the falls cascading down into a small, secluded beach below. However, access to the beach itself is prohibited to protect the delicate ecosystem and preserve the area's natural beauty.

The history of McWay Falls is equally fascinating. The waterfall gets its name from the nearby McWay family, who once owned a large piece of land in the area. In the 1930s, the land was sold to the state of California and became part of Julia Pfeiffer Burns State Park. The falls have since become one of the most popular and photographed features of the Big Sur coastline, drawing photographers, nature enthusiasts, and tourists from around the world.

The natural setting of McWay Falls is equally impressive. Big Sur is renowned for its rugged cliffs, dramatic coastal views, and diverse flora and fauna, and McWay Falls embodies these elements perfectly. The falls are framed by towering coastal redwoods, chaparral, and dense forest, creating a lush, vibrant environment. In contrast to the vivid greenery, the deep blue of the Pacific Ocean creates a striking visual contrast, with the shoreline and cliffs adding to the scene's dramatic impact.

One of the most notable aspects of McWay Falls is its seasonal changes.

Depending on the time of year, the falls can take on different characteristics. During the winter months, rain and snowmelt often make the waterfall even more dramatic, with increased water flow. In contrast, during the summer and fall, the falls may appear more tranquil, as the water flow slows down. Regardless of the season, McWay Falls remains a breathtaking sight throughout the year.

For visitors looking to explore further, Julia Pfeiffer Burns State Park offers a range of hiking trails that lead through the scenic wilderness of Big Sur. One of the most popular trails is the McWay Waterfall Trail, a relatively easy walk that offers incredible views of the falls and the ocean. The trail is about half a mile long and is wheelchair accessible, making it a perfect option for families, photographers, and those with mobility limitations. Along the way, visitors will encounter native plants, wildlife, and plenty of opportunities for taking photos of the falls and the surrounding coastline.

In addition to the trail, the area surrounding McWay Falls is home to various plant and animal species. Coastal sagebrush, cypress trees, and lush ferns cover the cliffs and hillsides, while the waters below are home to a variety of marine life, including sea otters, seals, and sea lions. The area is also an important stop for migratory birds, making it a great location for birdwatching.

The combination of McWay Falls' unique beauty, its dramatic setting, and the surrounding natural wonders makes it a must-visit destination along the Pacific Coast Highway. The falls offer visitors an opportunity to witness the raw power of nature in one of California's most picturesque regions. Whether you are simply stopping for a photo, taking a leisurely walk along the trail, or just appreciating the serene beauty of the landscape, McWay Falls provides a truly unforgettable experience.

Due to its remote location and the protected nature of the area, McWay Falls is best visited by car, with parking available at Julia Pfeiffer Burns State Park. However, visitors should be aware that the area can get crowded during peak tourist seasons, particularly in the summer months. For the most peaceful experience, it is recommended to visit early in the morning or during the off-season, when the park is less busy and the waterfall is less likely to be crowded.

In conclusion, McWay Falls is a must-see destination for anyone traveling along California's Big Sur Coast. With its spectacular natural beauty, dramatic waterfall, and serene environment, it's one of the most iconic landmarks in the state. Whether you're a nature lover, photographer, or simply someone seeking to experience the magnificence of California's coastline, McWay Falls offers an unforgettable experience that will stay with you long after you leave.

50

MEDIEVAL TORTURE MUSEUM

COUNTY: LOS ANGELES   CITY: LOS ANGELES

DATE VISITED: WHO I WENT WITH:

RATING: ☆ ☆ ☆ ☆ ☆   WILL I RETURN?   YES / NO

6757 Hollywood Blvd
Los Angeles, CA 90028
213-414-7777

The Medieval Torture Museum, located in Los Angeles, California, offers an intriguing and chilling glimpse into the darker aspects of history. This immersive museum takes visitors on a journey through the macabre and brutal methods of punishment, interrogation, and execution used during the Middle Ages. With its detailed recreations and vast collection of historical artifacts, the museum provides a stark reminder of humanity's capacity for cruelty while also serving as a fascinating exploration of medieval society, justice, and culture.

Spanning over 6,000 square feet, the Medieval Torture Museum is one of the largest attractions of its kind in the United States. The museum's exhibits are meticulously designed to recreate the atmosphere of the medieval era, immersing visitors in a world of dungeons, torture chambers, and judicial practices that shaped the period. Each exhibit features life-sized figures, authentic-looking replicas of torture devices, and detailed dioramas that depict the grim realities of medieval punishment.

Among the many artifacts on display are infamous instruments such as the Iron Maiden, the rack, the breaking wheel, and the thumbscrew. Each device is accompanied by informative descriptions that explain its historical context, intended use, and the psychological and physical torment it inflicted on its victims. The exhibits are both educational and evocative, shedding light on the methods used to extract confessions, punish criminals, and enforce religious or political power during a time of widespread superstition and fear.

The museum also explores the social and cultural factors that fueled the development of such methods, including the influence of the Inquisition, witch hunts, and feudal justice systems. Visitors can gain a deeper understanding of the ways in which fear and control were wielded as tools of governance and religion, often targeting marginalized or accused individuals. The detailed narratives and visual displays provide a sobering reflection on the consequences of unchecked authority and societal paranoia.

What sets the Medieval Torture Museum apart is its emphasis on interactivity. Many exhibits encourage visitors to engage with the displays through hands-on features and multimedia presentations. Virtual reality experiences are also available, allowing guests to step further into the past and witness reenactments of medieval scenes in a deeply immersive way. These elements add a modern twist to the museum, making it accessible and engaging for a wide audience.

While the museum's subject matter is undeniably dark, it is presented with the intent to educate and provoke thoughtful discussion rather than to sensationalize or glorify violence. Visitors are invited to reflect on the evolution of human rights and the ways in which society has progressed since the medieval era. By confronting the harsh realities of the past, the museum aims to foster a greater appreciation for the freedoms and protections enjoyed today.

Located in the heart of Los Angeles, the Medieval Torture Museum is easily accessible and makes for a unique addition to the city's diverse cultural attractions. It is suitable for history enthusiasts, fans of the macabre, and anyone interested in exploring the complexities of human nature and historical justice systems. However, due to its intense and graphic content, the museum is recommended for mature audiences.

A visit to the Medieval Torture Museum is a haunting and thought-provoking experience that leaves a lasting impression. It serves as both a stark reminder of humanity's darker chapters and a testament to the progress achieved over the centuries in the pursuit of justice and human dignity.

51

MENDOCINO COAST

COUNTY: MENDOCINO   CITY: MENDOCINO

DATE VISITED: WHO I WENT WITH:

RATING: ☆ ☆ ☆ ☆ ☆   WILL I RETURN?   YES / NO

The Mendocino Coast, located along Northern California's Pacific coastline, is one of the most picturesque and rugged regions in the state. Stretching over 90 miles, this scenic coastline is known for its dramatic cliffs, dense forests, charming towns, and abundant wildlife, making it a perfect destination for nature lovers, outdoor enthusiasts, and anyone seeking a peaceful escape. The Mendocino Coast encompasses a variety of landscapes, from towering redwood forests to pristine beaches, providing visitors with a diverse range of activities to enjoy.

One of the most popular features of the Mendocino Coast is its striking coastal scenery. The jagged cliffs that line the shore are dramatically shaped by the power of the Pacific Ocean, creating a stunning contrast against the clear blue waters below. Visitors can enjoy spectacular views from various points along the coast, such as Point Cabrillo Light Station or Mendocino Headlands State Park, where hiking trails offer access to breathtaking vistas of the coastline, rugged rocks, and crashing waves. Whether you're hiking along the cliffs or simply enjoying the view from a scenic lookout, the beauty of the Mendocino Coast is undeniable.

The coastal region is also famous for its charming towns, most notably Mendocino, a small, historic village perched on a bluff overlooking the ocean. Mendocino is known for its well-preserved Victorian architecture, with its colorful buildings, quaint shops, and art galleries. Strolling through the town, visitors can explore its unique boutiques, restaurants, and cafes while soaking in the atmosphere of this picturesque seaside village. The town also has a rich history, with many buildings dating back to the 19th century, when it was a key logging and shipping hub. Today, Mendocino is a popular spot for visitors looking to experience its artistic culture, historic charm, and coastal beauty.

Another key attraction along the Mendocino Coast is its natural beauty, especially its redwood forests. The area is home to some of the tallest trees in the world, which can be explored through numerous hiking trails in parks like Russian Gulch State Park and Navarro River Redwoods State Park. Walking among these ancient giants is a truly awe-inspiring experience, with their towering trunks and dense canopy creating a peaceful, otherworldly atmosphere. The towering redwoods, along with the surrounding lush vegetation and vibrant wildlife, make the Mendocino Coast a haven for those seeking a connection with nature.

In addition to its natural wonders, the Mendocino Coast offers a wide range of outdoor activities. The region is a prime destination for hiking, with miles of trails through forests, along the coastline, and through state parks. Kayaking and canoeing along the coast provide an opportunity to experience the area from a different perspective, while fishing, whale watching, and tidepooling are popular activities in the surrounding waters. The coastal region is also known for its excellent birdwatching opportunities, as many migratory species make stops along the coast, especially during the spring and fall.

The Mendocino Coast is also a haven for those interested in exploring its marine life. The nearby Mendocino Coast Marine Conservation Area is home to an incredible array of marine species, including seals, sea lions, otters, and an abundance of seabirds. Whale watching is a highlight, especially during migration seasons, when gray whales pass by the coast on their journey to and from Baja California. Guided whale watching tours offer visitors the chance to spot these magnificent creatures in their natural habitat, with the added bonus of seeing other marine wildlife along the way.

Food lovers will find much to enjoy in the Mendocino Coast as well. The region is known for its fresh, local seafood, particularly its Dungeness crab, oysters, and salmon, all of which can be enjoyed in the many excellent restaurants and markets that dot the coastline. Local wineries also thrive in the area, producing fine wines that pair perfectly with the region's culinary offerings. Mendocino County is home to several wineries, many of which are located in picturesque vineyard settings that provide wine-tasting experiences with views of the rolling hills and ocean.

The Mendocino Coast is a year-round destination, with each season offering its own unique charm. In the spring and summer, visitors can enjoy the mild temperatures, blooming wildflowers, and outdoor activities. Fall brings cooler temperatures and vibrant autumn foliage, while winter offers a quieter, more serene atmosphere, perfect for those looking to escape the crowds and enjoy the peaceful beauty of the coast.

Whether you are looking to relax and take in the breathtaking scenery, explore the outdoor adventures available, or immerse yourself in the history and culture of the charming towns, the Mendocino Coast has something for everyone. It's an ideal destination for a weekend getaway or a longer stay, offering visitors a chance to reconnect with nature and experience the best of Northern California's coastal beauty.

52 MINIATURE ENGINEERING CRAFTSMANSHIP MUSEUM (MECM)

COUNTY: SAN DIEGO   **CITY:** CARLSBAD

DATE VISITED: **WHO I WENT WITH:**

RATING: ☆ ☆ ☆ ☆ ☆   **WILL I RETURN?** YES / NO

3190 Lionshead Ave
Carlsbad, CA 92010
760-727-9492

The Miniature Engineering Craftsmanship Museum (MECM), located in Carlsbad, California, is a hidden gem for those with a passion for engineering, craftsmanship, and miniatures. This unique museum showcases an impressive collection of finely crafted miniature models, engines, and mechanical devices, all made with intricate detail and precision. It serves as a fascinating destination for visitors who appreciate the skill and artistry involved in creating miniature replicas of real-world machinery and engineering marvels.

One of the main attractions of the Miniature Engineering Craftsmanship Museum is its extensive collection of miniature engines, from steam-powered models to internal combustion engines, all meticulously constructed by talented craftsmen. Many of these miniatures are fully functional, demonstrating the same engineering principles used in their full-sized counterparts but in a much smaller scale. The museum features models of steam engines, engines from classic automobiles, and even working models of industrial machinery, all built with exceptional attention to detail and accuracy.

In addition to the engines, the museum houses an array of other engineering marvels, including miniature cars, airplanes, boats, and trains. These models are not just visually impressive; they also highlight the incredible skill required to construct such pieces. Visitors can view miniatures of early automobiles, classic airplanes, and even historical landmarks, all created with the precision and care of master artisans.

The museum's exhibits are organized in a way that allows visitors to explore the fascinating world of miniature engineering and craftsmanship at their own pace. Each display is accompanied by detailed information about the craftsmanship and engineering involved in creating the models, as well as the history behind each piece. Whether you're a mechanical engineer, a hobbyist, or simply someone who appreciates fine craftsmanship, the Miniature Engineering Craftsmanship Museum offers an enriching experience.

Another unique feature of the museum is its emphasis on education. The museum hosts demonstrations and educational programs, providing insights into the history of engineering and the techniques used to create these miniature works of art. These programs give visitors a deeper understanding of the technical skills required to create these models and the challenges faced by the craftsmen who build them.

For those visiting Carlsbad, the Miniature Engineering Craftsmanship Museum is a must-see destination, particularly for those interested in engineering, history, or miniatures. It's a perfect place for families, students, and anyone who enjoys learning about the world of engineering in a hands-on, engaging environment. The museum is a true testament to the incredible artistry and craftsmanship of model builders, and it offers a unique glimpse into the world of miniature engineering that's rarely seen elsewhere. Whether you're a casual visitor or a dedicated enthusiast, the MECM provides an unforgettable experience that showcases the beauty and ingenuity of miniature craftsmanship.

MISALIGNMENT MUSEUM

COUNTY: SAN FRANCISCO   **CITY:** SAN FRANCISCO

DATE VISITED: **WHO I WENT WITH:**

RATING: ☆ ☆ ☆ ☆ ☆   **WILL I RETURN?** YES / NO

1699 3rd Street Warriors Chase Center
San Francisco, CA 94158

The Misalignment Museum, located in Los Angeles, California, is an unconventional and thought-provoking museum that explores the concept of "misalignment" through art, objects, and interactive exhibits. The museum presents a collection of works that challenge traditional perceptions of order, symmetry, and alignment, encouraging visitors to consider the beauty and creativity that can arise from imperfection and disorder. This unique museum pushes the boundaries of what is typically expected in the art world, offering a fresh and playful perspective on the world around us.

At the Misalignment Museum, visitors will find a variety of exhibits that showcase the theme of misalignment in different forms. From visually distorted art pieces to objects that seem out of place or in unusual configurations, the museum explores how misalignment can be interpreted as both a physical and conceptual idea. These exhibits feature works by contemporary artists who embrace the idea that things don't always need to be perfectly aligned to be meaningful or beautiful. Many of the pieces encourage viewers to rethink their preconceived notions of order, highlighting how intentional or unintentional misalignment can be an important part of the creative process.

One of the key features of the Misalignment Museum is its interactive installations, which allow visitors to engage with the concept of misalignment in a hands-on way. These installations invite guests to participate in the creation of art, giving them the opportunity to experience how small changes or deviations can result in surprising and unexpected outcomes. The museum's interactive exhibits demonstrate how a shift in perspective or a slight misalignment can completely alter the perception of an object or image, offering a fun and immersive way to explore the concept.

The museum also features an array of sculptures, paintings, and photographs that play with visual dissonance, creating an engaging experience where nothing is exactly as it seems. The exhibits often incorporate elements of surrealism, abstraction, and optical illusion, allowing visitors to question the nature of alignment and symmetry in both art and life. By embracing the idea of misalignment, the museum offers a refreshing break from conventional art displays, where everything is typically expected to fit together perfectly.

Additionally, the Misalignment Museum fosters a sense of humor and lightheartedness, as much of the artwork invites playful interaction and exploration. It's a space where imperfections are celebrated, and visitors are encouraged to embrace the idea that not everything has to be perfect to be interesting or significant. This focus on the beauty of imperfection resonates with many who are tired of the rigid structures of traditional art spaces and are looking for something that feels more approachable and engaging.

For those visiting Los Angeles, the Misalignment Museum offers a unique and refreshing experience that stands out from more traditional art galleries and museums. It's a destination for anyone with an interest in contemporary art, creative expression, or simply those looking to see the world from a different perspective. The museum's approach to exploring the theme of misalignment challenges visitors to think outside the box and appreciate the quirky and unpredictable nature of the world around them. Whether you are an art enthusiast or someone simply looking for an unconventional museum experience, the Misalignment Museum promises to leave a lasting impression.

MONTEREY BAY AQUARIUM

COUNTY: MONTEREY   **CITY:** MONTEREY

DATE VISITED: **WHO I WENT WITH:**

RATING: ☆ ☆ ☆ ☆ ☆   **WILL I RETURN?**   YES / NO

886 Cannery Row
Monterey, CA 93940
831-648-4800

The Monterey Bay Aquarium, located in Monterey, California, is one of the most renowned aquariums in the world, offering visitors an immersive and educational experience centered around marine life and ocean conservation. Situated on the edge of the beautiful Monterey Bay National Marine Sanctuary, the aquarium provides a stunning view of the Pacific Ocean and serves as a gateway for learning about the rich and diverse ecosystem found beneath the waves. Founded in 1984, the Monterey Bay Aquarium has become a leading institution in marine research, conservation efforts, and public education.

One of the aquarium's main attractions is its incredible collection of marine species from the Monterey Bay and beyond. Visitors can explore a wide variety of exhibits that showcase everything from vibrant kelp forests to the depths of the ocean. The aquarium is home to more than 35,000 animals, representing hundreds of species, including sea otters, jellyfish, sea turtles, sharks, and a variety of colorful fish. The exhibits are carefully designed to mimic the natural habitats of these animals, creating an immersive experience that allows visitors to get up close and personal with the creatures of the sea.

Among the standout exhibits at the Monterey Bay Aquarium is the Kelp Forest exhibit, a towering 28-foot tank that simulates the underwater world of a kelp forest, complete with giant kelp and a wide range of marine life that thrives in this environment. Another popular attraction is the Sea Otter exhibit, where guests can observe these playful, charismatic creatures as they float and dive in their habitat. The aquarium also features interactive exhibits such as the Touch Pools, where visitors can gently touch sea stars, sea cucumbers, and other marine invertebrates, and the Open Sea exhibit, which houses large pelagic fish like tunas, sharks, and sardines, creating a stunning and dynamic display of ocean life.

The Monterey Bay Aquarium is also renowned for its commitment to ocean conservation and sustainability. The aquarium works tirelessly to promote awareness about the importance of protecting marine environments and the species that inhabit them. Through its exhibits and educational programs, the aquarium emphasizes the need for ocean preservation, sustainable fishing practices, and efforts to combat climate change and ocean pollution. It has launched numerous initiatives aimed at raising public awareness about the health of the oceans, including its work in marine animal rescue and rehabilitation.

In addition to its permanent exhibits, the aquarium offers a variety of special events, live presentations, and educational programs for visitors of all ages. These include guided tours, behind-the-scenes experiences, and seasonal events such as the annual Sustainable Seafood Festival. The aquarium also hosts a range of educational opportunities for schools, students, and families, fostering a deeper understanding of marine science and conservation.

The Monterey Bay Aquarium also features a fantastic café that offers ocean-friendly dining options, serving locally sourced and sustainable food while providing stunning views of the ocean and the surrounding coastline. The gift shop, located on-site, features unique ocean-themed products and souvenirs, many of which promote conservation efforts and the protection of marine life.

For anyone visiting Monterey or the surrounding areas, the Monterey Bay Aquarium is a must-see attraction. With its engaging exhibits, commitment to education and conservation, and the beauty of its location, the aquarium provides an unforgettable experience for visitors of all ages. Whether you're a marine enthusiast, a family looking for an educational outing, or simply someone who appreciates the beauty of the ocean, the Monterey Bay Aquarium offers a memorable and enriching experience that inspires a greater appreciation for the world beneath the waves.

55

MONTEREY BAY WHALE WATCH

COUNTY: MONTEREY   CITY: MONTEREY

DATE VISITED:	WHO I WENT WITH:

RATING: ☆ ☆ ☆ ☆ ☆   WILL I RETURN?   YES / NO

84 Fisherman's Wharf
Monterey, CA 93940
831-375-4658

Monterey Bay Whale Watch, located in Monterey, California, offers an unforgettable experience for nature lovers and adventure seekers looking to witness the incredible marine wildlife of the Pacific Ocean. Known for its exceptional whale watching tours, Monterey Bay Whale Watch provides an opportunity to see some of the world's most majestic marine creatures in their natural habitat. Situated near the entrance to the Monterey Bay National Marine Sanctuary, the company is perfectly positioned to offer a range of tours that explore the abundant ocean life of this rich and diverse marine ecosystem.

The primary attraction of Monterey Bay Whale Watch is the chance to observe the migration of various whale species, including the iconic Gray Whale, Humpback Whale, Blue Whale, and Fin Whale. Depending on the season, visitors may also encounter Orcas, dolphins, and other marine mammals, as well as a wide array of seabirds. The whale watching tours are conducted in comfortable, well-equipped vessels, guided by experienced naturalists who share their knowledge of marine life and the importance of ocean conservation.

One of the highlights of a whale watching tour with Monterey Bay Whale Watch is the stunning beauty of the Monterey Bay itself. The bay is one of the most productive marine environments in the world, and its waters are home to a wide variety of marine life. Tours depart from the scenic Monterey Harbor, where visitors can enjoy the panoramic views of the coastline before embarking on their journey. As the boat heads out into the open waters, guests are treated to breathtaking views of the rugged coastline, the surrounding mountains, and, of course, the incredible marine creatures that make this area so unique.

The naturalists on board provide valuable insights into the behavior and habits of the whales and other marine species, explaining the migration patterns, feeding behaviors, and the challenges these animals face in the ever-changing ocean environment. The tours are designed not only to showcase the whales but also to educate visitors about the delicate balance of marine ecosystems and the importance of preserving the ocean for future generations.

Monterey Bay Whale Watch operates year-round, with different species of whales migrating through the bay at various times of the year. During the winter and spring months, the Gray Whales pass through the area on their long migration from the Arctic to Baja California. Summer and fall bring the opportunity to see Humpback Whales, Blue Whales, and Fin Whales, as well as the chance to spot dolphins and sea lions. The tours are flexible and offer a variety of options, including both public and private tours, allowing guests to choose the experience that best fits their needs.

In addition to whale watching, Monterey Bay Whale Watch also offers wildlife-watching tours that focus on other marine animals, such as sea otters, seals, and a wide variety of seabirds. These tours are ideal for those who want to explore the full diversity of marine life in the area, beyond just the whales. For those interested in a more hands-on experience, the company also offers photography tours, where guests can take professional-quality photos of the marine wildlife in the bay.

The tour experience is designed to be both educational and exhilarating. As visitors venture out onto the water, they are immersed in the natural beauty of the Monterey Bay National Marine Sanctuary, a protected area that is home to a wealth of marine species and ecosystems. The sanctuary itself is a vital part of the region's biodiversity and is one of the reasons why the area is such a prime destination for whale watching.

For anyone visiting Monterey or the surrounding areas, Monterey Bay Whale Watch provides a unique and memorable way to connect with nature and experience the majesty of the ocean. Whether you're a seasoned whale-watching enthusiast or a first-time visitor, the tours offer a chance to witness the awe-inspiring sight of whales and other marine life in their natural habitat. With expert guides, comfortable vessels, and a commitment to sustainable wildlife viewing, Monterey Bay Whale Watch is a must-do experience for anyone looking to explore the marine wonders of the Pacific.

56

MOUNT SHASTA

COUNTY: SISKIYOU   CITY: MOUNT SHASTA

DATE VISITED: WHO I WENT WITH:

RATING: ☆ ☆ ☆ ☆ ☆   WILL I RETURN? YES / NO

Mount Shasta City Visitor Center
300 Pine Street
Mount Shasta, CA 96067

Mount Shasta is a majestic, dormant stratovolcano located in the Cascade Range of northern California, standing as one of the tallest peaks in the state at 14,179 feet (4,322 meters). It is a striking landmark that dominates the surrounding landscape, visible from miles around and offering breathtaking views. The mountain's snow-capped summit, glaciers, and pristine surroundings make it a popular destination for outdoor enthusiasts, photographers, and nature lovers. It is situated in Siskiyou County, near the town of Mount Shasta, which serves as a gateway for visitors seeking to explore the region's natural beauty. The mountain is deeply rooted in local history and Native American culture, with indigenous tribes considering it a sacred site. Mount Shasta is not only a visually stunning natural feature but also an important part of California's ecological and geological heritage.

For those with a love of outdoor adventure, Mount Shasta offers year-round recreational opportunities. During the winter months, the mountain is a prime destination for skiing and snowboarding, with several areas offering slopes suitable for both beginners and advanced skiers. The Mount Shasta Ski Park, located on the southern slopes of the mountain, provides an excellent winter experience with chairlifts, snowshoeing trails, and sledding areas. In the warmer months, the mountain becomes a haven for hikers, climbers, and mountaineers. The challenging climb to the summit of Mount Shasta is popular with experienced mountaineers, though the ascent is not to be taken lightly, requiring technical skill and proper preparation. The mountain is known for its glaciers, and routes to the summit typically pass by the Hotlum, Whitney, and Bolam glaciers, each offering a unique and challenging experience.

For those looking for less strenuous activities, Mount Shasta offers numerous hiking trails at various elevations, which allow visitors to enjoy the area's beautiful forests, alpine lakes, and meadows. The Pacific Crest Trail passes nearby, offering opportunities for long-distance hiking and backpacking. For an easier, more scenic experience, the Mount Shasta Wilderness offers an array of shorter hikes that provide sweeping views of the surrounding valleys and the mountain itself. Trails like Lake Siskiyou and Castle Lake offer a serene experience with opportunities for swimming, fishing, and picnicking. The surrounding forests, such as the Shasta-Trinity National Forest, provide ample opportunities for camping, wildlife viewing, and nature walks, making it a wonderful spot for families and casual hikers.

Beyond hiking and climbing, Mount Shasta is also a popular destination for spiritual seekers, as it is believed by many to be a sacred and energy-charged site. The mountain has been associated with mystical phenomena and has attracted those interested in metaphysical and spiritual experiences, including meditation and yoga retreats. The area's natural beauty, combined with its tranquil atmosphere, provides a peaceful setting for reflection and connection with nature.

The nearby town of Mount Shasta offers visitors a charming base for their adventures, with local shops, cafes, and accommodations providing everything from cozy lodges to luxurious hotels. The town is also home to several cultural attractions, including the Mount Shasta Fish Hatchery and the Mount Shasta Museum, which offers insight into the region's history, Native American culture, and the mountain's significance. The Mount Shasta Sisson Museum showcases exhibits on the mountain's geology and local wildlife, offering a deeper understanding of the area's unique ecosystem.

Mount Shasta is also part of the larger Shasta-Trinity National Forest, which spans over 2 million acres of wilderness and includes rivers, lakes, and forests, providing a wide range of outdoor activities. The McCloud River Falls, located just south of the mountain, is a particularly scenic spot, known for its multiple waterfalls and hiking opportunities along the river.

For those interested in local agriculture, Mount Shasta and the surrounding area offer opportunities to visit vineyards and farms. The region's climate and elevation are conducive to growing a variety of fruits, vegetables, and wine grapes, and visitors can enjoy local produce and wine tasting experiences at nearby wineries.

In addition to its recreational and cultural offerings, Mount Shasta is surrounded by a rich history, with the mountain being a key feature in the region's geological development. The mountain's volcanic activity over the past 300,000 years has left behind a diverse and unique landscape, including lava flows, crater lakes, and volcanic rock formations. Today, Mount Shasta remains an active geological site, with periodic seismic activity and the possibility of future eruptions, though it is currently dormant.

Whether you're seeking adventure on the slopes, a peaceful retreat in nature, or a deep connection to the region's spiritual energy, Mount Shasta offers an unforgettable experience. Its majestic beauty, outdoor activities, and tranquil atmosphere make it a must-visit destination in Northern California for adventurers, nature lovers, and those looking to explore one of the state's most iconic natural landmarks.

57

MUIR WOODS NATIONAL MONUMENT

COUNTY: MARIN   CITY: MILL VALLEY

DATE VISITED: WHO I WENT WITH:

RATING: ☆ ☆ ☆ ☆ ☆   WILL I RETURN?   YES / NO

1 Muir Woods Rd
Mill Valley, CA 94941
415-561-2850

Muir Woods National Monument is a serene sanctuary of ancient coastal redwood trees located just 12 miles north of San Francisco in Marin County, California. Renowned for its towering trees, tranquil atmosphere, and lush vegetation, Muir Woods offers visitors an unparalleled opportunity to experience one of the world's most magnificent ecosystems. Established in 1908 by President Theodore Roosevelt, the monument was named in honor of conservationist and naturalist John Muir, a pivotal figure in the American environmental movement.

The park is home to coastal redwoods (Sequoia sempervirens), the tallest tree species in the world. Many of the trees in Muir Woods are over 600 years old, with some reaching heights of more than 250 feet. Walking among these giants evokes a sense of awe and reverence, as the dense canopy creates a cathedral-like atmosphere. The quiet stillness is punctuated by the sounds of birds, rustling leaves, and flowing water, making it a perfect escape from the urban hustle of nearby San Francisco.

Visitors can explore the monument through a network of well-maintained trails that cater to all levels of hikers. The Main Trail, a flat and accessible loop, takes visitors through the heart of the redwood grove along wooden boardwalks and dirt paths. Along the way, interpretive signs provide insights into the park's ecology, history, and the vital role redwoods play in their environment. More adventurous visitors can venture onto longer trails such as the Ben Johnson Trail or the Dipsea Trail, which connect Muir Woods to Mount Tamalpais State Park and offer breathtaking views of the surrounding landscapes.

Muir Woods is also a haven for biodiversity. The shaded forest floor is covered in ferns, mosses, and wildflowers, creating a lush understory beneath the towering redwoods. The ecosystem supports a variety of wildlife, including deer, squirrels, and birds such as owls, woodpeckers, and warblers. The nearby Redwood Creek provides a habitat for Coho salmon and steelhead trout, which are key to the local ecosystem.

In addition to its natural beauty, Muir Woods has a rich cultural and historical significance. John Muir's advocacy for the preservation of wildlands inspired the creation of the National Park Service, and Muir Woods stands as a testament to his legacy. The monument is also part of the larger Golden Gate National Recreation Area, which encompasses several iconic natural and historical sites in the region.

Due to its popularity, Muir Woods can become crowded, especially during weekends and holidays. To ensure a smooth visit, reservations are required for parking or the shuttle service that runs from nearby locations. Arriving early in the morning or late in the afternoon provides a quieter experience and the chance to enjoy the forest in a more peaceful setting.

The park is open year-round, and each season offers a unique experience. Spring brings vibrant wildflowers, while the cool, misty mornings of summer highlight the redwoods' ethereal beauty. Fall offers warm hues in the deciduous plants, and winter brings a tranquil stillness that accentuates the monument's timeless character.

A visit to Muir Woods National Monument is a journey into an ancient world that inspires awe and deep appreciation for nature. Whether you're strolling along the Main Trail, hiking into the surrounding hills, or simply pausing to listen to the whispers of the redwoods, Muir Woods provides a rejuvenating and unforgettable experience that captures the magic of California's coastal forests.

58

NAPA VALLEY BALLOONS

COUNTY: NAPA   **CITY:** YOUNTVILLE

DATE VISITED: **WHO I WENT WITH:**

RATING: ☆ ☆ ☆ ☆ ☆   **WILL I RETURN?** YES / NO

7901 Solano Avenue
Yountville, CA 94599
800-253-2224

Napa Valley Balloons, located in the heart of Napa Valley, California, offers an unforgettable hot air balloon experience that lets visitors soar above the breathtaking landscape of one of the world's most famous wine regions. Known for its picturesque vineyards, rolling hills, and tranquil beauty, Napa Valley provides the perfect backdrop for a peaceful yet exhilarating adventure in the sky. The balloon rides offer a unique perspective of the valley, giving guests a chance to enjoy panoramic views of the lush vineyards, quaint towns, and distant mountain ranges, all while experiencing the serenity of flight.

The Napa Valley Balloons experience begins early in the morning, just as the sun starts to rise, offering a peaceful start to the day. Guests gather at the designated launch site, where the crew prepares the balloon, and the ride takes off just after dawn. As the balloon ascends, visitors are treated to a stunning visual feast. The valley's patchwork of vineyards, with their neat rows of grapevines, stretches across the land, while the morning fog begins to lift, revealing the scenic beauty of the surrounding Mayacamas Mountains and Vaca Range. The changing colors of the sky as the sun rises over the valley make for an enchanting experience, and the calm, quiet nature of the balloon ride allows passengers to fully take in the splendor of their surroundings.

A typical flight lasts about an hour, although it can vary depending on weather conditions. During the ride, guests can enjoy breathtaking views of some of Napa Valley's most famous wineries and estates, offering a rare and magical view of the region. The pilot guides the balloon through different altitudes, allowing guests to see Napa from various perspectives, whether it's a closer look at the vineyards or a higher view of the entire valley. The slow and peaceful nature of the flight creates an atmosphere of tranquility and awe, making it a truly memorable experience.

Upon landing, guests are treated to a traditional post-flight celebration, which typically includes a toast with champagne or sparkling wine. This celebratory moment is a wonderful way to mark the end of the flight and savor the joy of the adventure. Afterward, guests are often given the chance to take photos and reflect on the stunning views and unforgettable experience.

For those looking to extend their Napa Valley adventure, Napa Valley Balloons offers packages that combine the hot air balloon ride with other Napa Valley experiences. These may include wine tastings at world-class wineries, gourmet brunches, or vineyard tours, making it an ideal way to explore the region's rich culture and natural beauty. The combination of the balloon ride and wine tasting experience is especially popular, as guests can enjoy both the thrill of flight and the renowned wines of Napa Valley, all in one day.

The rides are operated with safety as a top priority, and the professional pilots have years of experience navigating the skies. The company is known for its commitment to providing a safe, smooth, and enjoyable experience for all passengers. Napa Valley Balloons is also recognized for its excellent customer service, with a team dedicated to ensuring guests feel comfortable and at ease throughout the experience.

Hot air balloon rides with Napa Valley Balloons are perfect for a romantic getaway, a special celebration like an anniversary or birthday, or simply for anyone looking to experience the beauty of Napa Valley in a unique way. Whether it's for a first-time visitor or a seasoned Napa enthusiast, the balloon ride offers a one-of-a-kind adventure that provides memories to last a lifetime. It's an exceptional way to see Napa Valley from a completely different perspective, offering unparalleled views and an experience that blends adventure, serenity, and the natural beauty of California's wine country.

59

NEVADA FALLS LOOP

COUNTY: MARIPOSA   **CITY:** MARIPOSA

DATE VISITED: _____   **WHO I WENT WITH:** _____

RATING: ☆ ☆ ☆ ☆ ☆   **WILL I RETURN?**   YES / NO

You can drive to Yosemite year-round and enter via Highways 41, 140, and 120 from the west. Tioga Pass Entrance (via Highway 120 from the east) is closed from approximately November through late May or June. Hetch Hetchy is open all year but may close intermittently due to snow. Please note that GPS units do not always provide accurate directions to or within Yosemite.
209-372-0200

The Nevada Falls Loop, located in Yosemite National Park, California, is one of the park's most popular and scenic hiking trails. Known for its breathtaking views and moderate level of difficulty, this 5-6 mile loop offers hikers an unforgettable experience as it weaves through lush forests, past rushing waterfalls, and up to panoramic vistas of the surrounding valley and peaks. The trail provides an ideal opportunity to witness the stunning natural beauty of Yosemite, offering a combination of lush greenery, towering granite cliffs, and majestic waterfalls.

Starting from the Happy Isles area in Yosemite Valley, the Nevada Falls Loop trail takes hikers through a variety of ecosystems, from forested paths to rocky outcroppings. The first part of the hike follows the Mist Trail, which is famous for the close-up views it offers of Vernal Falls. The Mist Trail is aptly named for the spray that rises from the falls, creating a refreshing mist that cools hikers as they ascend. The trail is steep and involves a series of well-maintained stone steps, but the reward is the impressive sight of the falls tumbling over the cliffside into the Merced River below.

After reaching the top of Vernal Falls, the trail continues to climb toward Nevada Falls, which is larger and even more spectacular. As hikers approach Nevada Falls, the roar of the waterfall becomes louder, and the views of the cascading water over granite cliffs are awe-inspiring. At 594 feet, Nevada Falls is one of the tallest waterfalls in Yosemite National Park, and the sight of the water plunging down into the river below is truly breathtaking. For many hikers, reaching the top of Nevada Falls is the highlight of the trail.

The Nevada Falls Loop offers two options for descending: hikers can either return the way they came via the Mist Trail or take the John Muir Trail, which provides a gentler, longer route back to Yosemite Valley. The John Muir Trail offers a less crowded, more tranquil descent, with fantastic views of the valley and the surrounding peaks, including the iconic Half Dome. Along this route, hikers are treated to stunning panoramas and a variety of flora and fauna as they make their way back down to the valley floor.

The Nevada Falls Loop is considered a moderate to challenging hike, particularly due to the steep incline on the Mist Trail, but it is highly rewarding for those who are up for the adventure. The best time to hike the Nevada Falls Loop is during the spring and early summer when the waterfalls are at their fullest, though it can also be hiked year-round. In the spring, the rushing water and mist create a refreshing atmosphere, while in the fall, the surrounding foliage adds vibrant colors to the scenery.

Hikers should come prepared with plenty of water, sun protection, and sturdy footwear, as parts of the trail can be slippery and uneven, especially near the waterfalls. It's also important to note that the Mist Trail can be crowded during peak tourist season, so early morning or late afternoon hikes are recommended for those seeking a quieter experience. The trail can also be strenuous, particularly if you plan to complete the full loop, so it's important to know your limits and pace yourself.

The Nevada Falls Loop is a must-do for anyone visiting Yosemite National Park who enjoys outdoor adventure and stunning natural beauty. With its sweeping views of waterfalls, forests, and granite peaks, it's a quintessential Yosemite experience that offers a chance to see some of the park's most iconic features up close. Whether you're a seasoned hiker or a first-time visitor to Yosemite, the Nevada Falls Loop will leave you with lasting memories of the park's awe-inspiring landscapes and natural wonders.

60

NEWPORT BEACH

COUNTY: ORANGE   CITY: NEWPORT BEACH

DATE VISITED: WHO I WENT WITH:

RATING: ☆ ☆ ☆ ☆ ☆   WILL I RETURN? YES / NO

Newport Beach is a premier coastal city in Orange County, California, known for its picturesque waterfront, luxurious lifestyle, and wide variety of recreational activities. Situated along the Pacific Ocean, this vibrant beach town offers a unique blend of natural beauty, world-class amenities, and a rich cultural scene, making it one of the most popular destinations on the California coast. The city's stunning coastline is one of its main attractions, with miles of sandy beaches that are perfect for sunbathing, surfing, swimming, and beach volleyball. Newport Beach is particularly famous for its iconic surf spots, including The Wedge, a world-renowned location known for its massive waves and challenging surf conditions, drawing surfers from all over the globe.

The heart of Newport Beach is its bustling Harbor, a hub for boating, kayaking, and paddleboarding. The harbor is home to a wide variety of yachts, sailboats, and small vessels, offering visitors the opportunity to enjoy scenic boat rides or rent a kayak to explore the waters up close. A popular attraction in the harbor is the Newport Beach Boat Parade, an annual event during the holiday season that showcases elaborately decorated boats and is one of the largest and oldest Christmas boat parades in the country. The harbor is also home to the Balboa Island Ferry, which transports passengers between Balboa Island and the mainland, providing a scenic and fun way to enjoy the area's waterfront views.

For those seeking more laid-back activities, Balboa Island is a must-visit. This charming, small community offers a relaxed atmosphere, with streets lined with quaint shops, cozy cafes, and delicious local eateries. Visitors can stroll along the island's boardwalk, rent a bicycle, or enjoy a famous Balboa Bar, a delicious treat consisting of a frozen chocolate-dipped ice cream bar with toppings. Balboa Island also features the Balboa Fun Zone, a family-friendly amusement area with an old-fashioned ferris wheel, arcade games, and a variety of souvenir shops.

A short distance from the harbor is the bustling Newport Pier, which is another iconic landmark of the city. The pier stretches out into the ocean, providing stunning views of the coastline and acting as a gathering place for locals and tourists alike. The pier is a popular spot for fishing and is home to several seafood restaurants that offer fresh, locally caught dishes. The surrounding Newport Beach boardwalk is perfect for walking, biking, or simply taking in the scenic beauty of the area.

Beyond its natural beauty, Newport Beach also offers a variety of cultural and shopping experiences. Fashion Island, an open-air shopping center, is home to some of the most luxurious retail stores in the country, as well as high-end dining options. This upscale shopping district offers a world-class shopping experience, with brands like Chanel, Louis Vuitton, and Tiffany & Co., as well as a variety of trendy boutiques. For those interested in the arts, the Orange County Museum of Art (OCMA) features a diverse collection of contemporary art exhibits and offers educational programs for visitors of all ages.

Newport Beach also has a rich culinary scene, with everything from casual beachside dining to elegant, fine dining experiences. The city's waterfront restaurants offer spectacular views of the harbor and the Pacific Ocean, with many serving fresh seafood dishes, locally inspired fare, and craft cocktails. Lido Marina Village, an upscale waterfront shopping and dining area, is another popular destination for food lovers, offering a variety of trendy cafes and restaurants with waterfront seating.

Outdoor enthusiasts can enjoy a variety of activities in the nearby Corona del Mar State Beach, which is perfect for picnics, sunbathing, and tide pool exploration, as well as Crystal Cove State Park, which offers hiking trails, beaches, and some of the best scenic vistas in the area. For golf lovers, The Balboa Bay Resort features a championship golf course that offers challenging greens and beautiful views.

Newport Beach also boasts an active and thriving social scene, with plenty of events, festivals, and activities throughout the year. From the Newport Beach Film Festival to the Newport Beach Jazz Festival, the city offers a wide range of events that cater to a variety of interests, including music, art, film, and food. For those seeking a more relaxed pace, the city's numerous spas and wellness centers provide a perfect retreat, offering massages, yoga classes, and other treatments that take advantage of the area's serene atmosphere.

For families, Newport Beach is home to a variety of kid-friendly attractions, including the Newport Dunes Waterfront Resort, which offers a range of water activities, beach rentals, and picnic areas. The Environmental Nature Center provides educational programs, nature trails, and an opportunity to experience the natural beauty of Orange County's coastal habitats. Families can also visit the nearby Irvine Park, which features playgrounds, bike rentals, and a small zoo.

With its beautiful beaches, luxurious shopping, fine dining, cultural experiences, and family-friendly attractions, Newport Beach has something for everyone. Whether you are looking to relax by the ocean, explore the city's rich history, or indulge in world-class shopping and dining, this coastal gem offers an unforgettable experience.

61 OAKLAND CALIFORNIA TEMPLE & VISITORS' CENTER

COUNTY: ALAMEDA   **CITY:** OAKLAND

DATE VISITED: _____ **WHO I WENT WITH:** _____

RATING: ☆ ☆ ☆ ☆ ☆   **WILL I RETURN?** YES / NO

4766 Lincoln Avenue
Oakland, CA 94602
510-328-0044

The Oakland California Temple & Visitors' Center, located in Oakland, California, is a significant religious and cultural landmark in the San Francisco Bay Area. As part of The Church of Jesus Christ of Latter-day Saints (LDS Church), the Oakland Temple stands as a beautiful symbol of faith and is the largest LDS temple in Northern California. Opened in 1964, the temple's striking architecture and its serene location atop a hill make it a must-visit destination for those interested in religious history, architecture, and the stunning views of the surrounding region.

The Oakland Temple is set against a backdrop of the picturesque East Bay hills, offering breathtaking panoramic views of the Bay Area, including San Francisco, the Golden Gate Bridge, and the surrounding cities. Its towering spire, adorned with a golden statue of the angel Moroni, is visible from many parts of the area and stands as a beacon of faith and peace. The temple's design combines modern and classical elements, with white granite walls and intricate architectural details that reflect both elegance and spiritual significance.

Visitors to the Oakland California Temple can enjoy exploring the adjacent Visitors' Center, which is open to the public and offers a variety of exhibits and interactive displays about the LDS Church's history, teachings, and worldwide activities. The center provides a welcoming environment for guests of all backgrounds to learn about the faith, and knowledgeable staff members are available to answer questions and provide information. The Visitors' Center also features multimedia presentations, displays on family history and genealogy, and artwork depicting scenes from the Bible and the Book of Mormon.

The Oakland California Temple itself is a sacred space, and as such, only members of the LDS Church in good standing are allowed to enter the temple for worship and religious ceremonies. However, the temple grounds are open to the public, and visitors are encouraged to walk around the beautifully landscaped gardens, which are meticulously maintained and provide a peaceful setting for reflection and contemplation. The gardens feature a variety of native and exotic plants, fountains, and statues that add to the temple's serene atmosphere.

In addition to the temple and Visitors' Center, the Oakland California Temple is an important hub for the LDS community in the Bay Area. It serves as a place for spiritual growth, community gatherings, and religious education. Many visitors come to the temple to learn more about the LDS faith, participate in religious events, or simply enjoy the tranquility of the temple grounds.

For those who are not familiar with the LDS Church or its beliefs, a visit to the Oakland California Temple & Visitors' Center offers a great opportunity to learn about the teachings of the church in an accessible and welcoming environment. Whether you are interested in the architecture, the history, or the religious practices of the LDS Church, the Oakland Temple is a place of beauty, peace, and education.

The Oakland California Temple and Visitors' Center are also popular during special events and holidays. During Christmas, the temple grounds are beautifully decorated with lights and festive displays, attracting visitors from all over the Bay Area. The temple and Visitors' Center host special holiday programs, including musical performances, and provide a unique way to experience the Christmas season in a spiritually uplifting way.

Overall, a visit to the Oakland California Temple & Visitors' Center offers a unique experience that combines spiritual reflection, historical education, and stunning views of the Bay Area. Whether you're interested in the religious significance, the peaceful surroundings, or simply the opportunity to enjoy one of the area's most iconic landmarks, the Oakland Temple is a must-see destination for visitors to the San Francisco Bay Area.

COUNTY: MONTEREY   **CITY:** PACIFIC GROVE

DATE VISITED: **WHO I WENT WITH:**

RATING: ☆ ☆ ☆ ☆ ☆   **WILL I RETURN?** YES / NO

Pacific Grove Oceanview Boulevard, located in Pacific Grove, California, is one of the most scenic and serene drives along the California coast. Known for its breathtaking ocean views, the boulevard runs along the rugged coastline of the Monterey Peninsula and offers visitors a picturesque experience of natural beauty, wildlife, and historic landmarks. Stretching for approximately 2.5 miles, the road provides access to several popular spots, including Lovers Point, Asilomar State Beach, and the Pacific Grove Municipal Golf Course.

One of the main attractions of Oceanview Boulevard is the stunning views of the Pacific Ocean. Visitors can enjoy panoramic vistas of the sparkling blue waters, rocky shorelines, and the occasional glimpse of local wildlife, such as sea otters, seals, and migrating whales. The road winds through Pacific Grove's famous coastline, offering scenic outlooks and opportunities to stop and take in the beauty of the Pacific Ocean.

As you drive along Oceanview Boulevard, the surrounding landscape changes with the rhythm of the coastline. The views are diverse, from calm sandy beaches to rugged, craggy cliffs, making it a favorite spot for both casual sightseers and avid photographers. The stretch near Lovers Point is particularly popular, offering expansive views of the ocean, and is a favorite spot for picnics, kayaking, and relaxing by the water.

A particularly unique feature of Oceanview Boulevard is its proximity to Asilomar State Beach, which provides a mix of sand dunes, coastal bluffs, and tide pools. The beach is a perfect spot for walking, picnicking, or watching the waves crash against the shore. For those interested in local flora and fauna, the area surrounding the boulevard is home to a variety of coastal plants and birds, making it an excellent destination for nature enthusiasts.

In addition to its natural beauty, Oceanview Boulevard is steeped in history. The road passes through neighborhoods filled with charming historic cottages, many dating back to the early 20th century. This gives visitors a chance to experience the town's old-world charm while enjoying the modern amenities that Pacific Grove has to offer. One of the most notable spots along the boulevard is the Pacific Grove Museum of Natural History, which is located nearby and offers exhibits about the local wildlife and history of the area.

For those visiting the area during certain times of the year, Oceanview Boulevard is also a great location for experiencing the migration of monarch butterflies. The town of Pacific Grove is famous for being a winter haven for these butterflies, and during the fall and winter months, you can often see thousands of monarchs in the trees near the boulevard. The Monarch Butterfly Sanctuary located off the boulevard is an ideal place to stop and learn more about this natural phenomenon.

Whether you are taking a leisurely drive, stopping at one of the many viewpoints, or exploring the nearby parks and beaches, Pacific Grove Oceanview Boulevard offers a tranquil escape and a memorable way to experience the beauty of the Monterey Peninsula. With its rich combination of coastal vistas, wildlife sightings, and local history, this iconic roadway is a must-see destination for anyone visiting the Pacific Grove area.

PALACE GAMES

COUNTY: SAN FRANCISCO   **CITY:** SAN FRANCISCO

DATE VISITED: **WHO I WENT WITH:**

RATING: ☆ ☆ ☆ ☆ ☆   **WILL I RETURN?** YES / NO

3362 Palace Drive
San Francisco, CA 94123
415-997-8522

Palace Games, located in San Francisco, California, offers a unique and immersive escape room experience that brings history to life through thrilling, puzzle-filled adventures. Situated inside the historic Palace of Fine Arts, a stunning Beaux-Arts landmark built for the 1915 Panama-Pacific Exposition, Palace Games provides a mix of historical intrigue and challenging puzzles set in one of the most iconic buildings in San Francisco.

The attraction is known for its elaborate escape rooms, each designed with intricate attention to detail and tied to historical themes, providing participants with a chance to step back in time while solving mysteries. One of the most popular experiences at Palace Games is the "Escape from the Palace of Fine Arts" room, where players are tasked with solving a series of puzzles to escape from a replica of the Palace's original architecture, which adds a layer of historical context and realism to the experience.

What makes Palace Games particularly special is its emphasis on storytelling. Each game is crafted to incorporate elements of San Francisco's rich cultural and historical heritage, making the puzzles not only fun but also educational. The settings are meticulously designed with props and decorations that transport players into a different era. Whether you're solving complex puzzles, unlocking hidden secrets, or racing against the clock to complete your mission, Palace Games offers an exciting challenge for both beginners and seasoned escape room enthusiasts.

For those who enjoy teamwork, Palace Games provides an excellent opportunity to collaborate with friends, family, or colleagues. The games require participants to think critically, communicate effectively, and work together to solve each puzzle, making it a great bonding experience. The rooms are designed to accommodate groups of various sizes, ensuring that every visitor has an enjoyable experience, whether they are new to escape rooms or escape room veterans.

In addition to its escape room experiences, the Palace of Fine Arts itself is a must-see landmark, making Palace Games a perfect destination for tourists. The Palace's stunning architecture and surrounding parkland provide a beautiful setting for visitors to relax before or after their escape room adventure. The building's grand rotunda and lagoon are often photographed, and visitors can take a leisurely walk around the scenic park and enjoy the iconic structure.

Whether you're looking to test your puzzle-solving skills, learn more about the history of the Palace of Fine Arts, or just enjoy a fun and engaging activity with friends and family, Palace Games is a memorable destination in San Francisco. With its historical themes, detailed environments, and immersive storytelling, it's an escape room experience that stands out in the city's vibrant tourism scene.

PANORAMA TRAIL

64

COUNTY: MARIPOSA   CITY: MARIPOSA

DATE VISITED: WHO I WENT WITH:

RATING: ☆ ☆ ☆ ☆ ☆   WILL I RETURN?   YES / NO

You can drive to Yosemite year-round and enter via Highways 41, 140, and 120 from the west. Tioga Pass Entrance (via Highway 120 from the east) is closed from approximately November through late May or June. Hetch Hetchy is open all year but may close intermittently due to snow. Please note that GPS units do not always provide accurate directions to or within Yosemite.
209-372-0200

The Panorama Trail, located in Yosemite National Park, California, is one of the most rewarding and scenic hikes in the park, offering breathtaking views of some of the most iconic landmarks in Yosemite Valley. This 8.5-mile trail takes hikers on a journey through diverse landscapes, providing an incredible vantage point for viewing waterfalls, granite cliffs, and the lush, forested valley floor below. The Panorama Trail is a moderately strenuous hike that offers visitors an unforgettable way to experience the grandeur of Yosemite.

The trail begins at Glacier Point, which itself is a popular viewpoint offering sweeping panoramic views of Yosemite Valley, Half Dome, and the High Sierra peaks. From this starting point, hikers descend along the trail, following the contours of the mountainside. The path is well-maintained and mostly downhill, though there are some uphill sections, especially near the end. The trail provides a variety of vistas, each more stunning than the last, offering up-close views of Half Dome, Illilouette Basin, and Vernal Falls. As hikers make their way down the trail, they are treated to changing scenery, from the high alpine environment near Glacier Point to the lush forests closer to Yosemite Valley.

One of the highlights of the Panorama Trail is the chance to see Vernal Falls and Nevada Falls up close. The trail passes near both of these spectacular waterfalls, giving hikers the opportunity to hear the thundering roar of the water and feel the refreshing mist as it sprays into the air. The views of these waterfalls from the Panorama Trail are particularly impressive, as they drop dramatically down granite cliffs, surrounded by dense forest and the expansive Yosemite Valley.

As you approach the end of the trail, you'll reach Yosemite Valley, where the trail intersects with the Mist Trail and the John Muir Trail, offering access to additional hiking opportunities. From this point, you can either continue on to other destinations in the park or take the shuttle back to the starting point, depending on your time and energy.

The Panorama Trail is known for its diverse terrain, which includes a mix of shaded forests, open meadows, and rocky outcroppings, as well as its rich flora and fauna. Hikers may spot wildlife such as mule deer, black bears (from a safe distance), and a variety of bird species, including eagles and peregrine falcons.

Because of its length and elevation change, the Panorama Trail is best suited for hikers with some experience. It is typically a one-way trail, with most visitors opting to shuttle or arrange for transportation back to their starting point at Glacier Point. The trail can be hiked year-round, but the best time to visit is in late spring and early summer, when the waterfalls are at their fullest and the wildflowers are in bloom. However, it is important to note that portions of the trail may be closed in the winter due to snow and ice, so checking trail conditions before embarking on your hike is recommended.

For those seeking a unique way to experience the beauty of Yosemite National Park, the Panorama Trail provides an exceptional opportunity to see the park's most iconic features from a stunning perspective. The hike is not only visually striking but also offers a sense of accomplishment and connection to the natural world, making it a must-do adventure for nature lovers and avid hikers visiting Yosemite.

----

65 PCPA - PACIFIC CONSERVATORY THEATRE

COUNTY: SANTA BARBARA   CITY: SANTA MARIA

DATE VISITED: WHO I WENT WITH:

RATING: ☆ ☆ ☆ ☆ ☆   WILL I RETURN?   YES / NO

800 S College Dr
Santa Maria, CA 93454
805-922-8313

PCPA – Pacific Conservatory Theatre, located in Santa Maria, California, is one of the region's most renowned professional theater companies, offering a diverse array of performances throughout the year. Established in 1953, PCPA has a long history of producing high-quality productions that showcase the rich talent of its performers and technical crew. With its commitment to excellence in theater, PCPA has become a cornerstone of Central Coast culture, providing exceptional live theater experiences to audiences of all ages.

The theater company produces a wide range of performances, including classic plays, contemporary works, and musicals. PCPA is particularly well known for its innovative adaptations and interpretations of classic works, as well as its commitment to bringing new and contemporary stories to life on stage. Its productions are characterized by strong performances, creative direction, and impressive sets and costumes, which combine to create an immersive and engaging theater experience.

A hallmark of PCPA – Pacific Conservatory Theatre is its unique role as a conservatory for emerging theater professionals. The company provides training for students in its prestigious theater conservatory program, where aspiring actors, directors, and technicians have the opportunity to hone their craft while working alongside seasoned professionals. This educational aspect enriches the company's productions, allowing audiences to experience the work of both seasoned performers and up-and-coming talent.

PCPA's main stage performances are held at the Marjorie Luke Theatre, located in the heart of Santa Barbara, and the Solvang Festival Theater, a charming, outdoor venue that provides a beautiful setting for summer performances. The Solvang Festival Theater is especially popular for its open-air productions, where attendees can enjoy a warm summer evening under the stars while watching a high-quality theater performance. This unique venue adds a magical element to the experience, especially for outdoor productions such as Shakespeare plays, which are a regular feature in PCPA's lineup.

In addition to its regular season of performances, PCPA also offers educational outreach programs that engage the local community. These programs aim to introduce the joys of theater to students, families, and underserved communities, helping to foster a love of the arts and providing opportunities for artistic expression and growth. PCPA's educational programs are designed to cultivate young talent, inspire creativity, and provide audiences with a deeper appreciation for the arts.

For theater lovers visiting Santa Maria and the Central Coast, PCPA provides a rich and varied theatrical experience. Whether you're attending a classic drama, a contemporary work, or a family-friendly musical, the performances at PCPA are always professionally produced and expertly executed. The company's commitment to both the art of theater and the development of new talent ensures that each production is a memorable and enriching experience.

With its combination of professional productions, educational programs, and community engagement, PCPA – Pacific Conservatory Theatre is a vibrant and essential part of California's cultural landscape. Whether you are a local resident or a visitor, experiencing a show at PCPA is a must for anyone who appreciates the magic of live theater.

66

PIER 39

COUNTY: SAN FRANCISCO   CITY: SAN FRANCISCO

DATE VISITED: WHO I WENT WITH:

RATING: ☆ ☆ ☆ ☆ ☆   WILL I RETURN? YES / NO

Beach Street & The Embarcadero
San Francisco, CA 94133

Pier 39, located in San Francisco, California, is one of the city's most iconic and vibrant waterfront destinations, offering a unique blend of shopping, dining, entertainment, and breathtaking views of the bay. Situated along the northern edge of San Francisco Bay, Pier 39 has become a must-visit spot for both tourists and locals, offering a lively and engaging experience for visitors of all ages.

The pier itself is home to a wide variety of shops, restaurants, and attractions, making it an ideal place to spend an afternoon or evening. Visitors can stroll along the bustling walkways, browse through a diverse range of stores selling everything from souvenirs and clothing to artisanal goods and local crafts. Whether you're looking for a gift, a snack, or a unique piece of art, Pier 39 offers something for every taste and budget. In addition to its shops, the pier features a variety of restaurants, offering everything from casual bites to fine dining, with many eateries providing beautiful views of the bay and Golden Gate Bridge.

One of the most famous features of Pier 39 is the large population of sea lions that gather on the docks near the pier. These playful marine mammals can often be seen lounging in the sun or frolicking in the water, drawing large crowds of visitors who come to watch them bask and interact. The sea lions became a beloved symbol of the area after they first appeared in large numbers in the late 1980s, and they continue to attract visitors from around the world.

In addition to shopping and dining, Pier 39 is home to several attractions that make it a popular family destination. Visitors can explore the Aquarium of the Bay, which showcases the rich marine life of the San Francisco Bay, offering an up-close look at local sea creatures, including rays, sharks, and colorful fish. The San Francisco Carousel, a beautifully designed hand-carved carousel, is a hit with children, while the Magowan's Infinite Mirror Maze challenges visitors to navigate through a fun, twisting maze of mirrors. For those seeking panoramic views of the bay, Pier 39 offers an observation deck with stunning vistas of the Golden Gate Bridge, Alcatraz Island, and the San Francisco skyline.

Pier 39 is also a hub for entertainment, with street performers, live music, and seasonal events adding to the festive atmosphere. Throughout the year, the pier hosts a variety of special events and festivals, including the San Francisco Symphony's Waterfront Concerts, holiday celebrations, and New Year's Eve fireworks over the bay. The pier's waterfront setting and lively environment make it a great place to enjoy a meal, take in the sights, or simply relax and people-watch.

For those exploring San Francisco's waterfront, Pier 39 is conveniently located near other famous attractions, such as Fisherman's Wharf, Ghirardelli Square, and the Embarcadero. The area is easily accessible by public transportation, including the historic Cable Cars, and offers ample parking for those driving into the city.

Whether you're looking for shopping, dining, family-friendly fun, or simply a place to relax and enjoy the views, Pier 39 provides an unforgettable experience in the heart of San Francisco. Its combination of natural beauty, vibrant entertainment, and iconic attractions make it a must-see destination for anyone visiting the city.

67

PINNACLES NATIONAL PARK

COUNTY: SAN BENITO   CITY: PAICINES

DATE VISITED: WHO I WENT WITH:

RATING: ☆ ☆ ☆ ☆ ☆   WILL I RETURN? YES / NO

5000 East Entrance Road
Paicines, CA 95043
831-389-4486

Pinnacles National Park, located in central California, is a stunning and unique landscape that showcases the dramatic effects of volcanic activity and erosion over millions of years. As one of the newest national parks in the United States, designated in 2013, Pinnacles has quickly become a favorite destination for hikers, rock climbers, and nature enthusiasts drawn to its towering spires, lush valleys, and diverse wildlife.

The park's most striking feature is its rugged rock formations, known as pinnacles, which were formed by ancient volcanic eruptions and the movement of the San Andreas Fault. These jagged peaks, cliffs, and monoliths create a surreal and awe-inspiring backdrop for outdoor adventures. The High Peaks Trail offers hikers an up-close encounter with the park's dramatic rock spires, with panoramic views and sections of the trail that require navigating narrow passages and steep staircases carved into the stone.

Pinnacles National Park is divided into two distinct areas, the East and the West, with no road connecting them. The East Side is known for its shaded oak woodlands, flowing creeks, and access to popular caves, while the West Side features dramatic cliffs and rock formations. Visitors can explore both sides by hiking the trails that traverse the park's heart, such as the Condor Gulch Trail and the Bear Gulch Trail, which connect to the High Peaks area.

One of the park's unique attractions is its talus caves, created by boulders that have fallen into narrow canyons. These caves, such as Bear Gulch Cave and Balconies Cave, are exciting to explore, with dimly lit passageways, cascading water, and eerie echoes. Bear Gulch Cave is home to a colony of endangered Townsend's big-eared bats, and sections of the cave may be closed during the bat breeding season to protect these remarkable creatures.

Pinnacles is also a sanctuary for the California condor, one of the most endangered birds in the world. The park's rugged cliffs and remote terrain make it an ideal habitat for these massive birds, with wingspans of up to 10 feet. Spotting a condor soaring above the pinnacles is a highlight for many visitors, and the park plays a crucial role in the ongoing recovery efforts for this species.

Wildlife enthusiasts will find a rich variety of animals in the park, including golden eagles, peregrine falcons, bobcats, and foxes. The diverse plant life ranges from chaparral-covered slopes to seasonal wildflower blooms that paint the landscape with vibrant colors in the spring. The park's ecosystem thrives in the unique microclimates created by its rugged terrain.

Rock climbers are drawn to Pinnacles' challenging routes, which range from beginner-friendly climbs to advanced ascents. The park's volcanic rock, while brittle in some areas, provides unique climbing opportunities amidst breathtaking scenery. Climbers should follow park regulations to ensure safety and minimize impact on the environment.

Camping is available at the Pinnacles Campground, located on the East Side of the park. The campground offers tent and RV sites, along with amenities such as a swimming pool and picnic areas. Stargazing is another highlight of a visit, as the park's remote location provides dark skies free from light pollution, revealing a dazzling view of the Milky Way.

Pinnacles National Park is accessible year-round, but the best times to visit are in the spring and fall when temperatures are moderate. Summers can be hot, with temperatures often exceeding 90°F (32°C), while winters bring cooler weather and the chance to see the park's landscape dusted with snow.

Whether you're climbing the rocky pinnacles, hiking through wildflower-filled valleys, or watching a condor soar across the sky, Pinnacles National Park offers a unique and unforgettable experience. Its combination of dramatic geology, rich biodiversity, and opportunities for adventure make it a must-visit destination for anyone exploring California's natural treasures.

68

POINT LOBOS

COUNTY: MONTEREY   **CITY:** CARMEL-BY-THE-SEA

DATE VISITED: **WHO I WENT WITH:**

RATING: ☆ ☆ ☆ ☆ ☆   **WILL I RETURN?**   YES / NO

Hwy 1
Carmel, CA 93923

Point Lobos State Natural Reserve, located along the rugged central coast of California, just south of Carmel-by-the-Sea, is one of the most scenic and ecologically diverse areas in the state. Known for its dramatic coastal views, rich marine life, and diverse landscapes, Point Lobos is often referred to as "the crown jewel of the state park system" and is a must-visit destination for nature lovers, hikers, photographers, and anyone seeking to experience the natural beauty of California's coastline.

The reserve is a stunning 700-acre park that spans along a stretch of the Monterey Peninsula, offering panoramic views of the Pacific Ocean, rocky cliffs, and lush forests. Its diverse habitats range from rugged coastline and tide pools to dense forests of Monterey pine, cypress, and coastal scrub, providing a haven for both wildlife and visitors. Point Lobos is a popular spot for a variety of outdoor activities, including hiking, birdwatching, tidepooling, photography, and scuba diving. The area is rich in wildlife, with frequent sightings of sea otters, harbor seals, sea lions, and various seabirds. The reserve is also home to a variety of plant species, including rare and endangered species that thrive in this protected environment.

One of the highlights of Point Lobos is its extensive network of trails, which offer easy to moderate hikes with spectacular views. The most popular trail, the Cypress Grove Trail, takes visitors through a scenic forest of coastal cypress trees, with breathtaking views of the coastline and the opportunity to spot wildlife such as deer and birds of prey. The China Cove and Bird Island Trail offer stunning vistas of the coastline, with views of sea otters and seals sunbathing on the rocks. For those interested in marine life, the Carmel River State Beach Trail leads to a sandy beach where visitors can explore tide pools and watch the waves crash against the shore. Many of the trails are accessible year-round and provide opportunities to witness the changing seasons, from wildflower blooms in spring to the vibrant colors of fall.

The area is also a prime location for marine enthusiasts, with opportunities for kayaking, snorkeling, and scuba diving in the crystal-clear waters surrounding the reserve. The marine protected areas around Point Lobos are home to kelp forests, marine life, and underwater caves that attract divers from around the world.

Point Lobos is a designated California State Natural Reserve, which means it is protected to preserve its natural beauty and biological diversity. As such, visitors are encouraged to respect the park's rules, including staying on designated trails, avoiding disturbance to wildlife, and following Leave No Trace principles. The park offers a visitor center with educational exhibits about the local flora and fauna, as well as information about the park's history and conservation efforts.

The Reserve is also a great spot for photographers, with stunning views of the coastline, dramatic cliffs, and wildlife offering countless opportunities for striking photos. The reserve's relatively untouched beauty has made it a favorite subject for landscape photographers and artists alike.

Whether you're an avid hiker, a wildlife enthusiast, or someone just looking for a peaceful retreat into nature, Point Lobos State Natural Reserve provides a remarkable experience with its unmatched beauty, wildlife, and natural splendor. With its combination of dramatic vistas, diverse ecosystems, and recreational opportunities, it's easy to see why Point Lobos is considered one of the most beautiful spots in California.

---

69 PRAIRIE CREEK REDWOODS STATE PARK

COUNTY: HUMBOLDT   CITY: ORICK

DATE VISITED: _____   WHO I WENT WITH: _____

RATING: ☆ ☆ ☆ ☆ ☆   WILL I RETURN?   YES / NO

127011 Newton B. Drury Parkway
Orick, CA 95555
707-464-6101

Prairie Creek Redwoods State Park, located in Humboldt County, Northern California, is a majestic and serene destination that offers visitors a chance to experience some of the tallest trees in the world. Part of the Redwood National and State Parks system, the park spans over 14,000 acres of old-growth redwood forest, featuring towering trees, lush ferns, and diverse wildlife. Known for its stunning natural beauty, Prairie Creek Redwoods State Park provides a peaceful escape into nature and is a must-see for anyone interested in the awe-inspiring redwood trees that have made this region famous.

The park is home to some of the most iconic and impressive redwood trees, with many towering over 300 feet in height. Some of the trees in the park are over 2,000 years old, standing as silent witnesses to the ancient history of the California coastline. The dense forests of giant trees create a mystical atmosphere, where sunlight filters through the canopy and casts dappled shadows on the forest floor. In addition to the majestic redwoods, visitors will encounter a variety of other plant species, including ferns, mosses, and wildflowers, that contribute to the park's lush and vibrant environment.

Prairie Creek Redwoods State Park offers numerous hiking trails that allow visitors to explore its diverse landscapes. The park's trails range from easy, paved pathways to more challenging backcountry routes. One of the most popular hikes is the Newton B. Drury Scenic Parkway, a 10-mile drive through the heart of the redwood forest, offering breathtaking views of the towering trees. For those who prefer to stretch their legs, the Redwood Creek Trail is a beautiful, moderate trail that takes hikers deep into the forest and along the banks of the Redwood Creek. For a more immersive experience, the James Irvine Trail leads visitors through ancient groves of redwoods, offering stunning views of the lush landscape.

Another highlight of the park is Fern Canyon, a narrow, moss-covered gorge that's surrounded by towering ferns and lush vegetation. The canyon features a creek that runs through it, creating a stunning natural landscape that feels like something out of a fairy tale. Fern Canyon has been featured in several films, including the popular Jurassic Park: The Lost World, due to its otherworldly beauty.

The park is also home to a rich diversity of wildlife. Visitors may encounter a variety of animals, including Roosevelt elk, black bears, and coyotes, as well as over 200 species of birds. Roosevelt elk, in particular, are often seen grazing in the meadows of the park, adding to the park's unique charm. The elk are most commonly seen in the early morning or late afternoon when they venture into the open fields to feed.

Prairie Creek Redwoods State Park offers a range of activities for visitors to enjoy. In addition to hiking, there are opportunities for birdwatching, photography, and wildlife viewing. The park also provides several campgrounds, including the Prairie Creek Campground, which is situated in the heart of the redwood forest and allows visitors to camp among the towering trees. The campgrounds offer both tent and RV sites, making it a great option for those looking to experience the park's beauty overnight. The park's visitor center provides educational exhibits about the park's natural history, including the importance of redwood forests and conservation efforts.

For those who are interested in exploring the surrounding areas, Prairie Creek Redwoods State Park is located near other attractions in the Redwood National and State Parks, such as Jedediah Smith Redwoods State Park and the Redwood National Park. These nearby parks also offer opportunities to explore more old-growth forests, hike scenic trails, and learn about the unique ecosystem that defines the region.

As a designated state park, Prairie Creek Redwoods State Park is committed to preserving its natural beauty for future generations. The park's combination of ancient redwood forests, diverse wildlife, and rich history makes it a must-visit destination for nature lovers, hikers, and anyone seeking to experience the grandeur of California's coast redwoods. Whether you're visiting for a day hike, a camping trip, or simply to immerse yourself in the peaceful beauty of the redwoods, Prairie Creek Redwoods State Park offers an unforgettable experience that will stay with you long after you leave.

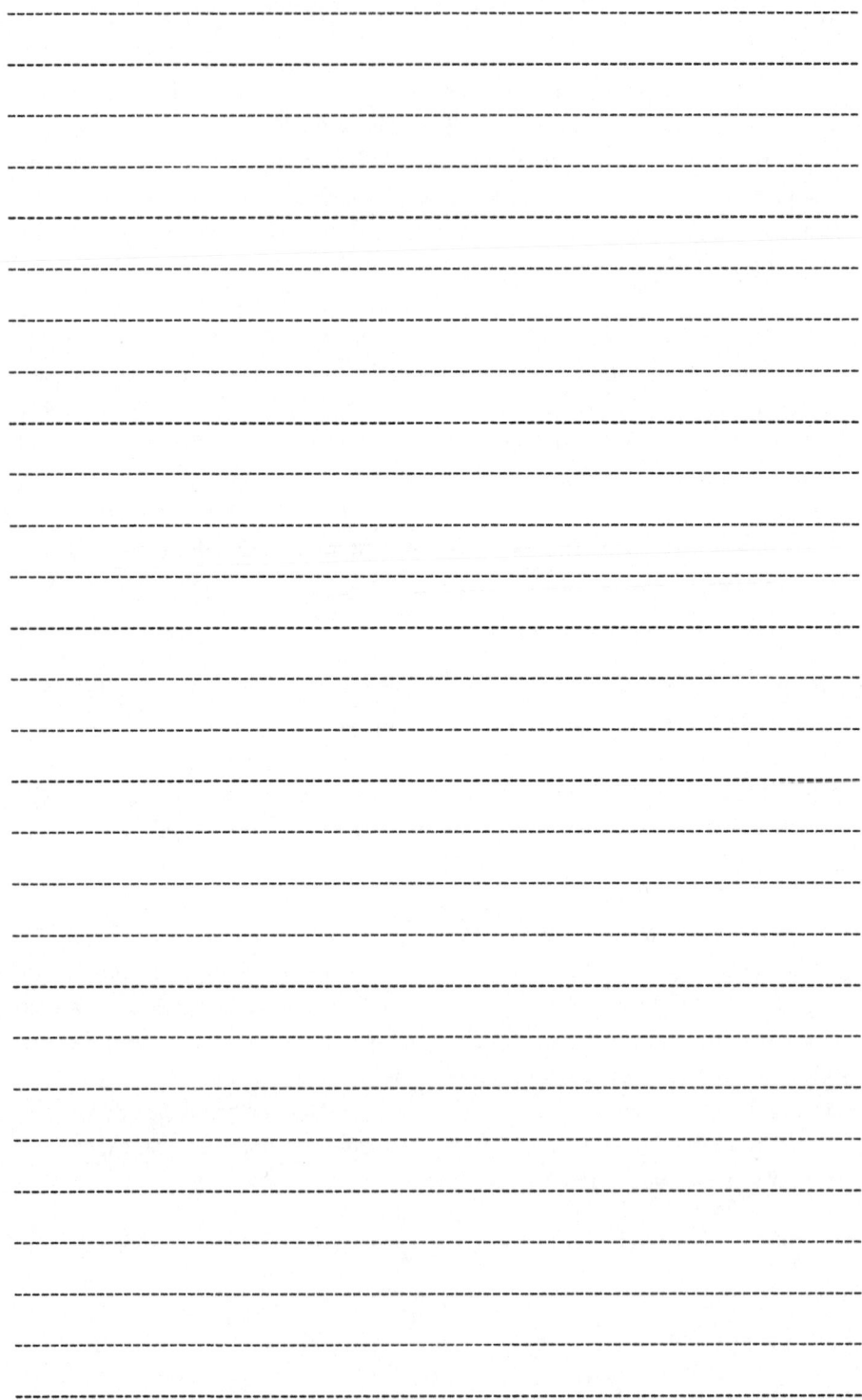

70

PRIDE MOUNTAIN VINEYARDS

COUNTY: NAPA   CITY: ST. HELENA

DATE VISITED: WHO I WENT WITH:

RATING: ☆ ☆ ☆ ☆ ☆   WILL I RETURN?   YES / NO

4026 Spring Mountain Rd
St. Helena, CA 94574
707-963-4949

Pride Mountain Vineyards, located on the crest of the Mayacamas Mountains in Napa County, California, offers one of the most stunning winery experiences in the region. Situated at the boundary between Napa Valley and Sonoma Valley, the vineyard is renowned for its exceptional wines, breathtaking panoramic views, and unique location. The vineyard sits at an elevation of over 2,100 feet, making it one of the highest-altitude wineries in the area. This elevation provides a cooler climate ideal for growing premium grapes and offers visitors an unparalleled view of the surrounding valleys and vineyards, adding to the winery's appeal as a top destination for wine enthusiasts.

The history of Pride Mountain Vineyards dates back to 1989 when it was established by the Pride family. The vineyard has become known for producing award-winning wines and its commitment to sustainable farming practices. The estate spans 235 acres, with approximately 85 acres dedicated to vineyards. The combination of diverse soil types, cool mountain temperatures, and high elevation allows the vineyard to cultivate a wide range of grape varieties, including Cabernet Sauvignon, Merlot, Syrah, and Chardonnay.

The winery is especially known for its red wines, particularly its Cabernet Sauvignon and Merlot blends, which are celebrated for their depth, complexity, and rich flavors. These wines showcase the quality of the terroir, with the high-altitude environment contributing to the development of intense flavors and a balanced structure. Pride Mountain Vineyards' winemaking philosophy emphasizes minimal intervention, with the goal of allowing the natural qualities of the fruit and the land to shine through in each bottle. The winery's commitment to sustainable viticulture practices ensures that the land is maintained with care, respecting the environment while producing wines that reflect the unique character of the region.

Visitors to Pride Mountain Vineyards are treated to more than just excellent wines. The winery offers a variety of tour and tasting experiences, many of which include visits to the winery's production facilities and caves. The cave tour is one of the highlights, as it takes guests through the winery's impressive underground caves where the wines are aged. These caves provide the ideal environment for maturing wines, and visitors can learn about the winemaking process and the winery's history while enjoying tastings of the estate's wines in the cool, intimate setting. In addition to the cave tours, the winery offers guided tours through the vineyards, giving guests the opportunity to learn about the farming practices that contribute to the quality of the wines. These tours often include tastings of the winery's signature wines, paired with an in-depth discussion of the flavors and aromas that define each wine.

For those looking for a more private experience, Pride Mountain Vineyards offers private tastings in beautiful, exclusive locations on the property. These tastings provide an intimate setting for guests to enjoy wines paired with local cheeses and charcuterie, all while taking in the breathtaking views of the valley below. The outdoor terrace is a particularly popular spot for enjoying wine, offering sweeping views of the vineyards and the surrounding mountains.

In addition to its renowned wines, Pride Mountain Vineyards has also made a name for itself through its commitment to sustainability and conservation. The vineyard utilizes organic and biodynamic farming practices, with a focus on preserving the health of the soil and the surrounding ecosystem. The winery works closely with nature, using sustainable water management systems and promoting biodiversity on the property to ensure that the vineyard remains healthy and productive for generations to come.

Whether you are a connoisseur of fine wines or simply someone looking to enjoy the beauty of Napa Valley, Pride Mountain Vineyards offers an unforgettable experience. With its incredible location, excellent wines, and warm hospitality, it is a perfect destination for anyone looking to immerse themselves in the world of California wine. The combination of scenic views, top-tier wines, and educational experiences makes a visit to Pride Mountain Vineyards a must for any wine lover exploring the Napa and Sonoma regions.

71

REDWOOD NATIONAL PARK

COUNTY: DEL NORTE, HUMBOLDT   CITY: CRESCENT CITY

DATE VISITED: WHO I WENT WITH:

RATING: ☆ ☆ ☆ ☆ ☆   WILL I RETURN?   YES / NO

1111 Second Street
Crescent City, CA 95531
707-464-6101

Redwood National Park, located in the northern part of California, is one of the most awe-inspiring natural wonders in the United States. Spanning over 139,000 acres, this UNESCO World Heritage Site is home to some of the tallest trees in the world, including the towering coast redwoods (Sequoia sempervirens) that can reach heights of over 370 feet. The park is part of the larger Redwood National and State Parks complex, which includes several state parks such as Prairie Creek Redwoods State Park and Jedediah Smith Redwoods State Park. Together, these parks protect a vast, diverse landscape of ancient forests, lush ferns, wild rivers, and coastal bluffs, offering an unparalleled natural experience.

The main draw of Redwood National Park is its magnificent redwood trees, which have been growing for thousands of years. Some of the trees here are more than 2,000 years old, and their massive size, towering above visitors, creates a truly humbling and surreal experience. These ancient trees form dense, majestic groves that are often shrouded in mist, adding to the park's ethereal and mystical atmosphere. Visitors to the park are encouraged to take their time exploring the forests, appreciating the peace and tranquility that these ancient trees offer.

In addition to its famous trees, Redwood National Park offers a wide range of activities for nature lovers, outdoor enthusiasts, and those seeking a peaceful retreat. The park is home to several hiking trails that wind through its towering forests, along rivers, and out to the Pacific coast. Popular trails include the Lady Bird Johnson Grove Trail, a relatively short loop through a beautiful redwood grove, and the more challenging Tall Trees Grove Trail, which leads to one of the tallest known redwood trees in the world. For those who want to experience a true wilderness adventure, the Redwood Creek Trail offers a multi-day backpacking journey through remote areas of the park.

The park also offers a variety of opportunities for wildlife viewing. The dense forests, diverse plant life, and wide range of ecosystems support an impressive variety of animal species, including black bears, Roosevelt elk, coyotes, and over 200 species of birds. Visitors may also spot smaller animals like squirrels, raccoons, and the elusive marbled murrelet, a seabird that nests in the tall trees. The park is an important habitat for many species, and its preservation is vital to the health of the ecosystem.

For those interested in exploring the rugged coast, Redwood National Park also features dramatic coastal bluffs and expansive beaches. The Gold Bluffs Beach area is a popular spot for picnicking, beachcombing, and enjoying the stunning views of the Pacific Ocean. The Kuchel Visitor Center, located near the beach, offers educational exhibits about the park's history, ecology, and the efforts to protect the redwood forests. The visitor center also provides information about the various trails, ranger-led programs, and activities available to visitors.

The park's climate is another unique feature, with cool, foggy weather being common throughout the year. This fog plays an essential role in the health of the redwood trees, as it provides moisture to the ecosystem, even during the dry summer months. The combination of fog, lush vegetation, and towering trees creates a magical and serene environment, making it a perfect location for photography, nature walks, and peaceful reflection.

Redwood National Park is also a place of historical and cultural significance. The area has been home to Native American tribes for thousands of years, with the Yurok and Karuk tribes being among the most prominent in the region. Today, visitors can learn about the park's cultural heritage and the history of these indigenous peoples through interpretive programs and exhibits at the visitor centers. The park has worked closely with local Native American tribes to ensure that their traditions, knowledge, and connection to the land are respected and preserved.

Whether you're seeking adventure, tranquility, or simply a chance to connect with nature, Redwood National Park offers something for everyone. It's a place where visitors can experience the grandeur of the natural world, from the towering redwoods to the rugged coastline and diverse wildlife. The park provides an immersive experience in one of the most beautiful and ecologically important regions of California, and its beauty is sure to leave a lasting impression on all who visit. Whether you're hiking through ancient groves, driving the scenic Avenue of the Giants, or simply standing in awe beneath the towering redwoods, Redwood National Park is a must-see destination for nature lovers and outdoor enthusiasts.

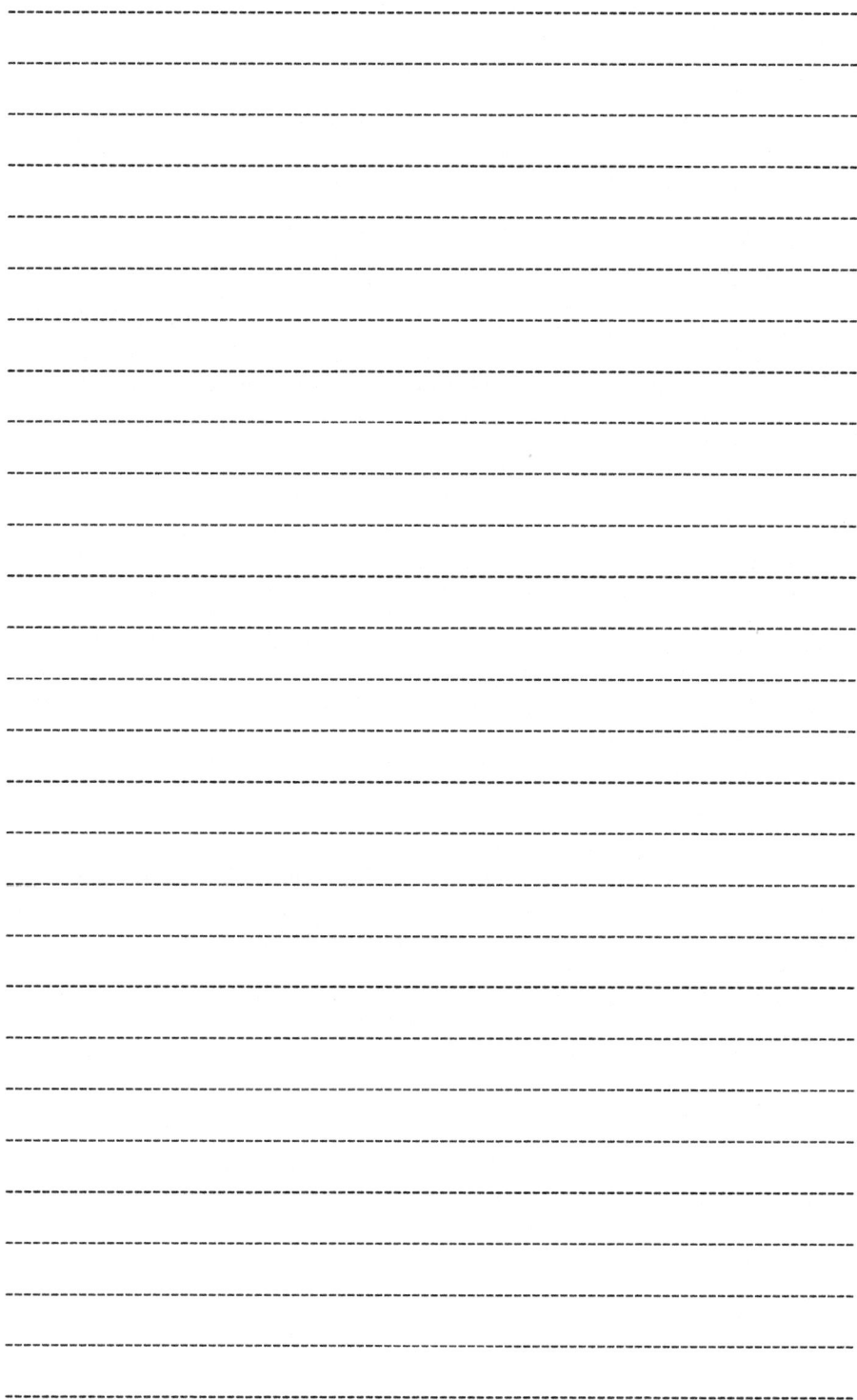

72

ROBERT BIALE VINEYARDS

COUNTY: NAPA   CITY: NAPA

DATE VISITED: WHO I WENT WITH:

RATING: ☆ ☆ ☆ ☆ ☆   WILL I RETURN?   YES / NO

4038 Big Ranch Rd
Napa, CA 94558
707-257-7555

Robert Biale Vineyards, located in the heart of Napa Valley, California, is renowned for producing some of the finest Zinfandel wines in the region. The winery's rich history, commitment to quality, and passion for crafting exceptional wines have earned it a dedicated following among wine lovers and connoisseurs. Founded in 1991 by Robert Biale, a third-generation Napa Valley farmer, the winery is known for its unique approach to Zinfandel production, producing wines that reflect the region's rich heritage and distinct terroir.

The vineyard is situated in the Rutherford area of Napa Valley, a renowned wine-growing region famous for its fertile soils and ideal climate for grape cultivation. Robert Biale Vineyards is particularly noted for its old-vine Zinfandel, sourced from some of Napa Valley's most historic and revered vineyards. The winery specializes in small-batch, hand-crafted wines, and its focus on quality and meticulous vineyard management has allowed it to consistently produce world-class wines that showcase the full potential of the Zinfandel grape.

Zinfandel is the winery's signature varietal, and Robert Biale Vineyards has become a leading producer of this iconic California wine. The winery's Zinfandel wines are known for their bold flavors, rich texture, and complex character. The vineyards that produce these wines are planted with some of the oldest and most well-established Zinfandel vines in Napa Valley, many of which date back to the late 1800s. These old vines are known for producing fruit with concentrated flavors, deep color, and a unique sense of place, all of which contribute to the exceptional quality of Robert Biale's wines.

In addition to Zinfandel, Robert Biale Vineyards also produces a variety of other red and white wines, including Sangiovese, Petite Sirah, Cabernet Sauvignon, and Chardonnay. Each wine is crafted with the same attention to detail, and the winemaking team uses traditional methods to ensure that the true expression of the grapes shines through in every bottle. The winery also takes a sustainable approach to farming, using organic and environmentally friendly practices to maintain the health of the vineyards and the surrounding ecosystem.

Visitors to Robert Biale Vineyards can enjoy a variety of tasting experiences that showcase the winery's exceptional wines and the beauty of Napa Valley. The tasting room offers intimate and educational experiences, where guests can taste a selection of wines paired with insights from the knowledgeable staff. The vineyard's picturesque setting provides an ideal backdrop for enjoying wine, with views of the surrounding vineyards and the rugged hills of Napa Valley. Private tours and tastings are also available, offering a more personalized experience for wine lovers looking to learn more about the winemaking process and the unique history of the winery.

In addition to its exceptional wines, Robert Biale Vineyards is known for its welcoming and friendly atmosphere. The winery prides itself on providing a warm, inviting experience for all visitors, whether they are seasoned wine enthusiasts or newcomers to the world of wine. The staff at Robert Biale Vineyards is passionate about sharing their knowledge and love of wine, and they strive to create an educational and enjoyable experience for every guest. The winery also hosts special events, including wine dinners, tastings, and educational seminars, providing opportunities for guests to deepen their knowledge of wine and the winemaking process.

The winery's commitment to quality and innovation, combined with its deep respect for Napa Valley's winemaking traditions, has earned Robert Biale Vineyards a reputation as one of the top wineries in the region. The winery has garnered numerous accolades and awards for its wines, and its Zinfandel in particular has received widespread recognition for its exceptional quality and character. Whether you are visiting Napa Valley for the first time or are a seasoned wine aficionado, a visit to Robert Biale Vineyards is a must for anyone looking to experience the best of what the valley has to offer. With its beautiful vineyards, exceptional wines, and warm hospitality, Robert Biale Vineyards offers an unforgettable wine country experience.

73

RUNYON CANYON PARK

COUNTY: LOS ANGELES   **CITY:** LOS ANGELES

DATE VISITED: _____   **WHO I WENT WITH:** _____

RATING: ☆ ☆ ☆ ☆ ☆   **WILL I RETURN?** YES / NO

2000 N Fuller Ave Hollywood
Los Angeles, CA 90046
323-644-6661

Runyon Canyon Park is one of Los Angeles' most beloved urban parks, offering an ideal escape from the hustle and bustle of the city. Located in the Hollywood Hills, this scenic park is a favorite among locals and tourists alike, thanks to its proximity to Hollywood Boulevard and its stunning views of the Los Angeles skyline, downtown LA, and the iconic Hollywood Sign. Whether you're seeking a peaceful walk, a challenging hike, or simply a place to enjoy the outdoors, Runyon Canyon has something to offer everyone.

The park features several hiking trails of varying difficulty levels, making it a popular destination for both beginner and seasoned hikers. The Main Trail, the most popular route, is an easy-to-moderate hike that winds through the canyon and offers beautiful views of the city below. For a more challenging experience, visitors can take the East Ridge Trail, which offers steeper climbs and even better panoramic views of LA, including the Santa Monica Mountains and the Pacific Ocean on a clear day.

One of the park's most attractive features is its accessibility, with trails that are just a short drive from downtown Los Angeles. Hikers can easily make their way to Runyon Canyon from neighborhoods like Hollywood, West Hollywood, and Beverly Hills. Visitors often come to Runyon Canyon for a workout, as the park is known for attracting fitness enthusiasts who jog, power-walk, or even do yoga on the scenic trails. The park's elevation offers a great challenge for those looking to get in a cardiovascular workout, while the incredible views make the effort all the more rewarding.

Aside from the physical benefits of hiking, Runyon Canyon provides a peaceful atmosphere, allowing visitors to connect with nature while being just minutes away from the urban environment. The park is home to a variety of native plants and wildlife, including California scrub oak, sagebrush, and wildflowers that bloom in spring. On any given day, hikers might catch sight of local wildlife like squirrels, rabbits, or even the occasional coyote.

For pet lovers, Runyon Canyon is particularly special, as it is one of the most dog-friendly parks in Los Angeles. The park features off-leash areas where dogs can run freely and enjoy the open space. Many locals bring their dogs to enjoy the trails, and the off-leash areas allow pets to socialize with other dogs while their owners explore the park. The off-leash policy makes it a unique space for both dog owners and non-dog owners to appreciate the outdoors.

Runyon Canyon is also a popular location for those looking to practice yoga, thanks to its serene setting and panoramic vistas. Many people bring mats and set up in quiet spots to enjoy outdoor yoga and mindfulness practices. The tranquility of the park makes it an ideal location for relaxation and reflection. Additionally, the park regularly hosts group fitness classes, such as boot camps, yoga sessions, and guided hikes, which are a fun way to explore the trails while staying active.

At the top of the park, visitors are rewarded with expansive views of Los Angeles, making it a favorite spot for taking photos, picnicking, or simply soaking in the sights. The views of the Hollywood Sign from the park's upper reaches are particularly stunning, with the sign perfectly framed against the backdrop of the canyon. The sight of the city stretching out below is equally impressive, providing a unique perspective of one of the world's most iconic urban landscapes.

While Runyon Canyon is a haven for hikers and fitness enthusiasts, it also serves as a cultural landmark. Over the years, it has gained a reputation as a gathering place for celebrities, influencers, and artists, adding a touch of Hollywood glamour to the otherwise natural setting. It's not uncommon to spot local celebrities walking their dogs or enjoying a quiet moment in the park. This blend of nature and entertainment gives Runyon Canyon an unmistakable energy and makes it a must-see destination for anyone visiting Los Angeles.

In addition to hiking and outdoor activities, the park offers a sense of community. Many people come to the park to meet up with friends, attend fitness classes, or simply relax and enjoy the views. The park's peaceful yet vibrant atmosphere allows visitors to connect with nature while also engaging with the diverse community of people who frequent the park.

Runyon Canyon is open year-round, and its trails can be enjoyed in all seasons. However, it's worth noting that the park can get busy, particularly on weekends and holidays, as it is a popular spot for both locals and tourists. There are parking lots nearby, but they can fill up quickly, so visitors are encouraged to arrive early to secure a spot or consider using public transportation to reach the park.

In conclusion, Runyon Canyon Park is an urban oasis that combines the best of nature and city life. With its stunning views, dog-friendly environment, and accessible hiking trails, it provides a perfect setting for outdoor activities and relaxation. Whether you're hiking, practicing yoga, enjoying a picnic, or simply taking in the sights, Runyon Canyon is an essential Los Angeles experience that offers something for everyone.

74

SAN DIEGO HARBOR CRUISE

COUNTY: SAN DIEGO   CITY: SAN DIEGO

DATE VISITED: WHO I WENT WITH:

RATING: ☆ ☆ ☆ ☆ ☆   WILL I RETURN?   YES / NO

990 North Harbor Dr.
San Diego, CA 92101
619-234-4111

San Diego Harbor Cruise offers visitors a relaxing and informative way to explore the stunning coastline and vibrant maritime activity of San Diego Bay. This popular attraction provides a unique perspective on the city's bustling harbor, iconic landmarks, and natural beauty, making it a must-do experience for visitors of all ages.

The cruises typically depart from the downtown area, near the historic Embarcadero. As you board the comfortable and spacious vessel, you're welcomed by knowledgeable crew members who provide commentary throughout the journey, sharing fascinating insights about the area's history, marine life, and notable sights. Depending on the tour operator, you can choose from various cruise options, including one-hour, two-hour, or sunset cruises.

During the tour, passengers are treated to unparalleled views of San Diego's skyline, complete with its modern skyscrapers, historic buildings, and waterfront attractions. One of the highlights is the opportunity to see the iconic USS Midway Museum, a retired aircraft carrier turned museum that stands proudly along the harbor. Other notable landmarks include the Coronado Bridge, a sweeping architectural marvel that connects downtown San Diego to the picturesque Coronado Island.

As the cruise navigates the bay, passengers often spot active naval ships, as San Diego is home to one of the largest naval fleets in the world. You might even catch sight of massive aircraft carriers, destroyers, or submarines docked at the nearby naval base. The commentary provides a deeper understanding of the city's strategic military importance and its rich maritime heritage.

Nature lovers will appreciate the abundant wildlife visible from the boat. San Diego Bay is home to playful seals and sea lions that bask on buoys and docks, as well as a variety of seabirds such as pelicans, cormorants, and gulls. With some luck, you might also spot dolphins swimming alongside the boat, adding an element of excitement to the journey.

For those seeking a romantic or serene experience, sunset cruises are a popular option. As the sun dips below the horizon, the bay transforms into a palette of vibrant colors, offering a picture-perfect backdrop for memorable photos. Many cruises also offer beverages and light snacks on board, allowing passengers to unwind and enjoy the views with a drink in hand.

Some operators provide specialty cruises, such as whale-watching tours or dinner cruises, for an even more immersive experience. Whale-watching cruises, typically available in the winter months, offer the chance to see gray whales as they migrate along the Pacific Coast.

Whether you're a first-time visitor or a local looking for a fresh perspective on the city, the San Diego Harbor Cruise is an ideal way to explore the area's highlights in comfort and style. With its combination of natural beauty, cultural landmarks, and maritime charm, it's an experience that captures the essence of San Diego's coastal allure.

75

SAN DIEGO SAND CASTLES

COUNTY: SAN DIEGO   CITY: SAN DIEGO

DATE VISITED: WHO I WENT WITH:

RATING: ☆ ☆ ☆ ☆ ☆   WILL I RETURN?   YES / NO

4306 Ocean View Boulevard
San Diego, CA 92113
619-200-0565

San Diego Sand Castles offers a one-of-a-kind experience for visitors to the coastal city of San Diego, California, by providing expert-led sandcastle building lessons and unique beach activities. Whether you're looking to learn the art of sculpting sand or simply enjoy a fun and creative group activity, San Diego Sand Castles offers the perfect opportunity to explore your artistic side on the beautiful sandy beaches of San Diego.

San Diego's beaches are ideal for sandcastle building, with their expansive stretches of soft sand and warm weather. Under the guidance of professional sand sculptors, guests are introduced to the secrets of crafting intricate sand sculptures. The lessons start with basic techniques and gradually build up to more advanced skills, allowing participants of all ages and abilities to create stunning works of art. From simple designs to elaborate, detailed sculptures, each session provides step-by-step instructions that ensure everyone leaves with the confidence to continue sculpting.

The sandcastle lessons are not just about learning techniques but also about fostering teamwork and creativity. Participants often work together in small groups, making it an excellent activity for families, friends, and even corporate team-building events. San Diego Sand Castles can cater to a wide variety of events, offering customized sandcastle building experiences for birthday parties, corporate outings, or even weddings. These events provide an opportunity for guests to bond over a shared creative experience while enjoying the beautiful beach surroundings.

The lessons are held at various iconic beaches in San Diego, including Coronado Beach, Mission Beach, and Pacific Beach, each offering its unique backdrop and charm. Whether you are a local resident or visiting the city for the first time, the beaches of San Diego provide the perfect canvas for sand art. In addition to the sculpting lessons, San Diego Sand Castles also hosts special events such as sandcastle competitions, where talented builders and enthusiasts come together to showcase their best creations in a fun, competitive environment.

Beyond sandcastle building, San Diego Sand Castles offers additional beach activities, such as beach games and guided tours, making it an ideal destination for a memorable day out by the ocean. For those looking to enjoy the beauty of the beach without getting their hands too sandy, there are also opportunities for photography and beachcombing, as the coastal areas around San Diego are known for their stunning natural scenery.

For those who want to take their experience to the next level, San Diego Sand Castles also offers advanced sand sculpting workshops. These workshops dive deeper into the art of sand sculpting, providing expert guidance on creating detailed and complex sculptures that can withstand the forces of nature for longer periods. This is a perfect experience for those who want to explore the craft of sand sculpture in more depth or for enthusiasts who are looking to improve their skills.

San Diego Sand Castles provides a relaxing yet creative way to experience the beauty of the coastline while learning something new. The experience is fun for people of all ages, and many participants leave with a greater appreciation for the artistry of sand sculpting. Whether you are building sandcastles for the first time or have experience with sand art, San Diego Sand Castles offers a unique and memorable beach activity that combines creativity, nature, and fun in one perfect experience.

For anyone visiting San Diego, a sandcastle building session is a must-try activity, offering both an enjoyable and relaxing way to spend time by the sea. It's an unforgettable way to make the most of San Diego's sun, sand, and surf while learning the art of sand sculpting from experienced professionals who are passionate about sharing their craft. Whether you're a beginner or an experienced artist, San Diego Sand Castles provides a wonderful way to explore your creativity and make lasting memories on the stunning beaches of California's Southern Coast.

76

SAN DIEGO ZOO

COUNTY: SAN DIEGO   **CITY:** SAN DIEGO

DATE VISITED: **WHO I WENT WITH:**

RATING: ☆ ☆ ☆ ☆ ☆   **WILL I RETURN?** YES / NO

2929 Zoo Drive Balboa Park
San Diego, CA 92101
619-231-1515

San Diego Zoo, located in Balboa Park in San Diego, California, is one of the most famous and visited zoos in the world. Known for its expansive and innovative exhibits, the zoo is home to more than 3,500 animals representing over 650 species. The zoo is renowned for its commitment to animal conservation, education, and providing a naturalistic environment for its inhabitants. It is a must-see attraction for visitors of all ages, offering an immersive and exciting experience that showcases the beauty and diversity of wildlife from around the globe.

The San Diego Zoo was founded in 1916 and has since grown into a world leader in animal care, conservation efforts, and research. The zoo is renowned for its pioneering work in creating open-air exhibits that mimic natural habitats, allowing animals to live in environments that closely resemble their native homes. The zoo's exhibits are designed to provide visitors with a glimpse into the lives of animals in a way that is both educational and engaging, giving them the opportunity to learn about conservation efforts and how they can help protect wildlife.

Among the zoo's most notable exhibits are its panda, koala, elephant, and tiger habitats. The Giant Panda Research Station is particularly famous, as the San Diego Zoo has been home to giant pandas for many years. Although the pandas have since returned to China, the zoo continues to contribute significantly to panda conservation efforts. The Koala Exhibit allows visitors to see these iconic Australian marsupials up close, while the Elephant Odyssey provides a fascinating view of African and Asian elephants, offering insights into the behaviors and needs of these majestic animals.

Another highlight of the zoo is the Safari Park, located a short distance from the main zoo, which is a larger, more expansive wildlife sanctuary. The Safari Park offers a unique experience where visitors can see animals in a more open setting that simulates the wild, with animals roaming freely across vast, natural habitats. Visitors can take part in safari tours that bring them up close to animals such as rhinos, giraffes, and cheetahs in a more expansive setting than the traditional zoo. The Safari Park also emphasizes global conservation efforts, supporting wildlife protection programs in various countries and working to preserve endangered species.

The San Diego Zoo also offers a variety of interactive experiences and educational programs that enhance visitors' understanding of the animals and the importance of conservation. Guided tours, animal encounters, and behind-the-scenes experiences provide deeper insights into the animals' lives and the zoo's conservation work. The zoo's Education Department runs numerous programs throughout the year, designed for school groups, families, and individuals, all focused on teaching about wildlife and environmental sustainability.

For those looking to get a closer look at the animals, the zoo offers special feeding sessions, where visitors can observe keepers feeding and interacting with the animals. These sessions provide an incredible opportunity to learn more about the animals' diets, behaviors, and training. For example, watching a zookeeper feed the giraffes or care for the orangutans gives a unique perspective on the care and attention the animals receive.

The San Diego Zoo also places a significant emphasis on sustainability and environmental stewardship. The zoo employs eco-friendly practices throughout its operations, from using solar energy to employing water conservation techniques. The zoo's efforts to create a sustainable, green space are reflected in its beautiful gardens, including its world-renowned botanical gardens, which showcase thousands of plant species from around the world.

For families, the zoo offers a wealth of activities designed to engage children and adults alike. The Jungle Gym, an interactive play area, allows kids to learn about animal movements and habitats through hands-on play. Additionally, the zoo provides a variety of educational exhibits and activities tailored to young audiences, making it a fantastic place for children to learn about the animal kingdom.

Dining and shopping options are also plentiful, with a wide variety of eateries offering everything from snacks to full meals, including options that cater to all dietary preferences. Souvenir shops throughout the zoo sell unique items, from plush animals to educational books and games, allowing visitors to take a piece of their experience home with them.

The San Diego Zoo is open year-round, and its convenient location in Balboa Park, just minutes from downtown San Diego, makes it an easy and accessible destination. With its lush gardens, exciting animal exhibits, and innovative programs, the zoo offers something for everyone, whether you're an animal enthusiast, a nature lover, or simply looking for a fun family outing. Its commitment to animal welfare and environmental sustainability ensures that the San Diego Zoo remains not only a top tourist attraction but also a vital resource for wildlife conservation and education. Whether you're exploring the zoo for the first time or revisiting old favorites, the San Diego Zoo offers a captivating and enriching experience for all who visit.

SAN FRANCISCO BAY

COUNTY: SAN FRANCISCO   **CITY:** SAN FRANCISCO

DATE VISITED: **WHO I WENT WITH:**

RATING: ☆ ☆ ☆ ☆ ☆   **WILL I RETURN?** YES / NO

San Francisco Ferry Building (iconic waterfront location):
1 Ferry Building
San Francisco, CA 94111, USA

San Francisco Bay is a stunning and iconic natural harbor located in northern California, encompassing approximately 1,600 square kilometers of water. The bay is surrounded by the city of San Francisco, its peninsula, and the East Bay and North Bay regions, making it a significant geographical and cultural feature. Known for its breathtaking views, rich history, and vibrant ecosystem, San Francisco Bay offers visitors a variety of attractions and activities that showcase the beauty and significance of the area.

San Francisco Bay is not only a vital shipping and transportation hub but also an ecological treasure. Its waters are home to a diverse array of marine life, including various species of fish, sea birds, and marine mammals. The bay has a long history of being a vital waterway for trade, exploration, and settlement. Today, it stands as one of the most recognized and celebrated bodies of water in the world, with its iconic landmarks, including the Golden Gate Bridge, Alcatraz Island, and Angel Island, attracting millions of tourists every year.

One of the most popular ways to experience San Francisco Bay is by boat. Visitors can take a scenic bay cruise, which provides unparalleled views of the San Francisco skyline, the Golden Gate Bridge, and famous landmarks such as Alcatraz Island. Several tour operators offer cruises that explore different aspects of the bay, including history, wildlife, and the stunning views of the city and surrounding areas. Whether you're on a private charter, a ferry ride, or a group tour, these excursions provide the opportunity to explore the bay's beauty up close and enjoy its natural splendor.

San Francisco Bay is also known for its exceptional wildlife watching opportunities. The bay is an essential stop for migratory birds along the Pacific Flyway, making it a prime spot for birdwatching, especially in places like the Don Edwards San Francisco Bay National Wildlife Refuge. This refuge, the largest tidal salt marsh in the United States, offers more than 30,000 acres of wetlands, grasslands, and mudflats where visitors can observe a wide range of birds, including the endangered California clapper rail and California least tern. The wildlife refuge is also home to a variety of mammals, including river otters, harbor seals, and the occasional bat-eared fox.

For those interested in outdoor activities, San Francisco Bay offers an abundance of recreational opportunities. Kayaking and stand-up paddleboarding are popular ways to explore the bay at a more leisurely pace. Paddlers can enjoy the calm waters near the shore, or for a more adventurous experience, they can venture under the Golden Gate Bridge and into the open waters. With stunning views of the city, the bridge, and the hills surrounding the bay, these activities provide a unique perspective on the landscape.

The Golden Gate Bridge is arguably the most famous and photographed landmark in the area. Spanning the entrance to San Francisco Bay, the bridge is not only an engineering marvel but also an iconic symbol of the city. Visitors can enjoy stunning views of the bridge from multiple vantage points, including Crissy Field, Fort Point, and Baker Beach. For those who want an up-close experience, walking or biking across the bridge is a popular activity that allows you to take in panoramic views of the bay and the city.

In addition to its natural beauty, San Francisco Bay has a rich history that can be explored through a variety of museums and historical sites. Alcatraz Island, known for its former prison, is a must-visit for those interested in the area's past. The island has a fascinating history, not just as a notorious federal prison, but also as a site of military fortifications and the location of the Native American occupation in the 1970s. The island offers self-guided audio tours that bring the history of the prison and its infamous inmates to life.

Angel Island, another prominent island in the bay, is known for its beautiful hiking trails and panoramic views. It also has a historical significance, as it served as the Ellis Island of the West, processing immigrants, particularly from China, during the late 19th and early 20th centuries. Visitors can explore the island's many trails, enjoy picnics, and visit the Angel Island Immigration Station Museum to learn about the immigrant experience.

For those seeking a more serene experience, San Francisco Bay Area is home to numerous parks and beaches that offer an escape into nature. Marin Headlands, located just across the Golden Gate Bridge, provides stunning hiking trails with panoramic views of the bay, cliffs, and the bridge itself. China Beach and Baker Beach are both picturesque coastal spots perfect for relaxing, sunbathing, and taking in the beauty of the bay. Whether you're looking to explore rugged cliffs, calm coves, or sandy beaches, the Bay Area has something to offer everyone.

The San Francisco Bay Trail, a network of more than 500 miles of hiking and biking paths, encircles the entire bay, offering access to many of the bay's parks, beaches, and wildlife areas. It's a great way to see the region's natural beauty while engaging in outdoor exercise. The trail is a popular route for cyclists, runners, and walkers, offering stunning views of the bay, the surrounding hills, and the Golden Gate Bridge.

As one of the most recognizable landmarks in the world, San Francisco Bay offers something for everyone, whether you're interested in history, wildlife, outdoor adventure, or simply enjoying the natural beauty of the area. Its diverse ecosystems, iconic landmarks, and recreational opportunities make it one of the top destinations in California, and a must-see for anyone visiting the Bay Area. Whether you're cruising the bay's waters, hiking its hills, or soaking in its history, San Francisco Bay is sure to leave a lasting impression on all who visit.

SAN FRANCISCO MAGIC THEATER AT THE MARRAKECH

(78)

COUNTY: SAN FRANCISCO   **CITY:** SAN FRANCISCO

DATE VISITED:	WHO I WENT WITH:

RATING: ☆ ☆ ☆ ☆ ☆   **WILL I RETURN?**   YES / NO

419 O'Farrell Street
San Francisco, CA 94102
415-794-6893

San Francisco Magic Theater at the Marrakech, located in San Francisco, California, is a unique and intimate venue that offers a magical and unforgettable experience for visitors. Situated in the vibrant Marrakech Hotel, the theater provides an opportunity to witness world-class magic performances in an elegant and cozy setting. The San Francisco Magic Theater is renowned for its close-up magic, sleight-of-hand performances, and mind-bending illusions, making it a must-see for anyone interested in the art of magic and illusion.

The Magic Theater offers an immersive experience that engages the audience in a way that traditional theater performances cannot. The shows are designed to be interactive, allowing spectators to get up close to the magician and experience the tricks firsthand. This intimacy allows the audience to feel as though they are part of the performance, making the magic even more astonishing. Whether it's a card trick performed right in front of you or a complex illusion that defies logic, the San Francisco Magic Theater delivers an experience that is both entertaining and mystifying.

One of the highlights of the theater is its close-up magic shows, which are performed right in front of the audience, often with spectators seated at tables surrounding the magician. This setup creates a personal connection between the performer and the audience, heightening the sense of mystery and wonder. The theater regularly features performances by award-winning magicians from around the world, each specializing in different forms of magic, including card tricks, mentalism, and visual illusions.

In addition to its regular magic shows, the San Francisco Magic Theater at the Marrakech also hosts special events and themed performances throughout the year. These events often feature guest magicians, as well as unique performances tailored to specific holidays or occasions, such as Halloween or New Year's Eve. The theater's flexibility allows it to cater to a wide variety of audiences, from families with children to adults looking for an evening of sophisticated entertainment.

The venue itself adds to the charm of the experience. The Marrakech Hotel is known for its exotic, Moroccan-inspired decor, which complements the magical atmosphere of the theater. The intimate setting, combined with the intricate and detailed surroundings, transports visitors into a world of mystery and illusion. The theater's intimate size ensures that no matter where you sit, you'll have an excellent view of the magic as it unfolds right before your eyes.

The San Francisco Magic Theater at the Marrakech is not just a place to watch magic; it's an experience that brings together entertainment, mystery, and the thrill of the unknown. The performances are designed to challenge the audience's perception of reality, leaving them amazed and wondering how the impossible was made possible. Whether you're a longtime fan of magic or someone new to the world of illusions, the San Francisco Magic Theater offers a mesmerizing escape into a world of wonder.

For those seeking a memorable night out in San Francisco, attending a performance at the San Francisco Magic Theater is a must. Its blend of expert magic, intimate ambiance, and captivating illusions makes it a standout attraction in the city. Whether you're visiting for the first time or returning for another magical evening, the theater guarantees an experience that will leave you speechless and in awe.

SANTA MONICA PIER

COUNTY: LOS ANGELES   **CITY:** SANTA MONICA

DATE VISITED: **WHO I WENT WITH:**

RATING: ☆ ☆ ☆ ☆ ☆   **WILL I RETURN?** YES / NO

200 Santa Monica Pier
Santa Monica, CA 90401
310-458-8900

The Santa Monica Pier, located in Santa Monica, California, is one of the most iconic and beloved landmarks in the United States. Situated on the stunning coastline of Santa Monica Bay, the pier has been a symbol of California beach culture for over a century. Offering a mix of amusement, dining, shopping, and breathtaking views, the Santa Monica Pier is a must-visit destination for locals and tourists alike, providing a nostalgic yet vibrant experience for visitors of all ages.

First opened in 1909, the Santa Monica Pier has a rich history that dates back more than a century. Today, it remains a bustling hub of activity, blending classic attractions with modern entertainment. One of the main draws of the pier is the Pacific Park, an amusement park located at the end of the pier. With its colorful rides, games, and attractions, Pacific Park offers fun for the whole family. The centerpiece of the park is the Ferris wheel, which provides stunning panoramic views of the ocean, the coastline, and the city of Santa Monica. At night, the Ferris wheel lights up in a spectacular display, creating a dazzling sight that can be seen from miles away.

Another popular attraction on the pier is the Carousel, a historic ride that has been delighting visitors since 1922. The Looff Hippodrome building, where the carousel is housed, is a beautiful example of early 20th-century architecture and adds to the nostalgic atmosphere of the pier. The wooden carousel is a favorite for children and adults alike, with its charming hand-carved horses and lively music creating a whimsical and joyful experience.

For those seeking more adventurous experiences, the Santa Monica Pier also features a range of arcade games, including classic pinball machines, air hockey, and a variety of video games. The pier is also home to several family-friendly attractions like the Trapeze School and bowling alleys, ensuring that there's something for everyone to enjoy.

Beyond the amusement park, the pier offers a variety of dining options, from casual eateries to sit-down restaurants, making it a perfect place to grab a bite while enjoying the views of the Pacific Ocean. Visitors can dine at seafood restaurants like The Lobster or enjoy casual snacks at places like Pier Burger or the classic Ice Cream Shop. Many of the restaurants offer outdoor seating with views of the ocean, allowing guests to take in the sea breeze and the stunning coastal scenery.

The Santa Monica Pier Aquarium, located below the pier, is another great way to experience local marine life. This small but educational aquarium focuses on the ecology of Santa Monica Bay, with exhibits showcasing sea life such as starfish, sea cucumbers, and local fish species. It's a wonderful stop for families and anyone interested in learning more about the area's marine environment.

Visitors can also enjoy the beautiful beaches surrounding the pier. Santa Monica Beach is renowned for its golden sand, ideal for sunbathing, beach volleyball, and surfing. The beach stretches for miles along the coast, providing plenty of space for relaxation and outdoor activities. From the pier, you can take a leisurely walk along the beach or rent bikes and ride along the California Coastal Trail, which runs from Santa Monica to nearby Venice Beach.

The pier is also a great starting point for exploring the rest of Santa Monica. Just a short walk from the pier is Third Street Promenade, a pedestrian-only shopping and dining district filled with stores, boutiques, cafes, and street performers. Visitors can shop for souvenirs, enjoy local artwork, or simply stroll around the vibrant area, making it the perfect complement to a day at the pier.

Throughout the year, the Santa Monica Pier hosts various events, including live music, festivals, and seasonal celebrations. It's also a popular spot for watching sunsets, with many visitors gathering on the pier to take in the spectacular view as the sun dips below the horizon, painting the sky with hues of orange, pink, and purple.

Whether you're looking for thrills on the Ferris wheel, a relaxing day on the beach, or simply a fun place to hang out with friends and family, the Santa Monica Pier has something for everyone. Its unique blend of history, entertainment, and natural beauty makes it one of California's most beloved landmarks and a quintessential part of the Southern California experience.

COUNTY: LOS ANGELES   **CITY:** SANTA MONICA

DATE VISITED: **WHO I WENT WITH:**

RATING: ☆ ☆ ☆ ☆ ☆   **WILL I RETURN?** YES / NO

Ocean Ave & Colorado Ave
Santa Monica, CA 90401
310-458-8300

Santa Monica State Beach is one of the most iconic and beautiful beaches in California, located in the heart of Santa Monica, just west of downtown Los Angeles. With its wide expanse of golden sand, inviting waters, and scenic views of the Pacific Ocean, Santa Monica State Beach attracts millions of visitors each year, making it a must-see destination for beachgoers, surfers, and tourists alike.

This stunning beach stretches for over 3 miles along the coastline, offering plenty of space for visitors to relax, play, and enjoy the natural beauty of the area. Whether you're sunbathing, swimming, or just strolling along the shoreline, the beach provides a classic Southern California experience, complete with stunning views of the ocean and the Santa Monica Mountains in the distance.

One of the key features of Santa Monica State Beach is its proximity to the Santa Monica Pier, a historic and lively landmark that is home to various attractions, including an amusement park, aquarium, and family-friendly restaurants. The iconic Pacific Park amusement park on the pier is a highlight for visitors of all ages, featuring a Ferris wheel, roller coaster, and other rides, all with spectacular views of the beach and the ocean.

For those looking to stay active, the beach offers a variety of recreational activities. Surfers flock to Santa Monica State Beach to catch waves, while volleyball players take advantage of the many sand courts scattered throughout the beach. The South Beach area is particularly popular for biking and skating, with a designated path that runs along the shore. Rentable bikes and skateboards make it easy for visitors to explore the beach in style, and the path also connects to the Marvin Braude Bike Trail, a 22-mile coastal bike route that stretches from Pacific Palisades to Torrance.

Along the beach, visitors will also find ample space for picnicking, with picnic tables and grassy areas providing the perfect setting for a relaxed meal with family or friends. The beach is well-equipped with restrooms, showers, and concessions, making it convenient for day-long visits.

Santa Monica State Beach also has a rich history, serving as a major center of recreation and leisure since the early 20th century. The beach was once the site of the famous Santa Monica Pier Aquarium, which showcased marine life found along the coast. Today, the city of Santa Monica continues to prioritize environmental preservation and beach conservation, making the area a model for sustainable beach management.

For those looking for a more serene experience, the beach is also home to Palisades Park, a lush park that runs along the cliffs above the beach and offers panoramic views of the ocean. This park is ideal for a peaceful walk or a scenic photo opportunity, with benches, walking paths, and native plant gardens.

In addition to its natural beauty, Santa Monica State Beach is surrounded by an abundance of restaurants, shops, and attractions. The Third Street Promenade, a popular pedestrian shopping area, is just a few blocks away, offering everything from high-end boutiques to casual eateries. The vibrant downtown area also hosts art galleries, museums, and cultural events, adding to the area's diverse offerings.

The beach is easily accessible by public transportation, including buses and the Expo Line light rail, which connects Santa Monica to downtown Los Angeles. There are also ample parking facilities, although they can fill up quickly, especially on weekends and holidays.

Whether you're looking to soak up the sun, enjoy a variety of activities, or simply take in the breathtaking coastal scenery, Santa Monica State Beach provides a quintessential Southern California experience that offers something for everyone. With its blend of natural beauty, recreational opportunities, and proximity to local attractions, it's no wonder that this beach remains a favorite among locals and visitors alike.

81

SCOT NERY'S BOOBIETRAP

COUNTY: LOS ANGELES   **CITY:** LOS ANGELES

DATE VISITED: **WHO I WENT WITH:**

RATING: ☆ ☆ ☆ ☆ ☆   **WILL I RETURN?**   YES / NO

6555 Hollywood Blvd Back Of The Building Parking Lot Entrance
Los Angeles, CA 90028
323-632-6735

Scot Nery's Boobietrap, located in Los Angeles, California, is a one-of-a-kind comedy and variety show that offers a unique and outrageous entertainment experience. A blend of surreal humor, wild improvisation, and clever tricks, Scot Nery's Boobietrap has become a popular and iconic performance in the city's vibrant comedy scene. Known for its eccentricity and unpredictable nature, the show is a mix of burlesque, physical comedy, and absurd storytelling, designed to keep audiences on the edge of their seats.

Scot Nery, the mastermind behind the show, is a seasoned performer with years of experience in comedy, magic, and circus arts. His boisterous and larger-than-life personality shines through in every performance, creating a high-energy atmosphere where anything can happen. As the host of Boobietrap, Scot Nery invites the audience into a world where the ordinary meets the extraordinary, combining slapstick humor, clever wordplay, and visually stunning acts that range from comedic skits to jaw-dropping magic tricks.

The name Boobietrap itself hints at the offbeat and irreverent nature of the show. It plays on the unexpected and absurd, encouraging viewers to suspend disbelief and enjoy the chaos unfolding on stage. The performance is designed to be unpredictable, with each show offering something new, ensuring that no two performances are ever alike. It often features surprise guest performers, outlandish costumes, and interactive elements that invite audience participation, making it a truly unique and engaging experience.

One of the highlights of Scot Nery's Boobietrap is its ability to blend different genres of performance. From magic tricks and illusions to slapstick humor, acrobatics, and improv, the show keeps guests laughing and amazed from start to finish. The performers, including Scot Nery himself, bring an infectious energy to the stage, creating an immersive experience where the audience feels like they are part of the act.

While the show may be known for its quirky humor, it also has a creative and artistic side. The set design and costumes are often elaborate, adding an extra layer of flair to the performances. Whether it's the vibrant lighting, colorful costumes, or whimsical props, every detail is crafted to enhance the immersive and playful atmosphere.

For those looking for a night of laughter, surprises, and offbeat entertainment, Scot Nery's Boobietrap offers a show unlike anything else in Los Angeles. It's a chance to see a performer who doesn't take himself too seriously, yet still delivers top-notch comedy and entertainment. If you're in the mood for something truly unique and filled with unexpected fun, Scot Nery's Boobietrap is a must-see experience that will leave you laughing long after the show is over.

82

SEAWORLD

DATE VISITED: **WHO I WENT WITH:**

RATING: ☆ ☆ ☆ ☆ ☆   **WILL I RETURN?**   YES / NO

500 Sea World Drive
San Diego, CA 92109
619-222-4732

SeaWorld San Diego, located in San Diego, California, is one of the most famous marine life parks in the world, offering visitors an unforgettable combination of exciting rides, animal encounters, and educational experiences. With its unique blend of theme park thrills and wildlife conservation efforts, SeaWorld has long been a top destination for families and marine life enthusiasts. Founded in 1964, the park has evolved over the years into a world-class attraction, featuring a wide variety of animal exhibits, thrilling roller coasters, and entertaining live shows.

At the heart of SeaWorld San Diego is its diverse collection of marine animals, ranging from majestic orcas and playful dolphins to sea lions, penguins, and countless fish species. The park offers guests the opportunity to learn about these incredible creatures through up-close encounters and interactive exhibits. Shamu Stadium, where visitors can watch the iconic orca shows, is one of the park's most popular attractions. The performances showcase the intelligence and grace of these magnificent creatures, while also educating the audience about orca conservation and their natural behaviors.

In addition to the orcas, SeaWorld San Diego is home to many other fascinating animals. The Dolphin Point exhibit allows visitors to interact with and learn about dolphins in a stunning coastal setting. Penguin Encounter provides a cool and interactive experience, where guests can view a variety of penguin species in a climate-controlled environment that simulates their natural habitat. The Sea Lion & Otter Stadium features entertaining and educational shows that highlight the intelligence and agility of sea lions and otters, offering both fun and valuable insights into the lives of these playful creatures.

For those seeking more thrill-seeking experiences, SeaWorld also boasts a range of exciting rides and roller coasters. One of the most popular attractions is the Electric Eel, a high-speed roller coaster that features sudden twists, drops, and airtime, offering an adrenaline-packed experience. Another must-ride is Manta, a winged coaster that simulates the sensation of flying while weaving through sharp turns and thrilling drops. Journey to Atlantis, a combination water ride and roller coaster, takes visitors on a wild adventure through a mythical undersea world, complete with high-speed drops and water splashes.

The park is also home to the Wild Arctic exhibit, where guests can get a glimpse of polar bears, beluga whales, and other Arctic creatures. This immersive experience combines both animal exhibits and virtual reality, allowing visitors to feel like they are embarking on a daring Arctic expedition. For younger guests, Sesame Street Bay of Play provides a fun and safe area with family-friendly rides, water play zones, and opportunities to meet beloved characters from Sesame Street.

Aside from the animal exhibits and thrill rides, SeaWorld San Diego is deeply committed to marine conservation and education. The park works with a variety of conservation organizations and participates in marine research and rescue efforts. Educational programs, such as the SeaWorld Rescue initiative, highlight the importance of protecting ocean ecosystems and the animals that inhabit them. Throughout the year, the park hosts special events like Halloween Spooktacular, Christmas Celebration, and Summer Nights, where visitors can enjoy themed attractions, live entertainment, and seasonal activities.

With its blend of animal experiences, thrilling rides, and family-friendly entertainment, SeaWorld San Diego offers something for everyone. Whether you're looking to learn more about marine life, experience world-class shows, or seek out heart-pounding adventure, SeaWorld promises a fun and educational day for visitors of all ages.

COUNTY: SAN DIEGO   **CITY:** ENCINITAS

DATE VISITED: **WHO I WENT WITH:**

RATING: ☆ ☆ ☆ ☆ ☆   **WILL I RETURN?** YES / NO

215 W K St
Encinitas, CA 92024
323-225-2471

Self-Realization Fellowship Hermitage & Meditation Gardens, located in Encinitas, California, is a serene and beautiful retreat center offering a peaceful escape from the stresses of daily life. Nestled along the stunning coastline of San Diego County, the Hermitage and its lush gardens provide visitors with a tranquil environment to meditate, reflect, and connect with their inner selves. This sacred place, which is part of the worldwide Self-Realization Fellowship (SRF) organization founded by Paramahansa Yogananda, serves as a sanctuary for spiritual seekers and those seeking peace, inner calm, and spiritual renewal.

The Self-Realization Fellowship was established in 1920 by Paramahansa Yogananda, who brought the teachings of meditation and self-realization to the West. His mission was to help individuals find spiritual fulfillment through the practice of Kriya Yoga, meditation, and an understanding of the unity of all religions. The Hermitage & Meditation Gardens in Encinitas are part of this broader mission and offer visitors a chance to experience the peace and beauty that Paramahansa Yogananda sought to inspire in others.

The highlight of the Self-Realization Fellowship Hermitage is undoubtedly its Meditation Gardens, which are open to the public and provide a breathtaking setting for meditation and quiet reflection. The gardens are beautifully landscaped with lush tropical plants, vibrant flowers, and trees, many of which are native to Southern California. The gardens overlook the Pacific Ocean, providing stunning panoramic views of the coastline and adding to the sense of peace and tranquility. Visitors can wander through the gardens, taking in the serene atmosphere, and find quiet spots to meditate, reflect, or simply enjoy the beauty of nature.

The gardens are meticulously designed to create a harmonious and calming environment. The winding paths, peaceful fountains, and carefully tended plants encourage visitors to slow down, breathe deeply, and connect with their inner selves. The ponds and water features add to the soothing ambiance, offering a place for reflection and quiet contemplation. Throughout the grounds, you will find benches and secluded areas where you can sit and enjoy the natural beauty, away from the distractions of daily life.

In addition to the gardens, the Self-Realization Fellowship Hermitage also offers a temple where visitors can engage in spiritual practices such as prayer and meditation. The temple is a peaceful and sacred space where people can find a sense of spiritual connection and serenity. The SRF teachings emphasize the importance of meditation in achieving self-realization and inner peace, and the Hermitage provides an ideal place to practice these teachings.

The Self-Realization Fellowship also offers various events and programs, such as guided meditation sessions, spiritual lectures, and workshops that aim to deepen one's understanding of self-realization and spiritual growth. The serene surroundings of the Hermitage enhance these experiences, helping participants find a sense of peace and clarity during their time at the center. Visitors can also explore the SRF's library and bookstore, which offers a wide range of books, teachings, and spiritual materials authored by Paramahansa Yogananda.

For those looking for a retreat from the fast-paced world, the Self-Realization Fellowship Hermitage & Meditation Gardens in Encinitas provides a perfect refuge. The combination of natural beauty, spiritual teachings, and peaceful surroundings makes it an ideal location for anyone seeking relaxation, inspiration, and spiritual rejuvenation. Whether you are new to meditation or an experienced practitioner, this tranquil sanctuary offers an opportunity to reconnect with yourself, find inner peace, and experience the transformative power of meditation and self-realization.

84

SENTINEL DOME

COUNTY: MARIPOSA   **CITY:** MARIPOSA

DATE VISITED: **WHO I WENT WITH:**

RATING: ☆ ☆ ☆ ☆ ☆   **WILL I RETURN?**   YES / NO

Glacier Point Road
Yosemite National Park, CA 95389
209-372-0200

Sentinel Dome, located in Yosemite National Park, California, is one of the park's most popular and rewarding hiking destinations, offering visitors spectacular panoramic views and an unforgettable experience. Standing at an elevation of 8,122 feet, Sentinel Dome provides an incredible 360-degree view that spans across Yosemite Valley, including the famous Half Dome, El Capitan, and Yosemite Falls, as well as the distant peaks of the Sierra Nevada Mountain Range. The summit of this dome-shaped peak provides one of the best vantage points in the park, making it a must-visit for those seeking an awe-inspiring perspective of Yosemite's landscape.

The Sentinel Dome Trail is a relatively short but moderately strenuous hike, making it an accessible option for both experienced hikers and beginners looking to experience a summit hike with less physical demand. The trail is 2.2 miles round trip with an elevation gain of about 400 feet. Despite its shorter distance, the trail still offers a rewarding ascent, passing through a variety of ecosystems, including lush meadows, ancient conifer forests, and rocky outcrops. The path itself is well-maintained, and hikers are treated to a beautiful and serene environment as they make their way to the top. Along the trail, the sounds of rustling leaves and the scent of pine trees provide a peaceful and refreshing atmosphere.

As visitors approach the summit, the vegetation begins to thin out, revealing the smooth granite dome that gives the peak its name. The final portion of the trail involves a short, steep section, but it is well worth the effort, as the summit provides stunning, unobstructed views of Yosemite's natural beauty. From the top of Sentinel Dome, visitors can see some of Yosemite's most iconic landmarks. Half Dome dominates the skyline, its distinct granite face rising above the valley below. To the west, El Capitan looms majestically, and Yosemite Falls plunges dramatically down the cliffs in the distance. The Yosemite Valley spreads out below, with its granite cliffs, waterfalls, and green meadows stretching as far as the eye can see. The surrounding peaks of the Sierra Nevada mountains also form a dramatic backdrop, especially in the early morning or late afternoon when the sunlight casts long shadows over the landscape.

The summit of Sentinel Dome is often less crowded than some of Yosemite's other famous viewpoints, making it a peaceful place to take in the grandeur of the park. The wide-open granite dome provides plenty of space to sit, relax, and take in the views. It is an excellent spot for photographers looking to capture the beauty of Yosemite's landscapes or for those simply seeking a moment of tranquility surrounded by nature.

The Sentinel Dome Trail is also notable for its accessibility. The trailhead is located along Glacier Point Road, which is easily reached from Yosemite Valley during the summer months. This makes it a popular hike for visitors staying in the valley or those driving along the scenic route to Glacier Point. The road is typically open from late spring to early fall, and the hike can be done in a few hours, making it perfect for a half-day outing. Visitors often choose to hike Sentinel Dome in conjunction with a visit to Glacier Point, which offers stunning views and is just a short drive from the trailhead.

The beauty of Sentinel Dome is particularly striking at sunrise and sunset when the soft light of early morning or evening creates dramatic contrasts across the valley and mountains. The warm glow on the granite cliffs and the ever-changing shadows of the landscape make these times ideal for photography or simply appreciating the awe-inspiring surroundings. For those looking for an added challenge, the hike can be extended to include Taft Point, another viewpoint located nearby, offering additional views of Yosemite Valley.

For anyone visiting Yosemite National Park, a hike to Sentinel Dome is a relatively easy but highly rewarding adventure that provides some of the most breathtaking vistas in the park. Whether you are a seasoned hiker or a casual explorer, the hike offers an opportunity to experience the stunning beauty of Yosemite's natural landscapes from a unique perspective. The sense of accomplishment when reaching the summit, combined with the panoramic views, makes Sentinel Dome a highlight of any trip to Yosemite, leaving visitors with memories of the park's grandeur that will last a lifetime. Whether you visit in the height of summer or the crisp coolness of fall, Sentinel Dome remains a must-see destination for all who venture into the natural wonder of Yosemite National Park.

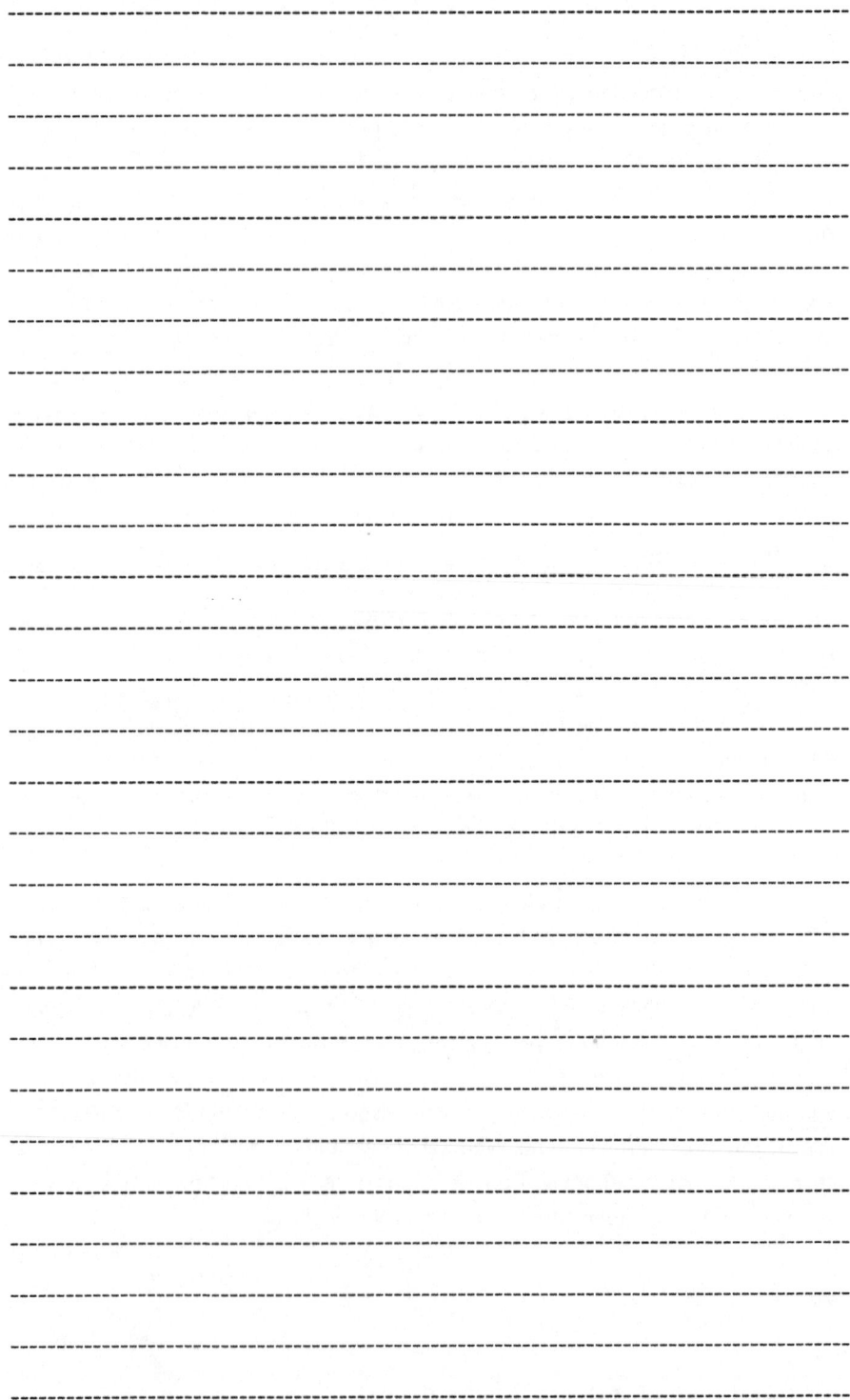

85

SEQUOIA & KINGS CANYON NATIONAL PARKS CALIFORNIA

COUNTY: TULARE   CITY: THREE RIVERS

DATE VISITED: WHO I WENT WITH:

RATING: ☆ ☆ ☆ ☆ ☆   WILL I RETURN?   YES / NO

47050 Generals Highway
Three Rivers, CA 93271
559-565-3341

Sequoia & Kings Canyon National Parks, located in the southern Sierra Nevada mountains of California, are a duo of breathtaking landscapes that together form one of the most awe-inspiring natural destinations in the United States. Covering over 1,300 square miles of rugged wilderness, these parks are renowned for their towering sequoia trees, dramatic granite peaks, and stunningly diverse ecosystems. Visitors to this region can expect unparalleled opportunities for exploration, adventure, and reflection amidst some of the most iconic scenery in North America.

The centerpiece of Sequoia National Park is the Giant Forest, home to the world-famous General Sherman Tree. At over 275 feet tall and with a base circumference of 103 feet, General Sherman is not only the largest living tree by volume but also one of the oldest living organisms on Earth, estimated to be over 2,200 years old. The Giant Forest contains numerous other massive sequoias, and its network of trails, such as the Congress Trail, allows visitors to wander through this majestic grove, feeling dwarfed by the ancient giants.

Adjacent to Sequoia, Kings Canyon National Park offers a slightly different, but equally stunning, natural experience. The canyon itself, carved by the Kings River, is one of the deepest in North America and is often compared to the Grand Canyon for its sheer scale and dramatic vistas. The Cedar Grove area at the canyon's base is a favorite spot for camping, hiking, and picnicking, while the Zumwalt Meadow Trail provides a gentle yet scenic loop with breathtaking views of the river, granite cliffs, and lush meadows.

Both parks are connected by the Generals Highway, a scenic road that winds through dense forests and offers panoramic views of the surrounding Sierra Nevada mountains. Along the route, visitors can stop at points of interest such as Tunnel Log, a fallen sequoia that has been hollowed out to allow cars to drive through, and Moro Rock, a massive granite dome with a steep staircase leading to its summit. From the top, visitors are rewarded with sweeping views of the Great Western Divide and the surrounding wilderness.

For those seeking solitude and adventure, the parks boast over 800 miles of hiking trails that range from easy nature walks to challenging backcountry treks. The High Sierra Trail and the Rae Lakes Loop are particularly popular with experienced hikers, offering access to pristine alpine lakes, cascading waterfalls, and rugged peaks. Mount Whitney, the tallest mountain in the contiguous United States at 14,505 feet, is also accessible from the parks and is a bucket-list destination for climbers.

The parks are rich in biodiversity, encompassing elevations from 1,370 feet in the foothills to over 14,000 feet in the high Sierra. This variation creates habitats for an array of wildlife, including black bears, mule deer, mountain lions, and an array of bird species. Seasonal wildflower blooms add bursts of color to the landscape, while groves of quaking aspens and alpine meadows provide additional scenic beauty.

Cultural and historical elements also enrich the experience of these parks. Native American tribes, including the Yokuts and Mono, have long histories in the region, leaving behind petroglyphs and other cultural artifacts. European settlers and early conservationists, such as John Muir, played pivotal roles in preserving the area, and their legacy is celebrated through interpretive programs and exhibits.

The parks are open year-round, with each season offering unique experiences. Spring brings wildflowers and rushing waterfalls, summer is ideal for hiking and camping, fall showcases colorful foliage, and winter blankets the higher elevations in snow, creating opportunities for snowshoeing and cross-country skiing.

Whether marveling at the towering sequoias, hiking through deep canyons, or simply enjoying the serenity of the wilderness, Sequoia & Kings Canyon National Parks are a testament to the grandeur and diversity of California's natural heritage. A visit to these parks is an unforgettable journey into the heart of the Sierra Nevada and a celebration of the wonders of the natural world.

86

SMOKE TREE STABLES

COUNTY: RIVERSIDE   **CITY:** PALM SPRINGS

DATE VISITED: **WHO I WENT WITH:**

RATING: ☆ ☆ ☆ ☆ ☆   **WILL I RETURN?** YES / NO

2500 S Toledo Ave, Palm Springs
Greater Palm Springs, CA 92264
760-327-1372

Smoke Tree Stables, located in Palm Springs, California, offers a unique and unforgettable equestrian experience, blending the beauty of the desert landscape with the thrill of horseback riding. Nestled at the base of the majestic San Jacinto Mountains, this family-owned and operated stable has been providing visitors with the opportunity to explore the stunning desert terrain on horseback for decades. With its expansive grounds and knowledgeable guides, Smoke Tree Stables offers a variety of riding experiences suitable for all levels, from beginners to seasoned riders, making it a perfect destination for equestrian enthusiasts and those looking to try horseback riding for the first time.

One of the key highlights of Smoke Tree Stables is its horseback riding tours, which take guests through the scenic Indian Canyons area. These guided rides allow visitors to immerse themselves in the breathtaking beauty of the desert landscape, which is filled with lush palm oases, rugged canyons, and striking rock formations. Riders can expect to encounter views of the towering San Jacinto Mountains, vast stretches of open desert, and tranquil streams that wind through the canyons. The experience offers a peaceful escape from the hustle and bustle of everyday life, with the rhythm of the horse's movements and the natural beauty of the surroundings creating a meditative atmosphere.

The stables at Smoke Tree Stables provide a selection of well-trained and well-cared-for horses, each chosen to match the experience and comfort level of the rider. Whether you are an experienced rider looking for a more challenging ride or a first-time rider seeking a gentle, leisurely trek, the stables have horses suited to every need. The knowledgeable guides, who are experienced equestrians themselves, ensure that each guest feels safe and confident on their ride. They provide helpful instructions for those who are new to horseback riding and are always on hand to answer any questions during the ride, ensuring a fun and enjoyable experience for all participants.

In addition to its scenic rides, Smoke Tree Stables offers a variety of packages and options for different types of riders. The Desert Ride is particularly popular, taking guests on a journey through the Indian Canyons with stunning views of the desert flora and fauna, while the Palm Springs Trail Ride offers a more relaxed, less challenging route through the tranquil desert terrain. For those looking for something extra special, Smoke Tree Stables also offers private rides, allowing guests to enjoy a more intimate experience with their guide. These private rides can be customized to suit the rider's preferences, whether that involves exploring different areas or focusing on a slower pace for a more leisurely ride.

Smoke Tree Stables is not just a place for horseback riding; it also provides a great opportunity for those looking to learn about the history and culture of the desert region. As guests ride through the canyons and desert landscapes, the guides share interesting facts about the local wildlife, plant life, and geology, giving visitors a deeper understanding of the desert environment. The stables also host a variety of special events throughout the year, including equestrian demonstrations and charity rides, making it a vibrant part of the Palm Springs community.

For those looking to take a break from the typical tourist attractions and experience something truly special, a visit to Smoke Tree Stables provides an authentic and memorable way to explore the natural beauty of Palm Springs. The peaceful and scenic atmosphere, combined with the opportunity to connect with nature on horseback, offers a rare and enriching experience that can be enjoyed by people of all ages.

The location of Smoke Tree Stables in Palm Springs makes it an easily accessible destination for both locals and visitors. Whether you're staying in the city for a weekend or just passing through, Smoke Tree Stables provides a fun and relaxing way to experience the desert's beauty from a unique perspective. The stables are also located near several other local attractions, including Indian Canyons, Joshua Tree National Park, and the famous Palm Springs Aerial Tramway, making it easy to combine a horseback ride with other outdoor activities.

Overall, Smoke Tree Stables offers a one-of-a-kind equestrian adventure in the heart of California's desert landscape. With its stunning location, experienced guides, and well-maintained horses, Smoke Tree Stables promises an unforgettable experience for anyone looking to explore the natural beauty of Palm Springs on horseback. Whether you're an experienced rider or a beginner, the stables ensure a safe, enjoyable, and memorable ride through one of California's most picturesque regions.

87

STOUT GROVE

COUNTY: DEL NORTE   **CITY:** CRESCENT CITY

DATE VISITED: **WHO I WENT WITH:**

RATING: ☆ ☆ ☆ ☆ ☆   **WILL I RETURN?**   YES / NO

1440 Highway 199
Crescent City, CA 95531
707-464-6101

Stout Grove, located in the Jedediah Smith Redwoods State Park in Del Norte County, California, is one of the most serene and awe-inspiring spots in the Redwood National and State Parks. This hidden gem is known for its breathtaking beauty, featuring towering ancient redwoods, lush ferns, and a peaceful atmosphere that invites visitors to step into a natural wonderland. The grove is accessible through an easy-to-navigate trail that provides visitors with an intimate experience among some of the tallest and oldest trees on Earth.

The main highlight of Stout Grove is the magnificent redwood trees, which can reach heights of over 350 feet and ages of over 2,000 years. The sight of these towering trees, with their massive trunks and canopy that stretches far above, is truly awe-inspiring. The trees in Stout Grove are part of a larger ancient forest, and the area offers a glimpse into the grandeur of these prehistoric giants. Walking among these colossal trees gives visitors a sense of scale and a deep appreciation for the power and longevity of nature.

The Stout Grove Trail, a short but rewarding hike, loops through the grove and offers visitors the chance to see the incredible diversity of plant life that thrives in the temperate rainforest of the region. Along the trail, visitors can spot lush ferns, moss-covered trees, and vibrant wildflowers, all set against the backdrop of the towering redwoods. The trail is easy enough for most visitors to navigate, making it suitable for families, photographers, and nature lovers of all ages. As you walk along the trail, the sunlight filtering through the high branches creates a mystical ambiance, with the forest floor illuminated by soft, dappled light.

In addition to its stunning beauty, Stout Grove is a haven for wildlife. The grove is home to a variety of species, including birds, deer, and other small mammals. The rich ecosystem provides a habitat for both terrestrial and aquatic creatures, as the nearby Smith River also adds to the area's ecological importance. Birdwatchers will find plenty to observe, with species like the Northern Spotted Owl and Steller's Jay often seen in the canopy. The combination of old-growth forest, diverse plant life, and the riverbank ecosystem makes Stout Grove a perfect destination for nature enthusiasts who enjoy wildlife observation and photography.

While Stout Grove is a serene and peaceful place to explore, it also holds a sense of historical significance. The Jedediah Smith Redwoods State Park, where Stout Grove is located, is named after the 19th-century American explorer Jedediah Smith, who was one of the first to travel through this region. The park was established in 1929 to protect this remarkable natural area, and today, it remains one of the most untouched and preserved sections of the California redwood forests. Visitors to Stout Grove are walking in the footsteps of early explorers, experiencing the same awe and wonder that those early travelers must have felt when encountering these massive trees.

For those interested in further exploring the area, Jedediah Smith Redwoods State Park offers several other trails and points of interest, such as the Hiouchi Trail and the Smith River, both of which offer a deeper connection to the natural environment surrounding the redwoods. After spending time in the grove, visitors can also explore the nearby Redwood National Park visitor centers, which provide educational displays about the natural history, cultural significance, and conservation efforts surrounding the redwood forests.

Getting to Stout Grove is relatively easy, as it is located just off the Howland Hill Road, a scenic route that winds through the redwood forest. The drive itself is a highlight, with several other viewpoints and groves to explore along the way. Parking is available near the grove, and the area is not usually as crowded as some of the other well-known spots in the Redwood National and State Parks, allowing visitors to experience the majesty of the redwoods in a more peaceful, reflective setting.

Whether you are a nature lover, photographer, or simply someone looking to experience the incredible natural beauty of Northern California, Stout Grove offers a truly memorable and awe-inspiring experience. The ancient redwoods, tranquil atmosphere, and rich biodiversity make it one of the most beautiful and iconic spots in the region, perfect for those seeking to connect with nature in its purest form. A visit to Stout Grove is a journey into one of the world's most extraordinary ecosystems, offering a rare opportunity to witness the timeless majesty of the redwoods.

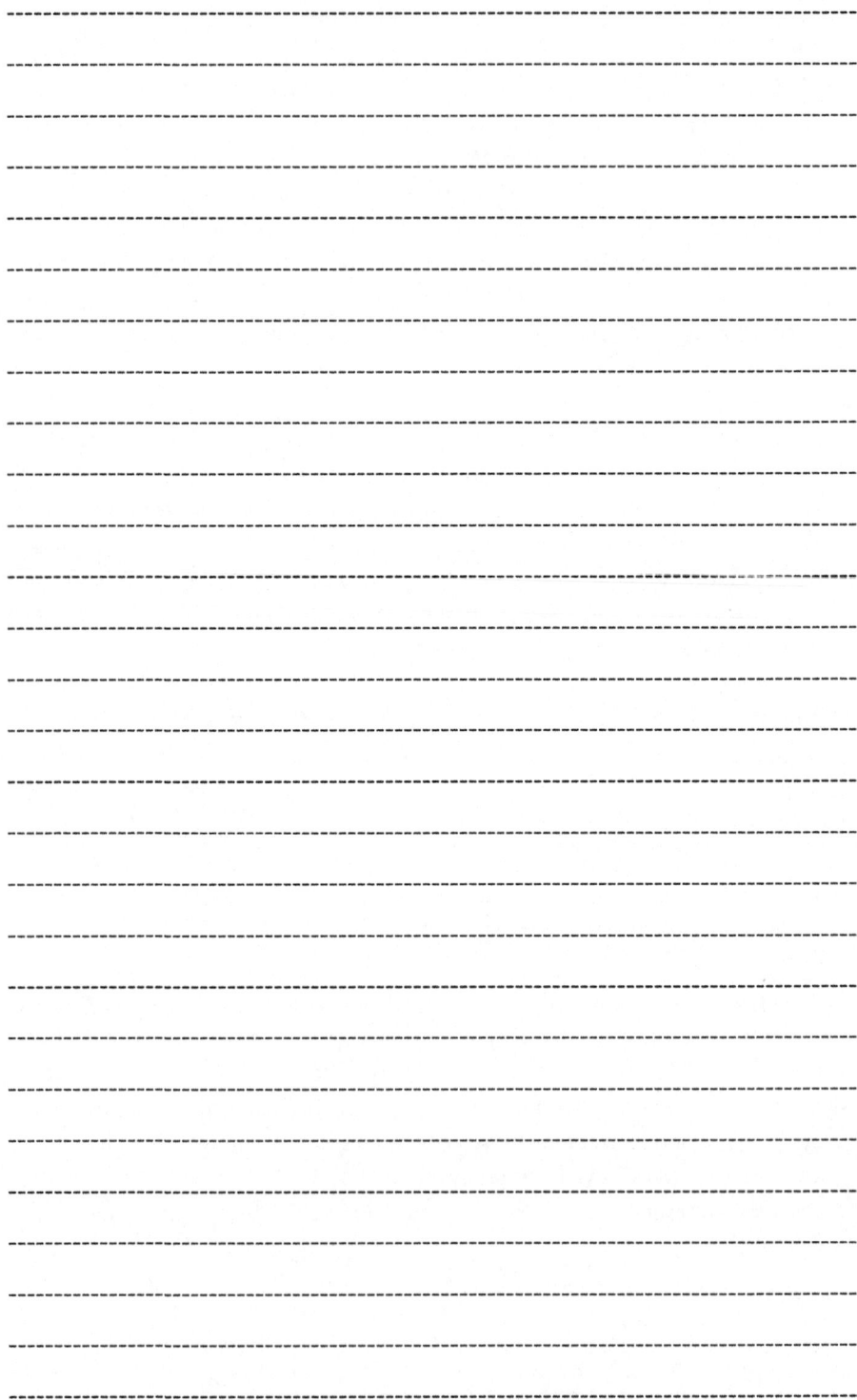

(88) # SUNSET CLIFFS NATURAL PARK

COUNTY: SAN DIEGO   **CITY:** SAN DIEGO

DATE VISITED: **WHO I WENT WITH:**

RATING: ☆ ☆ ☆ ☆ ☆   **WILL I RETURN?** YES / NO

Ladera St
San Diego, CA 92107

Sunset Cliffs Natural Park, located in San Diego, California, is a stunning coastal park known for its breathtaking views of the Pacific Ocean, dramatic cliffs, and vibrant sunsets. Situated along the western edge of the Point Loma Peninsula, this 68-acre park is a popular destination for locals and visitors alike, offering a mix of natural beauty, outdoor recreation, and the chance to experience the raw power of the ocean. The park is particularly famous for its panoramic vistas, making it one of the best spots in San Diego to watch the sun dip below the horizon.

The park's name, Sunset Cliffs, is a testament to the stunning sunset views it offers. Every evening, visitors flock to the cliffs to witness one of nature's most beautiful spectacles. As the sun sets over the Pacific, the sky is painted with brilliant hues of orange, pink, and purple, creating an unforgettable experience. The cliffs, which rise dramatically above the ocean, provide an ideal vantage point for watching this incredible natural phenomenon, and the park has become a beloved spot for photography, romantic strolls, and quiet reflection.

In addition to its sunset views, Sunset Cliffs Natural Park offers a variety of outdoor activities. The park features several walking trails that meander along the coastline, allowing visitors to explore the rugged terrain and enjoy breathtaking views of the ocean and cliffs. These trails vary in difficulty, from easy paths suitable for casual walks to more challenging routes that require a bit of hiking. The trails are well-maintained and provide access to some of the park's most scenic areas, including hidden coves, tide pools, and rock formations.

One of the most popular trails in the park is the Sunset Cliffs Trail, which runs along the top of the cliffs, offering sweeping views of the coastline and ocean below. This trail is relatively flat and is accessible to visitors of all fitness levels, making it a perfect choice for a leisurely walk. Along the way, visitors can enjoy the sound of crashing waves, the scent of saltwater, and the sight of seabirds soaring overhead. For those looking for a more adventurous hike, there are also steeper sections of the park that offer even more dramatic views and a sense of seclusion.

The park is also home to tide pools, which can be explored at low tide. These natural pools, formed in the rocky shoreline, are home to a wide variety of marine life, including sea anemones, crabs, starfish, and small fish. Exploring the tide pools is a fun and educational activity, especially for families and children. The rich marine ecosystem provides a fascinating glimpse into the underwater world, and visitors can learn about the diverse species that inhabit the waters off the coast of San Diego.

Birdwatching is another popular activity at Sunset Cliffs Natural Park. The park's cliffs and coastal habitats attract a variety of bird species, including seagulls, pelicans, and cormorants. The area is also a favorite stop for migrating birds, making it a great spot for bird enthusiasts to observe and photograph these winged creatures. Visitors may also spot marine mammals such as seals and sea lions off the coast, adding to the park's natural charm.

For those seeking a peaceful escape, Sunset Cliffs Natural Park offers plenty of quiet spots to relax and enjoy the surroundings. The park has several grassy areas perfect for picnics, as well as benches and lookout points where visitors can sit and take in the view. The sound of the ocean waves crashing against the cliffs and the sight of the sun setting over the horizon create a serene atmosphere that invites visitors to unwind and enjoy the beauty of nature.

Although Sunset Cliffs Natural Park is primarily known for its natural beauty, it also holds historical and cultural significance. The park is located near the Cabrillo National Monument and the Old Point Loma Lighthouse, two important landmarks in San Diego's history. The Cabrillo National Monument marks the spot where the first European, Juan Rodriguez Cabrillo, landed on the West Coast of the United States in 1542. Visitors to Sunset Cliffs can combine their visit to the park with a trip to these nearby historic sites, making it a great destination for both natural and cultural exploration.

Sunset Cliffs Natural Park is open year-round and is free to the public. It is easily accessible from the surrounding neighborhoods, with ample parking available along Sunset Cliffs Boulevard and in nearby parking lots. While the park is relatively small, its beauty and the variety of activities it offers make it a must-visit destination for anyone in San Diego. Whether you're looking for a scenic place to watch the sunset, a spot for a leisurely walk, or an opportunity to explore nature, Sunset Cliffs provides an unforgettable experience that showcases the rugged beauty of Southern California's coastline.

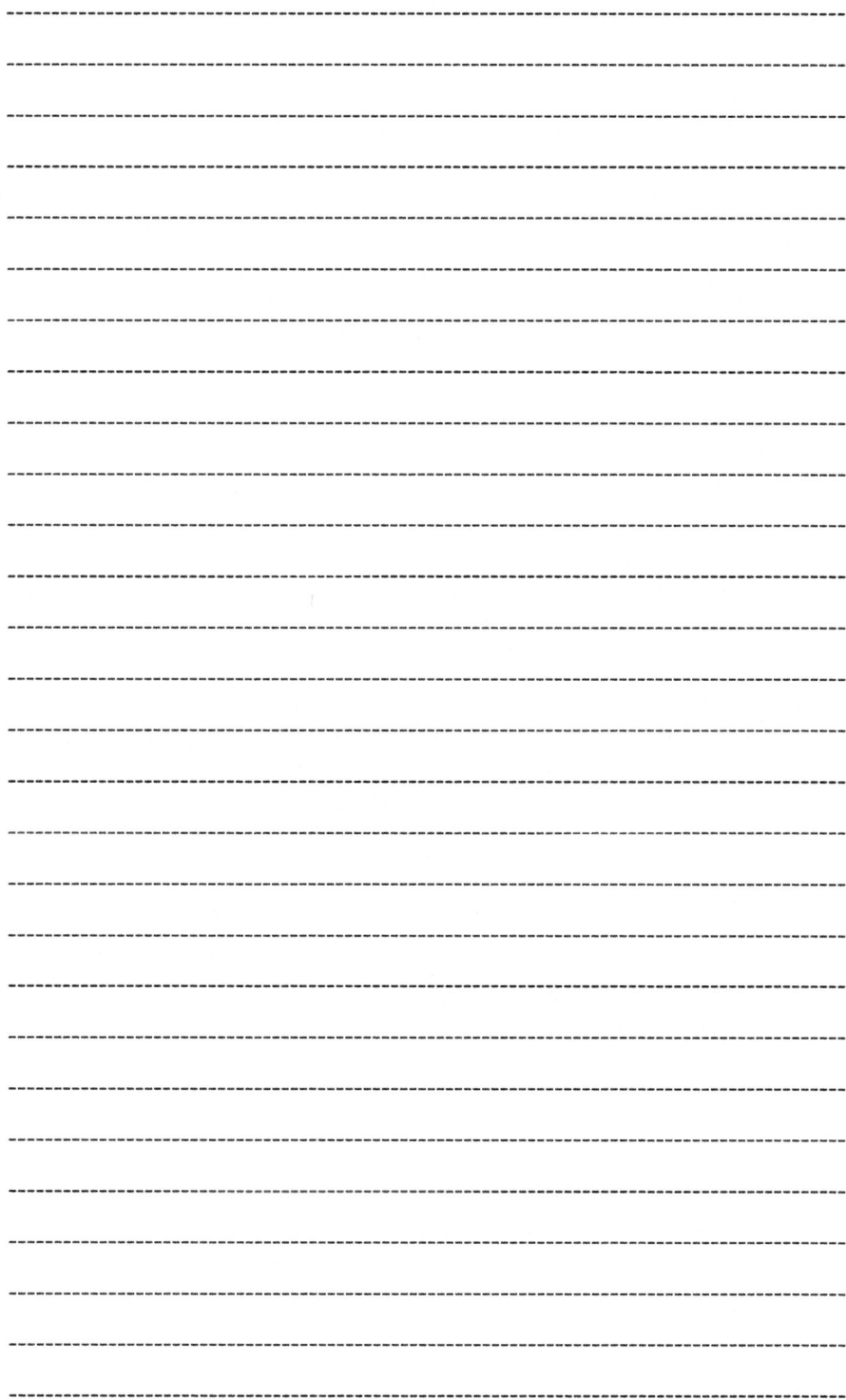

89

TAFT POINT

COUNTY: MARIPOSA   **CITY:** MARIPOSA

DATE VISITED: **WHO I WENT WITH:**

RATING: ☆ ☆ ☆ ☆ ☆   **WILL I RETURN?**   YES / NO

You can drive to Yosemite year-round and enter via Highways 41, 140, and 120 from the west. Tioga Pass Entrance (via Highway 120 from the east) is closed from approximately November through late May or June. Hetch Hetchy is open all year but may close intermittently due to snow. Please note that GPS units do not always provide accurate directions to or within Yosemite.
209-372-0200

Taft Point, located in Yosemite National Park, offers one of the most dramatic and stunning viewpoints in the entire park. Perched on the western edge of Yosemite Valley, Taft Point presents visitors with a breathtaking vista of towering granite cliffs, deep canyons, and the iconic El Capitan rock formation. Named in honor of former U.S. President William Howard Taft, this viewpoint has become a popular destination for hikers and nature enthusiasts seeking panoramic views of Yosemite's rugged landscape. The relatively short and moderate hike to Taft Point makes it accessible to a wide range of visitors, including those looking for a scenic adventure that offers some of the best photo opportunities in the park.

The hike to Taft Point is approximately 2.2 miles round-trip, starting from the Glacier Point Road and offering a moderate level of difficulty suitable for most visitors. Along the trail, hikers are treated to an array of spectacular views as they gradually approach the cliff's edge. The trail passes through forests of towering pines and granite outcrops before opening up to breathtaking vistas. As visitors near the point, the trees give way to unobstructed views of the valley below and the surrounding peaks, with El Capitan standing prominently in the distance. The stunning contrast of the deep valley, towering granite cliffs, and lush forested slopes creates a sense of awe that is unique to Yosemite National Park.

At Taft Point, the viewpoint itself is nothing short of mesmerizing. Standing at the edge of the cliff, visitors are rewarded with a spectacular panoramic view of the Yosemite Valley, with the Merced River winding through the valley floor far below. The expansive vista includes iconic landmarks such as Cathedral Spires, Sentinel Dome, and the aforementioned El Capitan, which is known worldwide for its challenging rock climbing routes. The view from Taft Point is especially striking at sunrise and sunset when the soft golden light bathes the landscape, casting long shadows over the valley and creating a breathtaking display of colors across the granite cliffs.

One of the highlights of Taft Point is the fissures, or deep cracks in the granite, that run along the edge of the cliff. These fissures, which drop hundreds of feet into the valley below, add to the dramatic feel of the area. The sheer drop from the viewpoint is not for the faint of heart, but for those with a head for heights, it provides an unforgettable experience. Visitors are encouraged to exercise caution and stay back from the edge, as the cliffs can be unstable in certain areas.

Taft Point is also a fantastic spot for photography. The sweeping views, dramatic landscapes, and the striking play of light and shadow make it a favorite among photographers looking to capture the essence of Yosemite. The changing seasons bring even more variety to the landscape, with spring wildflowers, summer greenery, fall foliage, and winter snow creating ever-changing scenes for visitors to enjoy.

For those looking for a more immersive Yosemite experience, Taft Point is often included in longer hikes that connect to other areas of the park. It is part of a network of trails that can be combined with a visit to Glacier Point, Sentinel Dome, or Yosemite Valley, providing visitors with the opportunity to explore more of the park's stunning scenery.

Access to Taft Point is generally seasonal, as the road to the trailhead is typically closed in winter due to snow. The trail is best visited in spring, summer, and fall, when the weather is mild and the views are at their most accessible. In winter, the area may be less crowded, but visitors should be prepared for challenging conditions and limited access.

Overall, Taft Point is one of Yosemite's most awe-inspiring and accessible viewpoints, offering hikers and nature lovers the chance to experience the grandeur of the park from a unique perspective. Whether you're visiting for a short day hike or planning a more extended trek through Yosemite, Taft Point should not be missed. Its dramatic beauty and unforgettable vistas make it a true gem within one of America's most beloved national parks.

90

TAHOE TREETOP ADVENTURE PARKS

COUNTY: PLACER   **CITY:** TAHOE CITY

DATE VISITED: **WHO I WENT WITH:**

RATING: ☆ ☆ ☆ ☆ ☆   **WILL I RETURN?** YES / NO

725 Granlibakken Rd
Tahoe City, CA 96145
530-807-1004

Tahoe Treetop Adventure Parks, located in South Lake Tahoe, California, offers an exciting and unique outdoor adventure that immerses visitors in the stunning natural beauty of the Sierra Nevada Mountains. The park features a series of aerial obstacle courses set high in the trees, giving participants a chance to explore the forest from a bird's-eye view while navigating through various challenges such as ziplines, rope bridges, climbing walls, and balance beams. The courses are designed for all skill levels, making it an ideal destination for families, friends, and adventure seekers of all ages. With its close proximity to Lake Tahoe, Tahoe Treetop Adventure Parks provides not only a thrilling outdoor experience but also a chance to enjoy the breathtaking scenery of the area, including views of the surrounding forests, mountains, and crystal-clear waters of the lake.

The park features multiple treetop adventure courses, each offering a different level of difficulty. From beginner to advanced courses, participants can choose the adventure that best suits their ability and comfort level. The beginner courses are designed for younger adventurers or those new to aerial courses, featuring easier obstacles and lower heights. As participants progress to more advanced courses, the obstacles become more challenging, with higher platforms, tighter rope courses, and faster ziplines. One of the park's highlights is the Treetop Challenge, which combines physical challenges and thrilling zipline rides for an adrenaline-pumping experience. The ziplines, some of which stretch for hundreds of feet, offer the perfect combination of excitement and stunning views of the surrounding forest canopy.

The park's Zipline Tour is another popular attraction, offering guests the chance to glide through the trees and over the beautiful terrain of the Tahoe Basin. Participants can soar over tree canopies and enjoy the thrill of high-speed ziplining while taking in the panoramic views of the lake, mountains, and forests. Whether you're zipping from one tree to another or carefully maneuvering through obstacles, the experience is sure to provide both excitement and a unique perspective on the surrounding wilderness.

In addition to the traditional treetop courses and zipline tours, Tahoe Treetop Adventure Parks offers a variety of family-friendly activities designed to keep everyone entertained. The courses are designed with safety in mind, and each participant is equipped with the necessary gear, including a harness and helmet, before embarking on their adventure. Trained staff members are always on hand to provide instructions and ensure that everyone is following proper safety protocols.

The park's location in the heart of the Lake Tahoe area makes it an ideal complement to other outdoor activities in the region. After a fun-filled day at the park, visitors can enjoy nearby activities such as hiking, mountain biking, and kayaking, or relax by the beautiful shores of Lake Tahoe. During the winter months, Tahoe Treetop Adventure Parks also transforms into a winter wonderland, offering snowshoe tours and other winter activities, making it a year-round destination for outdoor adventure enthusiasts.

Whether you're looking to challenge yourself on an aerial obstacle course, enjoy the thrill of ziplining, or simply soak in the breathtaking views of Lake Tahoe's landscape, Tahoe Treetop Adventure Parks offers an unforgettable experience that combines adventure, nature, and family fun. The unique combination of adrenaline-pumping activities and the natural beauty of the Tahoe region makes it a must-visit attraction for anyone looking for an exciting and memorable outdoor experience.

91

THE GETTY CENTER

COUNTY: LOS ANGELES   **CITY:** LOS ANGELES

DATE VISITED: **WHO I WENT WITH:**

RATING: ☆ ☆ ☆ ☆ ☆   **WILL I RETURN?** YES / NO

1200 Getty Center Dr N Sepulveda Blvd & Getty Center Dr
Los Angeles, CA 90049
310-440-7300

The Getty Center, located in Los Angeles, California, is one of the most renowned cultural destinations in the United States. Perched on a hilltop in the Brentwood neighborhood, the Getty Center offers breathtaking views of the city and the Pacific Ocean. This world-class museum and cultural complex is known for its impressive collection of art, architecture, gardens, and innovative exhibitions. It serves as the home of the J. Paul Getty Museum, which houses an exceptional array of Western art, spanning from the Middle Ages to the present day, including European paintings, sculptures, decorative arts, and manuscripts.

One of the most striking features of the Getty Center is its architecture. Designed by architect Richard Meier, the center's modernist buildings are made of travertine stone and glass, blending seamlessly with the surrounding landscape. The sleek, white structures stand in stark contrast to the natural beauty of the grounds, creating a visually stunning environment. The center's design includes expansive terraces, reflecting pools, and walkways, allowing visitors to enjoy panoramic views of Los Angeles, the Santa Monica Mountains, and beyond. The Getty Center itself is a work of art, with its open spaces and carefully designed courtyards providing a serene setting for visitors to explore.

The J. Paul Getty Museum at the Getty Center is home to a wide-ranging collection that spans over 1,000 years of art history. Highlights include paintings by Vincent van Gogh, Rembrandt, Claude Monet, and Paul Cézanne, as well as sculptures, drawings, and decorative arts from Europe and the Americas. The museum also features a significant collection of illuminated manuscripts, showcasing the skill and beauty of medieval art. Temporary exhibitions rotate throughout the year, offering new opportunities for visitors to experience diverse collections and explore different artistic movements, styles, and periods.

Another impressive aspect of the Getty Center is its beautiful gardens. The Central Garden, designed by landscape architect Robert Irwin, is a peaceful and lush space that complements the architecture of the museum. The garden features a variety of plant species, waterfalls, and winding paths, creating a tranquil oasis where visitors can relax and enjoy the natural beauty of the surroundings. The garden is a work of art in itself, offering an evolving landscape that changes with the seasons and provides a perfect setting for reflection and relaxation.

In addition to its art and gardens, the Getty Center offers a range of educational programs and resources. The museum provides visitors with access to scholarly resources, including lectures, symposia, and interactive experiences that engage visitors of all ages. The Getty Research Institute, housed within the Getty Center, is a leading research library dedicated to the study of art history, and it offers scholars and students valuable resources on a wide range of topics related to art, architecture, and culture.

The Getty Center is also known for its commitment to accessibility and public outreach. Admission to the museum is free, though parking is charged. The center is easily accessible by public transportation, and it provides an inclusive, welcoming environment for visitors from all walks of life. The Getty Center hosts a variety of public programs, including concerts, family activities, film screenings, and educational workshops, making it a dynamic and engaging cultural destination for both locals and visitors to Los Angeles.

For those seeking a deeper connection to art and culture, the Getty Villa, another museum in the Getty family, is located in Malibu, offering a focus on the art and cultures of ancient Greece, Rome, and Etruria. While the Getty Center provides a comprehensive experience of art history, the Getty Villa delves into the ancient world through its extensive collection of antiquities.

Overall, the Getty Center is a must-visit for anyone interested in art, architecture, and culture. Its stunning location, impressive art collections, and tranquil gardens make it one of the most iconic cultural institutions in Los Angeles, offering visitors a unique opportunity to engage with the world of art and history while enjoying one of the most beautiful settings in the city. Whether you're an art enthusiast, a history buff, or simply looking for a peaceful escape, the Getty Center promises an enriching and unforgettable experience.

92

THE HUNTINGTON LIBRARY, ART MUSEUM AND BOTANICAL GARDENS

COUNTY: LOS ANGELES   **CITY:** SAN MARINO

DATE VISITED: **WHO I WENT WITH:**

                    RATING: ☆ ☆ ☆ ☆ ☆   **WILL I RETURN?**   YES / NO

1151 Oxford Road
San Marino, CA 91108
626-405-2100

The Huntington Library, Art Museum, and Botanical Gardens is one of Southern California's most renowned cultural destinations, located in San Marino, just outside of Los Angeles. This expansive 207-acre estate is home to a vast collection of rare books, world-class art, and meticulously curated gardens, making it a unique and enriching experience for visitors of all ages and interests.

The Huntington Library is internationally known for its impressive collection of rare and historical manuscripts, including works by some of the world's greatest writers and thinkers. Among its treasures is the Gutenberg Bible, one of the earliest printed books, and the First Folio of Shakespeare's plays. The library's collection also includes early printed books, letters, and manuscripts from a wide range of historical periods and fields of study, from European history to American literature. Scholars from all over the world come to The Huntington to study its collections, making it a vital research institution.

The Art Museum at The Huntington houses an exceptional collection of European and American art, with a particular focus on 18th- and 19th-century works. Notable highlights include portraits by Thomas Gainsborough and John Singer Sargent, as well as a remarkable assortment of European and American landscapes, including works by Frederic Church and Thomas Cole. The museum also boasts a collection of decorative arts, including fine furniture, ceramics, and silver. The galleries provide a peaceful and inspiring space for visitors to explore these masterpieces, while rotating exhibits offer fresh perspectives on both classic and contemporary art.

Equally famous are the Botanical Gardens that surround the library and museum. These 16 specialized gardens showcase the diversity of plant life from around the world. The gardens are carefully designed to reflect various environmental regions, from the Desert Garden to the Japanese Garden, and offer visitors the chance to explore lush landscapes and serene environments. The Desert Garden is one of the largest and most significant collections of desert plants in the world, featuring cacti, succulents, and other arid-climate flora. The Japanese Garden, with its koi-filled ponds, tranquil pathways, and meticulously maintained flora, provides a peaceful retreat, evoking a sense of harmony and beauty. Other notable gardens include the Rose Garden, the Camellia Garden, and the Tropical Garden, each offering a different experience and showcasing a unique aspect of the botanical world.

The Huntington's gardens are not only a visual delight but also serve as a resource for horticulturists and botanists. The California Garden showcases the native flora of the region, while the Chinese Garden, designed to reflect the classical principles of Chinese garden design, features a beautiful blend of architecture, water features, and plant life. The gardens provide a peaceful setting for strolling, relaxing, or simply enjoying the beauty of nature. Seasonal displays of flowers and plant life, such as the blooming of camellias in winter or the springtime explosion of roses, add to the ever-changing splendor of the gardens.

The Huntington is also home to a variety of educational programs and events, making it an excellent destination for families, school groups, and lifelong learners. Visitors can take part in docent-led tours, attend lectures and workshops, or participate in hands-on activities in the gardens. The Children's Garden, a playful and interactive space, is especially designed for young visitors, allowing them to engage with nature through creative play and educational exhibits.

The estate also hosts several annual events, such as the Spring Garden Show and Holiday Celebrations, where guests can enjoy special programming, view seasonal garden displays, and partake in festive activities. The Huntington Tea Room offers a charming space for visitors to relax and enjoy a traditional English afternoon tea, complete with pastries, finger sandwiches, and other treats.

With its rich history, diverse collections, and tranquil gardens, The Huntington Library, Art Museum, and Botanical Gardens offers a peaceful escape and an opportunity for visitors to connect with art, literature, and nature in a single location. Whether you're a history buff, an art lover, or a nature enthusiast, The Huntington provides a wealth of experiences that inspire reflection, learning, and enjoyment.

COUNTY: LOS ANGELES   **CITY:** LOS ANGELES (SYLMAR)

DATE VISITED: **WHO I WENT WITH:**

RATING: ☆ ☆ ☆ ☆ ☆   **WILL I RETURN?** YES / NO

15151 Bledsoe Street Sylmar
Los Angeles, CA 91342
818-364-6464

The Nethercutt Collection, located in Sylmar, California, is an extraordinary museum that showcases an impressive array of vintage automobiles, mechanical musical instruments, and rare collectibles. Situated in the northern part of Los Angeles, this hidden gem offers a fascinating glimpse into the history of transportation, craftsmanship, and entertainment. The collection was founded by J.B. Nethercutt, an automotive enthusiast and businessman, and it is now managed by the Nethercutt Foundation. Known for its meticulous attention to detail, the museum is a testament to Nethercutt's passion for preserving history and fine craftsmanship, making it a must-visit for anyone interested in vintage cars, music, and mechanical artistry.

The centerpiece of the Nethercutt Collection is its extensive collection of over 130 classic automobiles, many of which are rare and meticulously restored to their original splendor. The collection includes some of the finest examples of pre-World War II cars, including Packards, Cadillacs, Duesenbergs, and Pierce-Arrows, as well as notable examples of Chrysler and Lincoln vehicles. These cars are not just aesthetically pleasing, but they are also significant pieces of automotive history, representing the peak of automotive design and innovation from the early 20th century. Many of the cars on display have won prestigious awards at international car shows and have been featured in notable films and exhibitions.

One of the most fascinating aspects of the collection is its focus on mechanical musical instruments. The Nethercutt Collection is home to a large number of self-playing pianos, orchestras, and player organs from the early 1900s. These beautifully crafted instruments, many of which were produced by companies like Wurlitzer and M. Schulz, offer a glimpse into the rich history of automatic music and entertainment. The collection also includes rare automated violins and music boxes, some of which are still operational and are occasionally demonstrated for visitors. The musical instruments are displayed in a grand, vintage setting, allowing guests to experience the incredible craftsmanship of these mechanical wonders, often accompanied by live demonstrations.

In addition to the cars and musical instruments, the Nethercutt Collection features an array of other rarities, including antique furniture, fine art, and historical artifacts. The museum's founder was passionate about preserving the artistry of the past, and the collection reflects this dedication. Visitors can explore beautifully restored furniture pieces, including French and English antiques, as well as other decorative items that showcase the craftsmanship of earlier centuries.

The museum's commitment to preservation and attention to detail is evident in every aspect of the Nethercutt Collection. The facility itself is designed to provide an intimate, high-end museum experience, where guests can wander through spacious galleries and admire the collection in a peaceful and elegant setting. Visitors are encouraged to take their time to explore the exhibits, and knowledgeable staff are available to share the stories behind the cars and musical instruments, as well as the history of the museum itself.

One of the highlights of the Nethercutt Collection is its exceptional ability to blend technology and art. The museum has carefully restored and maintained each piece in the collection, ensuring that it remains in pristine condition for future generations. The commitment to preservation is further exemplified in the way the museum operates, with detailed attention given to the care and conservation of each item in the collection. The Nethercutt Collection is not just a museum but a living tribute to the craftsmanship and innovation of past eras.

Visitors to the Nethercutt Collection will also have the opportunity to enjoy its Musical Automaton Gallery, where they can witness demonstrations of the mechanical musical instruments in action. These performances, accompanied by the elegant sounds of bygone music, offer an enchanting and immersive experience. The museum is open to the public for free, although visitors must schedule a reservation in advance to ensure access, as it is not a walk-in facility. This approach adds to the exclusivity and intimate atmosphere of the museum.

Overall, the Nethercutt Collection offers a unique and enriching experience that blends history, art, and technology. Whether you are an automotive enthusiast, a fan of mechanical music, or someone simply interested in fine craftsmanship, the Nethercutt Collection provides a rare opportunity to appreciate some of the finest examples of both modern and historic design. It is a hidden treasure in Los Angeles, offering a glimpse into the past while preserving these incredible works of art for the future.

COUNTY: SAN DIEGO   **CITY:** SAN DIEGO

DATE VISITED: **WHO I WENT WITH:**

RATING: ☆ ☆ ☆ ☆ ☆   **WILL I RETURN?** YES / NO

12600 N Torrey Pines Rd
San Diego, CA 92037

Torrey Pines State Natural Reserve is a stunning 2,000-acre coastal park located in San Diego, California, known for its dramatic landscapes, unique wildlife, and breathtaking views of the Pacific Ocean. Nestled along the cliffs of the La Jolla coastline, this reserve offers visitors a serene escape into nature, with scenic trails, pristine beaches, and one of the rarest species of pine trees in the world— the Torrey Pine.

The reserve is home to a variety of ecosystems, including coastal sage scrub, chaparral, and native plant species, as well as diverse animal life. The primary draw of the reserve is the Torrey Pine, which is found only in this area and on Santa Rosa Island off the coast of California. These trees are easily recognizable by their long, slender needles and their characteristic bark, which adds to the charm of the landscape.

Visitors to Torrey Pines State Natural Reserve can explore a network of hiking trails that wind through the park's diverse habitats. The trails range from easy to moderate in difficulty and offer incredible views of the ocean, coastal cliffs, and the surrounding hills. Popular hiking trails include the Guy Fleming Trail, which offers some of the best coastal views in the reserve, and the Razor Point Trail, which leads to a dramatic overlook of the Pacific Ocean and the jagged cliffs below. For a more challenging hike, the Beach Trail descends to the beach below, providing a direct route to the coast where visitors can relax, explore tide pools, or take in the scenic views of the surf.

One of the most unique features of Torrey Pines State Natural Reserve is its pristine environment, which has remained largely untouched for centuries. The reserve has been carefully preserved to protect its natural beauty and biodiversity, with efforts focused on the restoration of native plant species and the protection of endangered wildlife. Birds such as the California quail and red-tailed hawk are commonly seen throughout the reserve, and it is also home to a variety of small mammals, reptiles, and marine life that thrive in the surrounding ecosystems.

The reserve's Visitor Center provides informative exhibits about the natural history, geology, and wildlife of the area, offering educational opportunities for visitors of all ages. The center also has knowledgeable rangers available to answer questions and provide recommendations for exploring the park. Visitors can also pick up maps and brochures at the center to help navigate the trails.

For those interested in learning more about the reserve's history, the Torrey Pines area was once home to the Kumeyaay Native Americans, who lived in the region for thousands of years before European settlers arrived. Evidence of their presence can still be found in the area, including artifacts and shell middens.

At the top of the reserve, visitors will find the Torrey Pines Gliderport, a popular spot for hang gliders and paragliders to launch, providing a unique perspective of the cliffs and the ocean below. Watching these pilots soar above the reserve is a thrilling sight, adding to the reserve's allure and sense of adventure.

Additionally, Torrey Pines State Natural Reserve is situated near the Torrey Pines Golf Course, which is one of the most famous golf courses in the world, known for hosting the U.S. Open and offering panoramic views of the Pacific Ocean.

Torrey Pines State Natural Reserve is open year-round, with the best time to visit being during the spring and fall when the weather is mild and the wildflowers are in bloom. The park is accessible by car, and there is a parking lot at the reserve, though it can fill up quickly during peak times. Visitors can also access the reserve via public transportation or by bike.

Whether you are looking for a peaceful hike, an opportunity to observe rare wildlife, or simply a place to appreciate the natural beauty of California's coastline, Torrey Pines State Natural Reserve offers an unforgettable experience. With its unique landscape, diverse ecosystems, and stunning ocean views, it stands as one of the most beautiful and ecologically significant places in Southern California.

USS MIDWAY MUSEUM

95

COUNTY: SAN DIEGO   **CITY:** SAN DIEGO

DATE VISITED: | **WHO I WENT WITH:**

RATING: ☆ ☆ ☆ ☆ ☆   **WILL I RETURN?**   YES / NO

910 N Harbor Drive
San Diego, CA 92101
619-544-9600

The USS Midway Museum, located in San Diego, California, offers a unique and immersive experience aboard one of the most iconic aircraft carriers in U.S. naval history. The USS Midway was commissioned in 1945 and served in the U.S. Navy for over 47 years, participating in numerous military operations and playing a key role in the post-World War II era. After its decommissioning in 1992, the ship was transformed into a museum, allowing visitors to explore its rich history and learn about the lives of the sailors and pilots who served on it.

The museum is housed on the actual aircraft carrier, which is docked at the San Diego Bay waterfront, providing a stunning setting for this one-of-a-kind attraction. The USS Midway Museum offers a wide variety of exhibits and interactive displays that highlight the ship's history, military significance, and the role of naval aviation throughout the 20th century. Visitors can tour the vast deck of the aircraft carrier, where they can see a collection of over 30 restored aircraft, including helicopters and jets, many of which were used by the Navy during the ship's service.

One of the highlights of the museum is the Flight Deck, where guests can walk alongside historical aircraft, such as the F-14 Tomcat, A-6 Intruder, and F/A-18 Hornet, all of which played key roles in the Navy's air operations. The museum also offers a close-up look at the flight control center, where skilled officers and crew directed air traffic during military operations. The flight deck is a great place for taking photos, as visitors can get an up-close view of these powerful machines while enjoying breathtaking panoramic views of San Diego Bay.

Below deck, visitors can explore the USS Midway's interior, which has been meticulously preserved to give a sense of what life was like for the thousands of sailors who served aboard the ship. Guests can visit the Captain's Bridge, the Admiral's Cabin, and the Officer's Mess, as well as see the cramped sleeping quarters and working areas where crew members lived and worked. Interactive exhibits throughout the ship tell stories of daily life aboard the Midway, giving visitors a glimpse into the hardships and challenges sailors faced during long deployments.

The museum also offers a variety of educational programs, including guided tours and multimedia presentations, allowing guests to learn about the ship's history and its contributions to key moments in military history. Themed exhibits cover a range of topics, from aviation history to naval battles, and are complemented by personal stories and historical photographs that bring the ship's legacy to life. One of the most popular attractions is the Flight Simulator, where guests can experience the thrill of piloting a fighter jet through a series of aerial maneuvers, simulating the excitement of naval aviation.

Another notable feature of the USS Midway Museum is the collection of oral histories shared by former crew members. These personal accounts offer a rare, firsthand look at life aboard the carrier, providing emotional and insightful stories that deepen visitors' understanding of the ship's role in military operations.

For those interested in military history or aviation, the USS Midway Museum is a must-see destination in San Diego. It is a fascinating museum that tells the story of American naval aviation, the men and women who served in the U.S. Navy, and the Midway's legacy as one of the longest-serving aircraft carriers in U.S. history. Whether you're a history enthusiast, a military buff, or simply looking for an engaging experience during your visit to San Diego, the USS Midway Museum offers an educational and awe-inspiring adventure aboard a true piece of American history.

96

VENICE BEACH

COUNTY: LOS ANGELES　　　　　　　　　　　　**CITY:** LOS ANGELES (VENICE)

DATE VISITED:　　　　　　　　**WHO I WENT WITH:**

RATING: ☆ ☆ ☆ ☆ ☆　　　　　**WILL I RETURN?**　YES / NO

1800 Ocean Front Walk
Venice, CA 90291, USA

Venice Beach, located in the heart of Los Angeles, California, is one of the most iconic and eclectic beaches in the United States. Known for its vibrant atmosphere, diverse culture, and unique blend of art, fitness, and entertainment, Venice Beach is a must-see destination for both locals and visitors. The beach itself stretches for about two miles along the Pacific Ocean, offering beautiful views of the coastline, as well as a wide variety of activities and attractions for people of all ages.

One of the most famous features of Venice Beach is its Boardwalk, a bustling promenade that runs along the beach, filled with street performers, vendors, and tourists. The Venice Beach Boardwalk is a lively and colorful area where you can experience the free-spirited vibe of Venice. The boardwalk is lined with eclectic shops, tattoo parlors, food trucks, and artists selling their work, making it a great place to stroll, shop, and people-watch. Whether you're admiring the local artwork, watching skateboarders perform tricks, or sampling delicious food, the boardwalk is the heart of the Venice Beach experience.

At the Venice Beach Skate Park, visitors can watch some of the best skateboarders and BMX riders in the world showcase their skills. The park, located right on the sand, features a large bowl, ramps, and rails, providing a thrilling spectacle for those who love extreme sports. Nearby, the Muscle Beach Outdoor Gym is another highlight of Venice Beach. This historic open-air gym is known as the birthplace of modern bodybuilding, where famous figures like Arnold Schwarzenegger and Larry Scott trained. Today, it remains a popular spot for fitness enthusiasts, bodybuilders, and tourists who want to catch a glimpse of the action.

Another popular attraction is the Venice Canals, a serene and picturesque area designed by Abbot Kinney in the early 1900s. Inspired by the canals of Venice, Italy, this residential area features beautiful waterways lined with charming homes and lush greenery. Visitors can take a peaceful walk along the canals, enjoying the scenic beauty and unique architecture of the area. The Abbot Kinney

Boulevard, just a few blocks away, is also a trendy street filled with upscale boutiques, cafes, and restaurants, making it a great place to shop, dine, and explore the local culture.

For art lovers, Venice Beach offers a rich cultural experience. The area is home to a number of galleries, murals, and street art, reflecting the creative energy that has long defined Venice. The neighborhood has been a hub for artists, musicians, and performers for decades, and its creative spirit is on full display throughout the area. The Venice Art Walls, located near the boardwalk, is a designated space for graffiti and street art, where artists can paint and showcase their work, creating ever-changing murals that add to the area's colorful aesthetic.

Venice Beach is also a haven for outdoor activities, with plenty of opportunities for cycling, jogging, rollerblading, and beach volleyball. The Venice Beach Bike Path runs along the sand, allowing cyclists and skaters to cruise along the coast while enjoying the ocean breeze and scenic views. The beach itself is a great place to relax, swim, or soak up the sun, with lifeguard stations and volleyball courts available for beachgoers. The Ocean Front Walk provides a perfect vantage point to enjoy the ocean views while strolling along the shoreline, watching the surfers and beachgoers in action.

For those looking to relax and unwind, Venice Beach offers a laid-back atmosphere, with plenty of spots to kick back, people-watch, or enjoy a sunset. The iconic Venice Beach Pier is another must-see landmark, providing great views of the ocean and the surrounding coastline. Whether you're walking along the pier, fishing, or simply taking in the view, it's a peaceful spot to enjoy the beauty of the beach.

Venice Beach is not just a beach—it's a cultural hub, an artistic haven, and a place of boundless energy and creativity. Whether you're there to enjoy the beach, explore the boardwalk, admire the art, or take in the history, Venice Beach offers something for everyone. It's a place where people come to express themselves, relax, and celebrate the laid-back California lifestyle, making it one of the most iconic destinations in Los Angeles.

97

VGS CHATEAU POTELLE

COUNTY: NAPA   CITY: ST. HELENA

DATE VISITED: WHO I WENT WITH:

RATING: ☆ ☆ ☆ ☆ ☆   WILL I RETURN?   YES / NO

1200 Dowdell Ln
St. Helena, CA 94574
707-255-9440

VGS Chateau Potelle, located in the renowned Napa Valley of California, is a prestigious winery that offers a unique and intimate wine-tasting experience. Nestled in the heart of the valley, the winery provides visitors with an opportunity to explore some of the finest wines produced in one of the most celebrated wine regions in the world. The winery's picturesque setting, coupled with its exceptional wines and personalized service, makes it a must-visit destination for wine enthusiasts and tourists alike.

The history of VGS Chateau Potelle is deeply intertwined with the Napa Valley's winemaking tradition. Founded in the early 1990s, the winery was established with a vision to create wines that reflect the unique terroir of Napa Valley, particularly focusing on producing high-quality, handcrafted wines with a distinct sense of place. The winery is known for its commitment to sustainable farming practices, allowing the grapes to thrive in the ideal conditions that Napa Valley provides, ensuring exceptional quality in every bottle.

VGS Chateau Potelle is most famous for its carefully curated selection of Cabernet Sauvignon, Zinfandel, and Chardonnay wines, as well as its smaller lot, limited-edition offerings. The winemaking philosophy at VGS emphasizes small batch production, which allows the winery to focus on quality over quantity. The result is wines that are rich in flavor, complexity, and character, showcasing the nuances of Napa Valley's diverse microclimates and soils. Visitors can expect to taste wines that reflect the best of the valley's heritage, from bold and full-bodied reds to crisp, refreshing whites.

One of the standout features of VGS Chateau Potelle is its intimate and personalized wine tasting experience. The winery offers private tastings, where guests are guided through a selection of wines by knowledgeable staff who are passionate about the winery's history, philosophy, and wines. The tasting room, with its cozy and welcoming atmosphere, provides a perfect setting for enjoying the wines while learning about the intricate process of winemaking. Guests are often given the chance to sample rare or limited-edition wines that are not available to the general public, making the visit even more special.

The winery's beautiful grounds are also a major attraction, offering stunning views of the surrounding vineyards and the rolling hills of Napa Valley. The vineyard's location, high up in the hills, allows visitors to take in sweeping vistas of the valley below. Guests can enjoy a leisurely walk through the property, take in the landscape, and discover the winery's sustainable farming practices. The combination of breathtaking views and the serene environment makes VGS Chateau Potelle a perfect place to relax and enjoy a glass of wine.

In addition to its exceptional wines, the winery also offers a range of events and activities for visitors. These include wine-pairing dinners, wine and food events, and private tours of the vineyards and winery. These experiences provide a deeper insight into the winemaking process, from vineyard management to fermentation and aging, allowing guests to gain a full appreciation of what goes into each bottle of wine. For those looking to celebrate a special occasion, VGS Chateau Potelle also offers a variety of private event spaces where guests can host everything from small gatherings to large parties, all while enjoying the best wines that Napa Valley has to offer.

For those looking to take a piece of the Napa Valley home with them, the winery offers a selection of wines for purchase at the tasting room. Many of the wines are available exclusively to visitors, making it a great opportunity to stock up on rare bottles or discover new favorites. With its rich history, dedication to quality, and stunning location, VGS Chateau Potelle remains a true gem in Napa Valley's wine country. Whether you're a seasoned wine connoisseur or simply someone looking to experience the best of Napa, a visit to VGS Chateau Potelle is an unforgettable experience that captures the essence of California's renowned wine culture.

98

WELLINGTON CELLARS

COUNTY: SONOMA   **CITY:** GLEN ELLEN

DATE VISITED: _____   **WHO I WENT WITH:** _____

RATING: ☆ ☆ ☆ ☆ ☆   **WILL I RETURN?**   YES / NO

11600 Dunbar Rd
Glen Ellen, CA 95442
707-934-8604

Wellington Cellars, located in the stunning Napa Valley, California, is a boutique winery that offers a warm, welcoming experience for wine lovers seeking exceptional wines and a tranquil setting. Known for producing small-lot, handcrafted wines, the winery prides itself on its commitment to quality and craftsmanship, offering visitors a unique opportunity to explore some of the finest varietals in the region.

The winery's history dates back to the early 2000s when it was founded with the goal of producing wines that showcase the unique terroir of Napa Valley. Wellington Cellars focuses on creating limited-production wines with a distinct character and sense of place, carefully crafted to highlight the region's diverse soils and climates. By using sustainable farming practices and working closely with handpicked vineyards, the winery ensures that each bottle is a true reflection of the Napa Valley's exceptional growing conditions.

Wellington Cellars is known for its well-balanced, elegant wines, including its flagship varietals such as Cabernet Sauvignon, Merlot, and Sauvignon Blanc. The wines produced here are marked by their depth, complexity, and smooth finish, with each vintage showcasing the natural characteristics of the grapes. The winery also produces small-batch, limited-release wines, providing visitors with the opportunity to taste exclusive bottles that are not widely available, making it a truly special experience for wine enthusiasts.

The winery itself offers a relaxed and intimate atmosphere, providing a personal touch that many larger wineries can't match. Wellington Cellars offers private and by-appointment tastings, allowing guests to enjoy a personalized wine experience tailored to their tastes. Knowledgeable staff guide guests through the tasting, offering insights into the winemaking process, the vineyard's history, and the unique characteristics of the wines. The tasting room, located in a beautiful setting, provides a cozy and inviting space to sip wine while enjoying the peaceful surroundings.

Visitors to Wellington Cellars can take in the scenic beauty of Napa Valley, with vineyards and rolling hills providing a stunning backdrop. The winery's location in the valley offers breathtaking views, making it an ideal spot for a leisurely afternoon. The serene environment allows guests to connect with nature while sampling wines that capture the essence of Napa Valley's rich winemaking heritage.

In addition to the exceptional wine experience, Wellington Cellars offers special events and private tours for those who want to learn more about the winemaking process and the winery's history. The winery frequently hosts wine-pairing events, wine dinners, and other gatherings that highlight the relationship between wine and food, helping guests appreciate the nuanced flavors of the wines. Whether attending a special event or simply enjoying a quiet afternoon tasting session, visitors are treated to personalized attention and an intimate experience that is both informative and enjoyable.

For those looking to take home a bottle of Napa Valley's finest, Wellington Cellars offers a selection of wines for purchase at its tasting room. Guests can purchase exclusive wines that reflect the high-quality standards the winery is known for, with some bottles available only to those who visit the winery itself. This exclusivity adds to the allure of Wellington Cellars, as it allows visitors to enjoy rare wines that are difficult to find elsewhere.

With its commitment to producing high-quality wines, its intimate and inviting atmosphere, and its stunning Napa Valley location, Wellington Cellars provides a truly memorable experience. Whether you are a seasoned wine connoisseur or a first-time visitor to Napa Valley, Wellington Cellars is a must-visit destination for those seeking an authentic, personalized wine-tasting experience that celebrates the best of California's renowned wine country.

99

YOSEMITE NATIONAL PARK

COUNTY: MARIPOSA   **CITY:** MARIPOSA

DATE VISITED: **WHO I WENT WITH:**

RATING: ☆ ☆ ☆ ☆ ☆   **WILL I RETURN?** YES / NO

You can drive to Yosemite year-round and enter via Highways 41, 140, and 120 from the west. Tioga Pass Entrance (via Highway 120 from the east) is closed from approximately November through late May or June. Hetch Hetchy is open all year but may close intermittently due to snow. Please note that GPS units do not always provide accurate directions to or within Yosemite.
209-372-0200

Yosemite National Park, located in the western Sierra Nevada of California, is one of the most iconic and breathtaking natural destinations in the United States. Spanning over 1,200 square miles, this UNESCO World Heritage Site is celebrated for its dramatic granite cliffs, cascading waterfalls, ancient sequoia groves, and diverse ecosystems. Yosemite draws millions of visitors annually, offering them a chance to connect with nature and explore its awe-inspiring landscapes through a variety of activities and attractions.

One of the park's most famous features is El Capitan, a towering granite monolith that rises over 3,000 feet above the valley floor. Renowned as a mecca for rock climbers, El Capitan challenges even the most experienced athletes and has become a symbol of human perseverance and adventure. Nearby, the majestic Half Dome, with its distinctive shape and striking silhouette, is another iconic formation that lures climbers and hikers alike. The Half Dome hike, a strenuous trek with steel cables for the final ascent, offers panoramic views that are truly rewarding for those who undertake it.

Yosemite Valley, the heart of the park, is home to several of Yosemite's most popular attractions. The valley is framed by granite cliffs and features lush meadows, tranquil rivers, and historic lodges. Visitors flock to see Yosemite Falls, one of the tallest waterfalls in North America, which plunges nearly 2,425 feet in a dramatic three-tiered cascade. Other must-see waterfalls include Bridalveil Fall and Vernal Fall, each offering unique viewpoints and hiking opportunities.

The park is also known for its ancient sequoia trees, some of which are over 2,000 years old. Mariposa Grove, located in the southern part of Yosemite, is home to over 500 giant sequoias, including the Grizzly Giant, one of the largest and oldest trees in the grove. Walking among these towering giants is a humbling experience, providing a sense of timelessness and connection to the natural world.

For those seeking scenic drives, Glacier Point Road offers some of the most stunning vistas in Yosemite, including a breathtaking view of Half Dome, Yosemite Valley, and the surrounding high country. The Tioga Road, which traverses the park's high-elevation areas, provides access to serene alpine lakes, meadows, and trailheads leading to remote wilderness areas.

Yosemite also offers abundant opportunities for outdoor recreation. Hiking is a favorite activity, with trails ranging from easy walks like the Mirror Lake Trail to challenging backcountry routes like the John Muir Trail and the Mist Trail. Camping, fishing, horseback riding, and photography are other popular activities, while winter brings opportunities for snowshoeing, skiing, and ice skating.

Wildlife enthusiasts can spot a variety of animals within the park, including black bears, mule deer, bobcats, and numerous bird species. Yosemite's rich biodiversity is supported by its range of elevations and habitats, making it a vital sanctuary for flora and fauna.

The park is open year-round, but each season offers a unique experience. Spring showcases roaring waterfalls and blooming wildflowers, summer provides the best access to the park's higher elevations, autumn offers colorful foliage and fewer crowds, and winter transforms Yosemite into a snowy wonderland.

Yosemite National Park is more than just a place of extraordinary beauty; it is a testament to the enduring power of nature and a haven for those seeking inspiration, adventure, and tranquility. Whether exploring its iconic landmarks, embarking on thrilling outdoor activities, or simply soaking in its serene atmosphere, Yosemite remains an unparalleled treasure of natural wonder.

100

ZABRISKIE POINT

COUNTY: INYO, SAN BERNARDINO   **CITY:** FURNACE CREEK

DATE VISITED: **WHO I WENT WITH:**

RATING: ☆ ☆ ☆ ☆ ☆   **WILL I RETURN?** YES / NO

Route 190
Death Valley National Park, CA 92328
760-786-3200

Zabriskie Point is one of the most iconic and breathtaking landmarks within Death Valley National Park, located in Eastern California. It offers visitors a chance to witness some of the most surreal and striking landscapes in the United States, with its vivid colors, unique geological formations, and expansive views that seem to stretch endlessly into the horizon. Situated just a short drive from the park's main entrance, Zabriskie Point has become a must-see destination for nature lovers, photographers, and adventurers alike.

The area gets its name from Christian Zabriskie, a former vice president of the Pacific Coast Borax Company, who played a significant role in the development of the region during the early 20th century. Zabriskie Point itself is positioned along the Amargosa Range, which is part of the Mojave Desert. Its geology is one of the primary reasons the site has become such a popular attraction. The point offers visitors a view of the Badlands, a region filled with jagged hills, deep ravines, and erosion-carved ridges that create an otherworldly landscape.

One of the most notable features of Zabriskie Point is the dramatic mix of colors that paint the land. The slopes of the surrounding hills and valleys display shades of gold, brown, purple, and pink, a result of volcanic activity and the erosion of sedimentary rock formations over millions of years. These vibrant hues are most striking at sunrise and sunset when the soft light casts a warm glow over the landscape, making it a perfect time for photographers and nature enthusiasts to capture the beauty of the desert. The striking view of Gower Gulch and the Panamint Range in the distance adds to the allure of the location.

For those interested in exploring the area further, there are several hiking opportunities near Zabriskie Point. One of the most popular is the Gower Gulch Loop Trail, which begins at the viewpoint and leads hikers through the Badlands, offering an up-close experience of the stunning terrain. The trail is relatively short, about 2.5 miles round-trip, and provides visitors with the opportunity to explore the area's unique rock formations and the rugged desert environment. Along the way, hikers can enjoy a variety of desert flora and fauna, including creosote bushes, cactus, and possibly even desert wildlife such as jackrabbits or bighorn sheep.

Though the area around Zabriskie Point is a paradise for hikers, it's important to remember that temperatures in Death Valley can soar to extreme levels, especially in the summer months, making it crucial for visitors to plan their trips wisely. The best times to visit Zabriskie Point are during the cooler months of the year, from late fall to early spring. During the summer, temperatures can exceed 120°F, which is dangerous for anyone attempting to hike in the area without proper preparation. Even in cooler months, visitors should always carry plenty of water, wear sun protection, and be mindful of the desert's harsh conditions.

The viewpoint itself is accessible via a paved path that leads to an observation area, making it an ideal spot for visitors who may not want to hike but still want to experience the stunning vistas. The platform provides a safe and easy way to take in the panoramic views of the Badlands, with ample space for visitors to take photos and enjoy the landscape. The incredible visibility from this vantage point allows for sweeping views across Death Valley, including Furnace Creek, the Panamint Valley, and the Black Mountains. The view from Zabriskie Point provides a visual reminder of the extreme geological processes that have shaped this region over millions of years, from volcanic eruptions to the gradual erosion of rocks and minerals.

For those visiting Death Valley National Park on a more spiritual or reflective journey, Zabriskie Point offers a peaceful and awe-inspiring atmosphere. Its isolation, combined with the vastness of the surrounding landscape, evokes a sense of tranquility that allows visitors to appreciate the natural beauty of one of the most extreme and unique environments on Earth. The area's quiet serenity makes it an excellent spot for meditation or simply spending time in solitude, soaking in the expansive desert views.

Zabriskie Point is also known for its role in pop culture, having been featured in several films, including the 1970 film Zabriskie Point, directed by Michelangelo Antonioni. The film, which was named after the viewpoint, used the desert landscapes of the area to reflect the themes of social upheaval and rebellion, further solidifying the site's connection to the artistic world.

Overall, Zabriskie Point is an exceptional location to explore, offering visitors a glimpse into the natural wonders and geological history of Death Valley. Whether you're a photographer, hiker, or someone simply looking to enjoy a moment of tranquility in a stunning desert landscape, Zabriskie Point provides an unforgettable experience. Its striking geological formations, vibrant colors, and sweeping desert vistas make it one of the most photographed and celebrated landmarks in Death Valley National Park, truly showcasing the stark beauty of California's Mojave Desert.

PHOTOS

PHOTOS

PHOTOS

PHOTOS

PHOTOS

Thank you for reading my book!
I hope you enjoyed it.

If you have a moment, I would truly
appreciate it if you could share your
thoughts in an online review. Your feedback
not only helps me grow as an author but
also guides other readers in discovering new
books.

Feel free to reach out if you have any
suggestions:

✉ maxkukisgalgan@gmail.com

Thank you for your support!
Warm regards,

Max Kukis Galgan

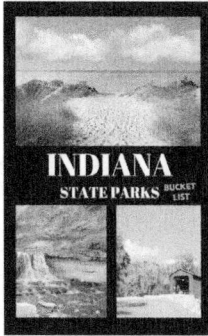

INDIANA
STATE PARKS BUCKET LIST

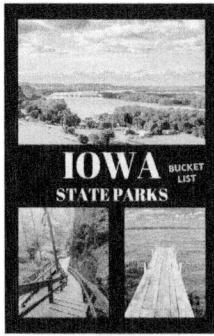

IOWA BUCKET LIST
STATE PARKS

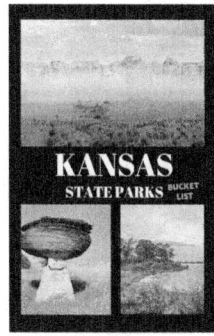

KANSAS
STATE PARKS BUCKET LIST

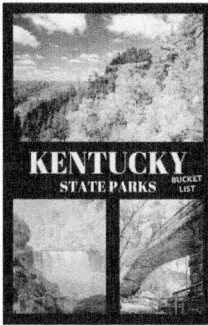

KENTUCKY
STATE PARKS BUCKET LIST

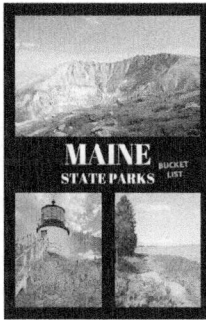

MAINE BUCKET LIST
STATE PARKS

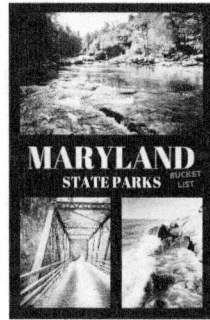

MARYLAND
STATE PARKS BUCKET LIST

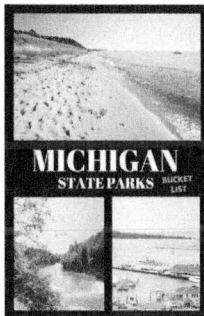

MICHIGAN
STATE PARKS BUCKET LIST

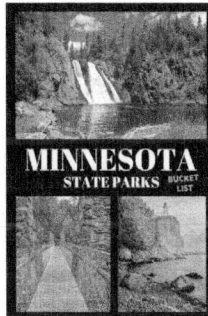

MINNESOTA
STATE PARKS BUCKET LIST

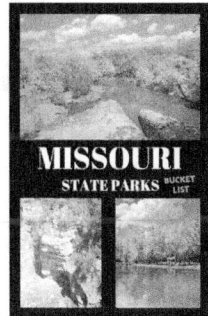

MISSOURI
STATE PARKS BUCKET LIST

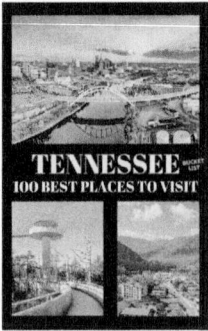

TENNESSEE
100 BEST PLACES TO VISIT

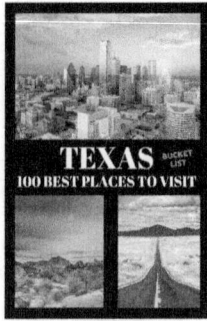

TEXAS
100 BEST PLACES TO VISIT

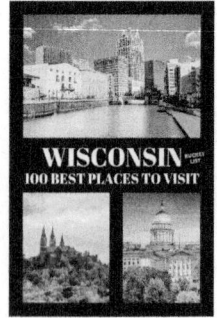

WISCONSIN
100 BEST PLACES TO VISIT

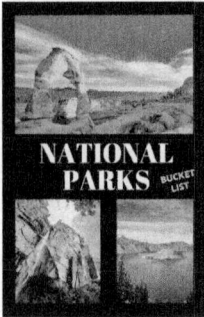

NATIONAL PARKS

Printed in Dunstable, United Kingdom

66924311R00157